The Foundations of History

The Foundations of History

Collingwood's Analysis of Historical Explanation

Stephen Leach

imprint-academic.com

Published in the UK by Imprint Academic
PO Box 200, Exeter EX5 5YX, UK

Published in the USA by Imprint Academic
Philosophy Documentation Center
PO Box 7147, Charlottesville, VA 22906-7147, USA

ISBN 9 781845 401771

A CIP catalogue record for this book is available from the
British Library and US Library of Congress

To My Parents

Contents

Part II

Preface

In my first years of studying philosophy at university I found myself in vague agreement with every different school of thought that I encountered. I imagine that this may be an experience held in common by many well-taught students. Realism, idealism, positivism, pragmatism—of every one I thought, 'there's something to it': but surely they could not all be right.

It was in the hope of better establishing my own position that I then turned to R.G. Collingwood's philosophy of history. For, knowing that Collingwood had worked in archaeology, and having worked for some years in archaeology myself, albeit at a humble level, I hoped that in reading his philosophy of history the criterion of this shared experience might help me to make up my mind upon philosophical problems with greater certitude than previously. Thus, it was not as a result of an immediate attraction to his philosophy that I came to study Collingwood's philosophy, nor was it the result of instruction from a favourite teacher.

Nonetheless, by the time I had finished the thesis upon which this book is based, I had come to think of Collingwood and, his modern-day expositor, my tutor Giuseppina D'Oro, as my mentors. Of course there are areas in which my ideas differ from theirs, but this is an opinion that I retain. I could not have asked for better teachers than R.G. Collingwood and Giuseppina D'Oro.

Acknowledgements

I would like to thank my tutor, Dr. Giuseppina D'Oro—for taking time to read the many different drafts of the thesis upon which this work is based and for her many constructive criticisms. Thanks also to my second tutors, Professor John Horton and Professor Hidemi Suganami; to Professor James Connelly and Dr. James Tartaglia, the referees of my thesis, for their comments and criticisms; to Professor David Boucher and to my first philosophy teacher, Dr. Katerina Reed-Tsocha.

A version of Chapter VI, 'The Ontological Argument', was first published in *Collingwood and British Idealism Studies* 14: 1, 2008 under the heading of 'Collingwood's Ontological Argument'. A version of the section of Chapter II under the heading of 'An Appreciation of R.G. Collingwood as an Archaeologist' was first published in *Bulletin of the History of Archaeology* 19: 1, 2009 under the heading of 'Appreciation of Collingwood as an Archaeologist'. I am grateful to the editors of both these journals for permission to reprint this work.

Finally, for providing inspiration, I would like to thank Ms. Kirsten Jarrett.

Stephen Leach, 2009

Abbreviations

Religion and Philosophy (1916) . . . . R.P.

Speculum Mentis (1924) . . . . S.M.

An Essay on Philosophical Method (1933) . . . E.P.M.

The Principles of Art (1938) . . . . P.A.

An Autobiography (1939) . . . . A.

First Mate's Log (1940) . . . . F.M.L.

An Essay on Metaphysics (1940) . . . . E.M.

The New Leviathan (1942) . . . . N.L.

The Idea of Nature (1945) . . . . I.N.

The Idea of History (1946) . . . . I.H.

The Principles of History (1999) . . . . P.H.

The Philosophy of Enchantment (2005) . . . . . . P.E.

Chapter I

Introduction

This book is intended to provide a thorough exposition and critical examination of R.G. Collingwood's philosophy of history and to locate Collingwood's views in relation to recent and current philosophy. My views are in general sympathetic to Collingwood's, though with several major caveats.

Part I is devoted to Collingwood's views on the nature and task of philosophy. Collingwood is relatively unusual among recent philosophers in that he devotes great attention to metaphilosophy, in particular to the question of the relation between philosophy and its subject matter. He argues that part of philosophy's subject matter is itself, for:

> If the first principles of philosophy are to be justified, they must be justified by philosophy itself.[1]

Collingwood is aware that this suggests circularity, since:

> This can only be done if the arguments of philosophy, instead of having an irreversible direction from principles to conclusions, have a reversible one, the principles establishing the conclusions and the conclusions reciprocally establishing the principles. But an argument of this kind, in which A rests on B and B rests reciprocally on A, is a vicious circle. Are we to conclude that philosophy is in a dilemma of either renouncing this characteristic function and conforming to the irreversible pattern of exact science, or else losing all cogency in a circular argument?[2]

Collingwood's answer is that, once the futile search for justified foundational beliefs is abandoned, what at first appeared as vicious circularity may be exploited to good effect. For it is by virtue of this trait — philosophy's reversible direction — that the philosopher, when he[3] turns his gaze outwards, is able to show us what, in an obscured sense, we already knew but had never made explicit. In particular, and as will be shown, philosophy is able to discover and bring to light other disciplines' 'absolute presuppositions', whilst yet retaining its own autonomy.

---

1 E.P.M., p.160
2 E.P.M. pp.160–61
3 Throughout this book, for 'he' read 'he or she' and for 'his' read 'his or hers'.

By 'absolute presuppositions' Collingwood refers to those presuppositions that are logically basic and distinctive to the particular disciplines that they underlie. Collingwood terms the attempt to recover these absolute presuppositions 'metaphysics without ontology'.[4] This term is intended to convey that the form of metaphysical inquiry proposed is a logical inquiry and is unconcerned with the ontological status of that which it studies.

However, despite advocating 'metaphysics without ontology', Collingwood also argues that the metaphysician must be committed to the existence of that which he studies—for the nature of his subject matter implies its existence. I argue, against Collingwood, that philosophical studies of the sort that he advocates can be productively pursued without any form of ontological commitment.

Part II is devoted to the exploration of Collingwood's philosophy of history and his attempt to recover the absolute presuppositions of history. In Collingwood's view to explain historically is to understand the reasons for which historical agents act. In historical explanation the connection between *explanandum* and *explanans* is a rational connection. In this fundamental respect, historians' explanations differ from natural scientists' 'causal' explanations in which events are explained when they are seen to follow as instances of general laws.

I argue that when Collingwood's views are reconstructed in the light of his 'metaphysics without ontology' it becomes clear that his *primary* concern is with the conceptual project of recovering history's absolute presuppositions, rather than with the provision of a methodology. I also make clear my sympathy for Collingwood's account of action explanation and in particular for his view that the mind-body problem in the philosophy of mind is essentially 'bogus'. (This view is discussed in relation to Donald Davidson's). However, in the penultimate chapter I argue that the subject matter of history may be wider than Collingwood suggests. I argue that there may be more to history than action explanation, and that it may be a mistake to regard the philosophy of history as synonymous with the philosophy of action. I also suggest that we should distinguish between the foundations of history and the foundations of archaeology.

In brief, in Part I, I argue that there is a valid core to Collingwood's metaphilosophy that is unaffected by his commitment to the ontological argument. In Part II, I argue that there is continued value in his approach to the philosophy of history that is unaffected by (apparent) relativism and historicism. However, whilst I am sympathetic to Collingwood's account of historical explanation, I suggest that the relation between history and archaeology requires further investigation.

The Structure of this Book

In some more detail, the structure of the book is as follows. Each chapter is intended to be self-contained but to also play a part in the project of providing an exposition and critique of Collingwood's philosophy of history.

In the first section of Chapter II I describe Collingwood's work as an archaeologist and historian. (As a philosopher, Collingwood viewed archaeology as his 'laboratory'[5]). In the second section I explain how, owing to his early death and the posthumous editing of his work, the overall structure of Collingwood's philosophical project is not as apparent as he would have wished. He envisaged his work as having a tripartite structure consisting of *An Essay on Philosophical Method* and *An Essay on Metaphysics*; *The Principles of Art* and *The Principles of History*; and *The Idea of History* and *The Idea of Nature*. In broad terms, *An Essay on Philosophical Method* and *An Essay on Metaphysics* may be seen as works of metaphilosophy; *The Principles of Art* and the unfinished *Principles of History* may be seen as examples of the practice of metaphysics; and *The Idea of History* (as originally conceived) and *The Idea of Nature* may be seen as, for the most part, describing the history of the concepts of 'history' and 'nature'.

In Chapter III I provide an overview of Collingwood's 'metaphysics without ontology'. I describe how his two principal works of metaphilosophy, *An Essay on Philosophical Method* (1933) and *An Essay on Metaphysics* (1940), were written in opposition to, respectively, Oxford realism and logical positivism. However, these works contain more than just negative criticisms: together they propose a new and constructive view of philosophy and metaphysics.

The arguments of *An Essay on Philosophical Method* and *An Essay on Metaphysics*, touched on in brief in Chapter III, are respectively expounded, in greater detail, in Chapters IV and V. In *An Essay on Philosophical Method* Collingwood advances the argument that the philosopher is well placed to analyse those beliefs and experiences whose origins lie outside of philosophy. Time is spent on the exposition of this work not only because it is a relatively neglected analysis of philosophical method but because it is the one work which Collingwood regarded as completed to the best of his ability.

In *An Essay on Metaphysics*, expounded in Chapter V, Collingwood argues against the logical positivists' verification principle — according to which all meaningful statements are either analytic (true or false in virtue of their meaning) or synthetic (true or false according to empirical evidence). Collingwood points out that an absolute presupposition is meaningful even though it does not fall within either of these categories. In the

---

5   A., p.121

argument that the metaphysician is ideally placed to recover the absolute presuppositions of other forms of inquiry, I note certain parallels between Collingwood's metaphilosophy and the metaphilosophies of Ludwig Wittgenstein, A.N. Whitehead, Nicholas Rescher and Bernard Williams.

Thus far the book is primarily expositional, but exposition makes way for criticism in Chapter VI, in which I argue that an underlying commitment to the ontological argument is unnecessary to the project of discovering absolute presuppositions. I argue that Collingwood's commitment to the ontological argument is an unnecessary aberration from what is fundamentally a conceptual project — the philosopher need not be committed to the existence of that which he studies, for his business is not to propound absolute presuppositions 'but to propound the proposition that this or that one of them is presupposed'.[6] Indeed, commitment to the ontological argument is at loggerheads with this project, for the metaphysician in search of absolute presuppositions will be placed at an advantage when he himself does not presume to stand upon firm ground.

In Chapter VII I discuss the difficulties of classifying Collingwood's 'idealism' — some scholars stress his affinity to Kant, others stress his affinity to Hegel. I suggest that it may be prudent to follow Collingwood's own example and to avoid the term 'idealism' altogether and to use instead the term 'metaphysics without ontology'.

The exposition and assessment of Collingwood's philosophy of history provide the subject matter of Part II in which I try to discover to what extent Collingwood, by his own lights, achieved his aim of discovering the foundations of history. Chapters VIII, IX, X and XI are primarily, though not entirely, expositional. The aim of Chapter XII is to reconnect aspects of Collingwood's thought with more recent trends in philosophy by contrasting his view of causation with that of Donald Davidson. Chapters XIII, XIV and XV suggest areas in which Collingwood's philosophy of history might be respectively clarified, criticised and revised.

More specifically, in Chapter VIII I present Collingwood's view of scientific history, in which the historian attempts to reconstruct the *rationale* underlying an agent's actions. He believes that this feature gives historians' explanations a fundamentally different character to those offered by the natural scientist. He contends that it is an absolute presupposition of history that 'all history is the history of thought'.[7] At the end of this chapter I suggest that, in order not to exclude historical agents such as Nero, this should be recast as 'the agent's reasoning should be recovered whenever possible'.

---

6   E.M., p.33
7   A., p.110; I.H., pp.215 &.317; P.H., pp.67, 98 & 100

Collingwood develops these ideas by provocatively claiming that the cause of an event is 'the inside of the event itself'[8] and that historical understanding consists of the re-enactment of the historical agent's reasoning. In Chapter IX I argue that 'the inside of the event' should be seen as a metaphorical presentation of the idea that the historian is interested in the historical agent's *rationale*.

In Chapter X, I examine 're-enactment' — the idea that 'the historian must be able to think over again for himself the thought whose expression he is trying to interpret'[9] — in the face of various criticisms, grounded upon misconceptions of Collingwood's aims. I argue that comparisons that have been drawn between Collingwood's views on understanding an historical agent and simulation theory, and between 're-enactment' and Quine's principle of charity, are misleading.

In Chapter XI I examine Collingwood's view of historians' distinctive use of the word 'cause' — as meaning 'that which affords the historical agent a motive'[10]; and his view that the word 'cause' has a different sense in history than in the practical sciences of nature (such as engineering or medicine) and the theoretical sciences of nature (such as physics). Collingwood argues that the word 'cause' has a different sense within each of these different areas. I relate these three different senses of 'cause' to three contemporary schools of thought on causation and explanation — advocating, respectively: 'rational explanation'; counterfactual, or contrastive, explanation; and 'causal explanation'.

In Chapter XII I consider Davidson's identification of reasons with causes and assess whether he has succeeded in overturning Collingwood's non-causalist view of action explanation. I argue that Collingwood's supporters are able to withstand Davidson's criticisms by challenging the idea that 'where there is causality, there must be a law'.[11]

Criticisms of 'relativism' and 'historicism' must also be faced before Collingwood's philosophy might be reconnected to the mainstream of contemporary philosophy. These are the subjects of the next two chapters.

In Chapter XIII, I attempt to defuse the charge of relativism that is raised against Collingwood's philosophy by the 'radical conversion hypothesis'. I argue that although philosophers and historians may study the same subject matter, they study it with different questions in mind. For the philosopher is interested in the absolute presuppositions of an area of inquiry, whereas the historian is interested in what attitudes predominated at certain times and places.

---

8   I.H., p.215
9   A., p.111
10   E.M., p.285
11   Davidson, Donald 'Mental Events' (1970) in *Actions and Events*, 1980, p.208

In Chapter XIV I consider the distinction between critical (or analytical) and speculative philosophy of history and argue that although Collingwood's intention—to recover the absolute presuppositions of history—would suggest that he is primarily engaged in a form of critical philosophy of history his work is not easily classifiable along these lines. There is also a speculative element to his philosophy and consequently the distinction between philosophy and history is not always clearly drawn. However, although, in both this and the previous chapter, I argue that in Collingwood's work the distinction between philosophy and history is sometimes blurred, this does not cast doubt upon the aims and methods of his overall project.

In Chapter XV I examine Collingwood's response to Bernard Bosanquet's view of history as 'the doubtful story of successive events'.[12] Collingwood replies in 'The Limits of Historical Knowledge' (1928): and this answer is later expanded via the exemplar of a miniature detective story entitled 'Who killed John Doe?' His interest in these passages shifts from the investigation of the distinctive characteristics of action explanation, as revealed in the work of historians, to the methodological question of how we can acquire knowledge of past events. Collingwood's answer is that the historian traces the logical connections between events in the same manner as the detective.

I argue that the analogy between the work of the historian and the work of the detective may be extended further than Collingwood realizes. However, there is a tension between the analogy made in 'Who killed John Doe?' and the rest of Collingwood's philosophy. I suggest ways by which this tension might be removed.

The principal conclusions of the book, already drawn, are briefly summarised in the final chapter, Chapter XVI.

---

12 Bosanquet, Bernard *The Principle of Individuality and Value*, 1912, p.79; quoted by R.G. Collingwood in 'The Limits of Historical Knowledge' *Journal of Philosophical Studies* 3 (1928), p.213

PART ONE

Chapter II

Collingwood's Writings

Collingwood's Work as an Archaeologist and Historian

In his short and busy life Collingwood found time to pursue two quite separate careers: as a philosopher and as an archaeologist. In the latter career
he followed in the footsteps of his father, W.G. Collingwood, whom as
well as being an artist, an historical novelist and a secretary to (and biographer of) John Ruskin was also an accomplished amateur archaeologist,
and a stalwart of the Cumberland and Westmorland Antiquarian and
Archaeological Society.[1] Collingwood writes in *An Autobiography* of growing up in 'a gradually thickening archaeological atmosphere'.[2]

R.G. Collingwood is the author of four major archaeological works:
Roman Britain (1923); *The Archaeology of Roman Britain* (1930); *Roman Britain
and the English Settlements* (with J.N.L. Myers, 1936); and *The Roman
Inscriptions of Britain* (edited by R.P. Wright, and published posthumously
in 1965).

Roman Britain (1923) 'was a short book; I wrote it in two days; it was
designed to be elementary, and it was full of faults ... it gave me a first
opportunity of finding out, more clearly than was possible within the limits of a short article, how my conception of historical research was developing'.[3] It was substantially revised in 1932 and revised again in 1934.

The Archaeology of Roman Britain (1930) was intended as a work of synthesis; as a summary of the growing number of archaeological papers that
had addressed specific problems relating to particular sites and particular
problems of chronology. As such it was written primarily for fellow
archaeologists. (The 1969 edition was revised by Collingwood's pupil, I.A.
Richmond, and credited to R.G. Collingwood and I.A. Richmond.)

Roman Britain and the English Settlements (1936) was written with J.N.L.
Myers. However, Collingwood emphasised: 'This work is not a work of
collaboration. It consists of two independent studies of two distinct,

---

1   See Johnstone, W.M. *The Formative Years of R.G. Collingwood*, 1967
2   A., p.80
3   A., pp.120–21

though interlocking subjects'.[4] Collingwood wrote on Roman Britain, and
its immediate aftermath; Myers wrote on the Anglo-Saxon invasions and
settlements. Collingwood saw this book as his historical and archaeological
magnum opus.

Roman Britain and the English Settlements, although supplemented and
modified by Sheppard Frere's *Britannia* (1967), stood as the authoritative
account of the subject until the Clarendon Press commissioned its replace-
ment, *Roman Britain* by I.A. Richmond's pupil, Peter Salway, published in
1981. Collingwood's history built on the previous authoritative works on
the subject *The Romanization of Britain*[5] and *The Roman Occupation of Britain*,[6] by Francis Haverfield. Something of the basic structure of Haverfield's
work remains in all these later works. Arguably this paradigm was only
finally superseded in 2006, by David Mattingley's *An Imperial Possession*.
(This history, like those by Haverfield, Collingwood, Frere and Salway,
was written both for archaeologists and for the general reader. A criticism
that Mattingley makes of all these predecessors is of their uncritical and
question-begging use of the term 'Romanization' — a term that is ultimately traceable to Theodor Mommsen).

Collingwood's *The Roman Inscriptions of Britain* (1965), completed by
R.P. Wright, consists of an illustrated catalogue of over 2,000 Roman
inscriptions. This work had been initiated by Mommsen and taken over by
Collingwood, from Haverfield, at the latter's death in 1919. Although regularly revised, this is still today the standard reference work on the subject.[7]

Other work includes the chapters on Roman Britain in *The Cambridge
Ancient History*[8]; and the chapter on 'Roman Britain' in *An Economic Survey
of Ancient Rome*,[9] and, as he mentions in *An Autobiography*, 'about a hundred articles and pamphlets mostly written between 1920 and 1930'.[10]
Collingwood also began work on the subject of the interpretation of folktales that he intended to publish as a book. This work, in which he argues
that folktales are of historical interest, both in themselves and as historical
evidence, has lately been published in *The Philosophy of Enchantment*
(2005). It was written over Christmas 1936 and in the early months of

---

4   Collingwood, R.G. and Myers, J.N.L. *Roman Britain and the English Settlements*, 1936, preface, v
5   Haverfield, F.J *The Romanisation of Britain*, 2nd ed., 1912
6   Haverfield, F.J. and George MacDonald *The Roman Occupation of Britain*, 1924
7   Collingwood, R.G. and Wright, R.P. *The Roman Inscriptions of Britain with Addenda and
     Corrigenda* by R.S.O. Tomlin 2nd ed. Stroud: Sutton, 1995
8   'The Romans and Britain' and 'The Conquest of Britain' in S.A. Cook et al (eds.) *Cambridge
     Ancient History* Vol. 10, 1934, pp.790–802; 'The Latin West: Britain' *Cambridge Ancient History*
     Vol. 11, 1936, pp.511–25; 'Britain' *Cambridge Ancient History* Vol. 12, 1939, pp.282–96
9   'Roman Britain' in T.Frank (ed.) *An Economic Survey of Ancient Rome* Vol.3, 1937, pp.1–118
10   A., p.145

1937,[11] until set aside 'partly through illness, and perhaps to focus more completely on *The Principles of Art*'.[12]

When he died at the age of fifty-three in January 1943 his pupil Ian Richmond wrote an 'Appreciation of R.G. Collingwood as an Archaeologist' in which he spoke of:

> a tendency which marked and sometimes marred his work, to drive the evidence hard and to build upon it a series of conclusions whose very artistry disguised the inherent weakness of foundation.[13]

It is not my intention to question this judgment, save to note that archaeology being a collaborative discipline devoted to the cumulative accretion of new data, it is hardly surprising that some of Collingwood's own most valued interpretations have been revised since his death (for example, his estimate of the total population of Roman Britain[14]). Others have been for the most part ignored (a prime example is his chapter on 'Art' in *Roman Britain and the English Settlements*).[15] Others have been incorporated into the latest work on Roman Britain (for example, his interpretation of Hadrian's Wall[16], his system of numbering of the milecastles on the Wall, and his work on the typology of Roman brooches and his work on Roman inscriptions[17]). Others yet have been neither revised nor incorporated into new work; but remain, as it were, 'on hold' (for example, his speculations concerning King Arthur and his interpretation of the bronze age site 'King Arthur's Round Table'[18]). Collingwood would not have expected otherwise.[19] For, granted his great works of synthesis, *Roman Britain* (1923) and *Roman Britain and the English Settlements* (1936), are imbued with a sense of authoritative finality — as though he had himself witnessed Caesar's invasions — nonetheless, although feint, the line between data and interpreta-

---

11 P.E. *lxiii* (Wendy James' introduction)

12 *Ibid. xxxii* (Philip Smallwood's introduction)

13 Richmond, I.A. 1943 'Appreciation of R.G. Collingwood as an archaeologist' *Proceedings of the British Academy* 29, pp.476–85 & 476. See also Birley, E. *Research on Hadrian's Wall*, 1961.

14 Collingwood, R.G. 'Town and Country in Roman Britain' *Antiquity* 1929, 3, pp.261–76. Collingwood's was the first such estimate. Martin Millett surveys the different approaches that have been taken towards this problem in *The Romanisation of Britain: An Essay in Archaeological Interpretation* 1990, pp.181–6.

15 Martin Hennig in *The Art of Roman Britain* (1997) suggests that there may be problems with the logical structure of this argument.

16 Collingwood's argues that the Wall should be seen not primarily as a 'fighting platform' but as an 'elevated sentry-line'. This argument is reiterated in David J. Breeze and Brian Dobson's *Hadrian's Wall* (4th ed.) 1999, pp.42–3

17 Collingwood, R.G. and Wright, R.P. *The Roman Inscriptions of Britain with Addenda and Corrigenda by R.S.O. Tomlin* 1995 2nd ed.

18 Collingwood's interpretations were challenged by Gerhard Bersu. See his 'King Arthur's Round Table' in *Transactions of the Cumberland and Westmorland Antiquarian and Archaeological Society*, 1940, 40, pp.169–206

19 As Richmond points out he had the grace to admit his mistakes. Richmond, I.A. 1943 'Appreciation of R.G. Collingwood as an archaeologist' *Proceedings of the British Academy* 29, p.476.

tion is rarely entirely absent.[20] Thus it is that good archaeologists create the conditions for their own supersession.

I would suggest however, with the benefit of hindsight, that Collingwood's greatest contribution to archaeology lies not in fieldwork and synthesis (although here his achievements are not slight); but rather – although the term was not then used – in archaeological theory.

According to his autobiography, upon going up to Oxford in 1908 Collingwood became aware of a 'Baconian revolution'[21] in archaeology, already in full swing. The guiding precept of this revolution was that no evidence need be taken at face value (as in 'scissors-and-paste history'), or classed simply as reliable or not; but rather, that the archaeologist should take the initiative in formulating specific questions of the evidence – with the aim of reconstructing the reason *why* the evidence took the form it did. In this way, when 'put to the question', the evidence might yield answers that a more passive approach could never have extorted. Flinders Petrie epitomised this attitude, when he wrote:

> The old saying that a man finds what he is looking for in a subject is too true; or, if he has not enough insight to ensure finding what he looks for, it is at least sadly true that he does not find anything he does not look for.[22]

As examples of what this new method might achieve Collingwood cited Sir Arthur Evans' work on Knossos and the work of Francis Haverfield on Roman Britain.[23]

Although only a few held such confident ambitious views,[24] other sources confirm the liveliness of the period.[25] Moreover, it was beginning to be argued that the same questions might be asked, with reasonable expectation of an answer, of a written document and of an unwritten artefact. The belief that non-written evidence is of equal worth as written was, for instance, explicitly stated by that 'bold revolutionary'[26] David George Hogarth, although it should be added that Hogarth claimed no originality for this idea.[27]

However, with the exception of Collingwood, all of this went on beneath the notice of contemporary philosophers, and archaeologists were

---

20 In *The Archaeology of Roman Britain* (1930), written primarily for his fellow archaeologists, the line between data and interpretation is more obvious than when he wrote for both archaeologists and the general reader.

21 A., p.115

22 Petrie, Flinders *Methods and Aims in Archaeology* 1904, p.49

23 A., pp.81–82

24 This is emphasised in Sir Leonard Woolley's autobiography *Spadework* 1953

25 Evans, Joan *A History of the Society of Antiquaries* 1956, pp.371-2

26 A., p.82

27 Hogarth wrote that the subject matter of archaeology should be taken as 'all documents, literary or material, all products of man, all things on which he has set his impress, and even all things which have set their impress on him' Hogarth, D.G. *Authority and Archaeology* 1899: v.

naturally content to leave them to their slumbers. For, then as now, archaeological theory was empirically driven—concerned, above all, with what does and does not work in practice.

Nonetheless, during the '20s and '30s, a small vocal minority including Collingwood, O.G.S. Crawford and Mortimer Wheeler did their best to propagate these ideas. In his autobiography, Collingwood summarised their methodology in the form of the following three principles.

1.   Never to dig 'either a five-thousand-pound site or a five-shilling trench without being certain that you can satisfy an inquirer who asks you "What are you doing this piece of work for?"'[28]

2.   'A second principle was that, since history proper is the history of thought, there are no mere "events in history": what is miscalled an "event" is really an action, and expresses some thought (intention, purpose) of its agent; the historian's business is therefore to identify this thought'[29]

3.   'A third principle was that no historical problem should be studied without studying what I called its second-order history; that is, the history of historical thought about it'.[30]

Arguably, realising the value of the above three principles, propagating them, and making them explicit, was Collingwood's greatest contribution to archaeology. (When, upon occasion, Collingwood drove his evidence too hard, it was not as a result of any of these principles).

The first principle is probably now more deep-rooted and widely recognised than ever before. Many would see it as one of the most basic presuppositions of archaeological theory. (Admittedly it is sometimes appropriate to ask relatively broad questions, but, nonetheless, few would now embark upon an archaeological career preferring to rely upon Mr Micawber's principle that something will turn up). The third principle is also now widely accepted.

The second principle is the most controversial, and, takes Collingwood to the heart of contemporary debates: for example, the debate surrounding the use of evolutionary theory. As an archaeologist Collingwood was eager to make use of any new theories that might prove useful, regardless of their origin, but he insisted that one still must ask *why* the people of the past acted as they did—what afforded them a motive, from their point of view. It is this feature that, he believed, distinguishes archaeology and history from natural science.

With respect to his fieldwork and works of synthesis contemporary archaeologists stand on Collingwood's shoulders but with respect to the above three principles Collingwood stands as our contemporary.

---

28   A. p.126
29   A. p.127
30   A. p.132

Closely linked to his work as an archaeologist is Collingwood's work as a conservationist — though I do not believe this has yet received attention in any book or paper. He was particularly concerned with the conservation of Hadrian's Wall. Much of the best preserved and archaeologically interesting stretches of Hadrian's Wall had, until the death of Mrs. N.J. Clayton in 1928, been safeguarded from destruction since the 1830s by the benevolent ownership of the Clayton estate. Upon Mrs. Clayton's death the Wall was scheduled in order to protect it from the possibility of future threats. But in 1930 archaeologists realized to their horror that this did not protect the Wall from the imminent prospect of stone being quarried just ten feet away from one of its best-preserved and impressive sections, immediately to the west of Housesteads fort. Existing legislation — the 1882 Ancient Monuments Act and the 1913 Ancient Monuments Consolidation and Amendment Act — served to protect the Wall itself but its immediate environment was left unguarded. The thought of the Wall being left perched on an artificial knife-edge led to numerous protests in the national press and to discussion at the highest level of government.

On 24 April 1930 *The Times* reported that the previous day the Cumberland and Westmorland Antiquarian and Archaeological Society (Collingwood's local society) had sent a resolution of protest to the Prime Minister and leader of the Opposition. Among numerous other protests that were recorded in *The Times*, On 3 May 1930 the paper reported that a number of the dons of Oxford University had sent an appeal to the First Commisioner of Works:

Hadrian's Wall
An Appeal from Oxford University

'The following letter has been addressed to Mr. Lansbury, First Commissioner of Works, by members of Oxford University:

University of Oxford, April 28

Sir, As members of the University of Oxford, we venture to express to you the hope that some means may be found to limit the proposed extension of quarrying works in the immediate neighbourhood of Hadrian's Wall. The stretch of the Wall, together with its associated works the Vallum and the Military Way, running from Chollerford to Gilsland, is, in our opinion, one of the most valuable of our national monuments. Both its beauty and its significance have already been impaired by the existing quarries; and we feel that the time has come when a binding and permanent limitation should be imposed on further disfigurement. We realize the importance of providing work, to the extent at present contemplated, for unemployed men in the Newcastle district; but we submit that it would be disastrous to permit the unlimited extension of such works, and so to leave the way open for the eventual destruction of a great historical monument.

We are, Sir; your obedient servants,

GREY OF FALLODEN, Chancellor.
F. HOLMES DUDDEN, Master of Pembroke, Vice-Chancellor.
HUGH CECIL } Burgesses
C.W.C. OMAN, Chichele Professor of Modern History } of the University
HERBERT L. WILD, Hon. Fellow of Exeter and
formerly Bishop of Newcastle.
H.A.L. FISHER, Warden of New College.
A.D. LINDSAY, Master of Balliol.
F.W. PEMBER, Warden of All Souls.
W.R. BUCHANAN RIDDELL, Principal of Hertford.
M.E. SADLER, Master of University College.
H.J. WHITE, Dean of Christ Church.
F.G.J. ANDERSON, Camden Professor of Ancient History.
GILBERT MURRAY, Regius Professor of Greek
JOHN L. MYRES, Wykeham Professor of Ancient History and
President of the Royal Anthropological Institute.
CHARLES S. SHERRINGTON, Waynflete Professor of Physiology and
President of the Royal Society.
CYRIL BAILEY, Fellow of Balliol.
R.G. COLLINGWOOD, Fellow of Pembroke'.

The fact that Collingwood's name appears last on the list, coupled with the style of writing, strongly suggests that Collingwood was the main orchestrator of this particular branch of the protest.

A file in the Public Record Office contains a short letter dated 14 May — from the official private secretary of George Lansbury, the Commissioner of Works, to an offical at 10 Downing Street — makes it clear that this appeal may have reached the desk of the Prime Minister, Ramsay MacDonald:

> Dear Mr Usher,
>
> I understand from Mr. Lansbury that the Prime Minister told him that he had not seen the representation from Oxford University published in the Times on the subject of the Roman Wall. I therefore send you a cutting which you may think it worth while to show to the Prime Minister.
>
> Yours sincerely
>
> R. Auriol Barker[31]

A similar appeal from dons at Cambridge, organized by the historian F.E. Adcock was sent directly to the Prime Minister and was also published in *The Times*.[32] It seems likely that the many different branches of this protest were closely co-ordinated. An additional concern expressed by Collingwood was that the break up the Clayton estate would lead to increasingly restricted public access to the Wall.[33]

---

31 P.R.O. 30/69/691

32 *The Times* 23 May 1930

33 Taylor, M.V. and Collingwood, R.G. 'Roman Britain in 1929' *Journal of Roman Studies* Vol. XIX 1929, p.185

The campaign of protest led to the passing of the 1931 Ancient Monuments Act, granting the First Commissioner of H.M. Works the power to make planning schemes and pay compensation. However, there were a series of delays before this act was implemented. When it was eventually implemented for the first and last time — it protected the surroundings of this particular section of the Wall by means of the Wall and Vallum Preservation Scheme — subsequently incorporated into Northumberland National Park.

The 1931 Ancient Monuments Act represents an intermediate stage between the impassioned but necessarily palliative and *ad hoc* protection of ancient monuments by groups of public spirited archaeologists and the more holistic and comprehensive approach to planning that has since been sought by local and national government. It is owing to the passing of this Act and to the vigilance and foresight of the campaigners that the four miles of the Wall immediately to the west of Housesteads fort — thought by many to be the finest stretch of the entire Wall[34] — traverse countryside that is still little changed since the Roman period. Our present day view of this bleak and rugged countryside remains a testament to the efforts of Collingwood and his fellow conservationists.[35]

This episode perhaps sheds some light on Collingwood's claim that in his addresses to the Cumberland and Westmorland Antiquarian and Archaeological Society he achieved a *rapprochement* between R.G.C. the theorist and R.G.C. the suppressed man of action:

> It may seem an odd form of 'release' for a suppressed man of action; but it was a very effective one. The enthusiasm for historical studies, and for myself as their leader in those studies, which I never failed to arouse in my audiences, was not in principle different from the enthusiasm for his person and his policy which is aroused by a successful political speaker.[36]

Clearly, Collingwood *was* genuinely appalled at the threat that faced the Wall, but at the same time as a suppressed man of action he would have relished the fight to save it. For, in his words:

> All thought exists for the sake of action.[37]

---

34 Collingwood, R.G. *A Guide to the Roman Wall*, 1930, p.27: 'The scenery, with its lakes, basalt crags, and distant views, is here at its best, and the remains of the Wall are very impressive, as they wind hither and thither to hold the edge of the crags or plunge into the gaps that separate one crag from the next'.

35 It should be added that, through tourism, the Wall today provides more employment than was offered by even the most ambitious quarry plans.

36 A., pp.151–2

37 S.M., p.15

The Overall Structure of Collingwood's Philosophical Project

It is apparent from letters written in 1939 to the Clarendon Press that Collingwood intended to explain his concept of metaphysics in a *series* of inter-related books. According to James Connelly:

> The final series was planned as a tripartite structure with each part comprising two books. Thus in the letter of 3 June the two *Essays* [*An Essay on Philosophical Method* and *An Essay on Metaphysics*] are brought into line as companion volumes under the general heading *Philosophical Essays*; *The Principles of Art* and the as yet unwritten *Principles of History* were to be companion volumes in the series *Philosophical Principles*; and in a later letter (October 19th) Collingwood wrote that *The Idea of History* and *The Idea of Nature* are to be companion volumes under the general title of *Studies in the History of Ideas*.[38]

However, at Collingwood's death in 1943 this scheme was forgotten. Collingwood's literary executor, Sir Malcolm Knox, extracted parts of the unfinished *Principles of History* and appended them (together with several other essays) to *The Idea of History*: Knox termed this final patchwork section of *The Idea of History* the 'Epilegomena'. Whilst the posthumous *Idea of History* (1946) became Collingwood's most widely read work, in a different form than he had ever intended, *The Principles of History* were lost and presumed destroyed—until the original manuscript was discovered in 1995[39] (together with two alternative conclusions to *The Idea of Nature*[40]). It then became apparent that *The Principles of History* was in fact never finished, although the completed first chapters are cohesive. The title page of *The Principles of History* has a note saying: 'To E.W.C. [Collingwood's first wife Ethel] If this ms. comes into your hands and I am prevented from finishing it, I authorise you to publish it with the above title, with a preface by yourself explaining that it is a fragment of what I had, for 25 years at least, looked forward to writing as my chief work'.[41]

The success of *The Idea of History*—in the form it took under the guidance of Knox—and the disregard of the original tripartite structure of his work, tended to obscure the idea that Collingwood was working on an essentially conceptual project. The move towards interpreting the aims of Collingwood's philosophy of history as conceptual rather than primarily methodological can be dated to W.H. Dray's *Laws and Explanation in History* (1957) and to Alan Donagan's *The Later Philosophy of R.G. Collingwood*

---

38 Connelly, James *Metaphysics, Method and Politics*, 2003, p.12

39 The full significance of this discovery is discussed in 'The Significance of R.G. Collingwood's *Principles of History*' Boucher, D. *Journal of the History of Ideas* vol. 58 no.2 1997, pp.309–30.

40 See Boucher, D. '*The Principles of History* and the Cosmological Conclusion to *The Idea of Nature*' *Collingwood Studies* 2 1995. Knox edited the *The Idea of Nature* so as to end with a conclusion (I.N.: 174–77) taken from Collingwood's lecture notes of 1940. Two alternative conclusions, 'the conclusion of 1934' and 'the conclusion of 1935' are appended to *The Principles of History* (1999).

41 P.H., p.3 f.n.

(1962).[42] (The first thorough analysis of *An Essay on Philosophical Method* did not appear until 1974[43]).

Outside of Collingwood's tripartite epistemological project, there stand six other books.

Religion and Philosophy (1916) was written 'in order to tidy up and put behind me a number of thoughts arising out of juvenile studies in theology ... '.[44]

Speculum Mentis (1924) 'is a record, not so very obscure in expression of a good deal of genuine thinking. If much of it now fails to satisfy me, that is because I have gone on thinking since I wrote it, and therefore much of it needs to be supplemented and qualified. There is not a great deal that needs to be retracted'.[45] It should be added that *Speculum Mentis* pre-dates 'Outlines of a Philosophy of History' (1928), the manuscript from which Collingwood dates the formulation of his mature philosophy of history.[46]

Outlines of a Philosophy of Art (1925) is a short work written at the request of the Clarendon Press. It was replaced by *The Principles of Art* (1938), as is made clear in the latter's preface.

First Mate's Log of a voyage to Greece in the schooner yacht 'Fleur de Lys' in 1939 (1940) was regarded by Collingwood as 'small beer', written 'to amuse'.[47] Known as Collingwood's 'happiest' work, its only philosophical interest is its brief discussion of utilitarianism and superstition.[48]

The New Leviathan (1942), Collingwood's final work, is 'an inquiry into civilization and the revolt against it'.[49] Whilst it does contain some interesting work on epistemology it is primarily a work of political philosophy. Although in failing health at the time of its writing Collingwood felt obliged to complete this work as his contribution to the war effort.

In *An Autobiography* (1939) Collingwood records the development of his thought. Its publication predates the publication of *An Essay on Metaphysics* (1940) although when he completed his final revision of *An Autobiography* he had already begun writing *An Essay on Metaphysics* and *The*

---

42   Also: Donagan, A. 'The Verification of Historical Theses' *Philosophical Quarterly*, 6 1956, pp.193–208

43   Martin, Rex 'Collingwood's Essay on *Philosophical Method*' *Idealistic Studies*, 4 1974, pp.224–50

44   A., p.43

45   A., p.56

46   A.,p.107 This manuscript is appended to *The Idea of History*. It may be inferred from *An Autobiography* that Collingwood dated the formulation of his mature philosophy of history to the years 1928 to 1930 — see A., pp.107 & 115.

47   F.M.L. Preface v

48   F.M.L. Chapter XVIII 'Monks and Morals', pp.145–53

49   N.L. 1.12.

Principles of History.[50] Therefore the only philosophical book begun after *An Autobiography* is *The New Leviathan.*

In the preface to *An Autobiography* Collingwood states that he wishes the reader 'to know that my rule in writing books is never to name a man except *honoris causa* – he criticises philosophies, but he aims to avoid criticism of named philosophers. It is generally acknowledged among Collingwood scholars that whilst Collingwood's account of his intellectual development is essentially accurate it is also somewhat terse. He does not, for example, acknowledge the philosophical influence of Giovanni Gentile, Benedetto Croce and Guido De Ruggiero, although he translated Croce's autobiography[51] and his *The Philosophy of Giambattista Vico;*[52] as well as De Ruggiero's *The History of European Liberalism;*[53] and (with Howard Hannay) De Ruggiero's *Modern Philosophy.*[54]

In *An Autobiography* Collingwood mentions two other works: *Truth and Contradiction,* written in 1917[55]; and *Libellus de Generatione, An Essay in Absolute Empiricism* written in 1920,[56] both of which he claimed to have destroyed – although *Libellus de Generatione* has since been recovered, as has chapter two of *Truth and Contradiction.*[57] (As both *Libellus de Generatione* and the surviving chapter of *Truth and Contradiction* are of the highest quality and interest, it is to be hoped that one day they might be published).

There also exists a relatively neglected dossier of lengthy correspondence between Collingwood and Gilbert Ryle upon Collingwood's support of the ontological 'proof', as set forth in *An Essay on Philosophical Method.* This correspondence is found in Ryle's *Collected Papers,*[58] and is also appended to the latest edition of *An Essay on Philosophical Method.*

In *An Autobiography* Collingwood states that his ideas on history were continually reworked and clarified:

> [They] were being worked out for nearly twenty years after I became a teacher of philosophy. They were repeatedly written down, corrected,

---

50 *An Essay on Metaphysics* was begun aboard the MV *Alcinous* on the outward leg of a voyage to Indonesia in October 1938 (see the editor's introduction to E.M. xv–xvi); *The Principles of History* was begun in Java in February 1939 (see the editors' introduction to P.H.lviii); and the last chapter of *An Autobiography* was re-written in March 1939 on the return voyage from Indonesia aboard the SS *Rhesus.*

51 Croce, Benedetto *An Autobiography,* 1927

52 Croce, Benedetto *The Philosophy of Giambattista Vico,* 1913

53 De Ruggiero, Guido *The History of European Liberalism,* 1927

54 De Ruggiero, Guido *Modern Philosophy,* 1920

55 A., pp.42 & 99

56 A., p.99

57 Boucher, D. 'The Significance of R.G. Collingwood's *Principles of History' Journal of the History of Ideas* vol. 58 no.2 1997, p.311

58 Ryle, Gilbert *Collected Papers,* Volume I, 1971

and rewritten; for whenever I have had a cub to lick into shape, my pen is the only tongue I have found useful.[59]

Hence the large quantity of unpublished essays, lecture notes and correspondence on this subject deposited at the Bodleian Library.

---

59   A., p.116

Chapter III

The Background to An Essay on Philosophical Method and An Essay on Metaphysics

Collingwood developed his views on metaphysics firstly in response to Oxford realism, and latterly in response to logical positivism. Contact with Oxford realism influenced the presentation of his ideas in *An Essay on Philosophical Method* (1933); and contact with logical positivism influenced the presentation of his ideas in *An Essay on Metaphysics* (1940). Collingwood's principal line of attack against both of these schools was that, in failing to examine the ground upon which they stood to criticise their predecessors, both Oxford realists and logical positivists were liable to anachronistically project their own preoccupations onto previous works of metaphysics: so that when Oxford realists criticised idealism and when logical positivists criticised metaphysics, they were in effect tilting against men of straw.

However, in making this point, Collingwood wished not simply to criticise his contemporaries for their lack of historical acumen: in exploring how his contemporaries had come to make naïve mistakes of historical interpretation, he *also* aimed to revise the concept of 'metaphysics'.

As I shall try to make clear in this chapter, it is the revision of metaphysics that unites *An Essay on Philosophical Method* and *An Essay on Metaphysics*. The concepts of philosophy and metaphysics discussed in these works form the respective subjects of Chapters IV and V — in relation to which the present chapter may be read by way of introduction.

The Critique of Oxford Realism

External things exist exactly as we know them.

This statement:

sounds realistic or idealistic according as one stresses the first three words of the dictum or the last four.[1]

Within a short space, it would be difficult to improve upon this summary of the seemingly perennial realism-idealism debate. However, the longevity of the debate, and the importance attached to it, is perhaps made more understandable if it is added that both idealists and realists have repeatedly charged their opponents with denying our knowledge of the external world.

In Oxford, at the time that Collingwood was writing, realists, under the unofficial leadership of John Cook Wilson, dominated the debate.

It was Collingwood's belief that, in their keenness to assert the ontological reality of the external world, the Oxford realists tended to neglect epistemological questions, questions of *how* we know what we do about the external world:

> The Oxford 'realists' talked as if knowing were a simple 'intuiting' or a simple 'apprehending' of some 'reality'. At Cambridge, Moore expressed, as I thought, the same conception when he spoke of the 'transparency' of the act of knowing; so did Alexander, at Manchester, when he described knowing as the simple 'compresence' of two things, one of which was a mind. What all these 'realists' were saying, I thought, was that the condition of a knowing mind is not indeed a passive condition, for it is actively engaged in knowing; but a 'simple' condition, one in which there are no complexities or diversities, nothing except just the knowing. They granted that a man who wanted to know something might have to work, in ways that might be very complicated, in order to 'put himself in a position' from which it could be 'apprehended'; but once the position had been attained there was nothing for him to do but 'apprehend' it, or perhaps fail to 'apprehend' it.[2]

Furthermore, Collingwood believed that, in dismissing their immediate predecessors[3] (sometimes erroneously) as absolute idealists, the Oxford realists tended to ignore their epistemological achievements.

It was against this background, standing as a maverick among the Oxford realists,[4] and seeking inspiration from an earlier generation of Oxford philosophers, that Collingwood wrote *An Essay on Philosophical Method* (1933).

> This I wrote during a long illness in 1932. It is my best book in matter; in style, I may call it my only book, for it is the only one I ever had the

---

1 Rescher, Nicholas 'Idealism' *The Cambridge Dictionary of Philosophy*, 2nd ed., 1999, p.412
2 A., pp.25–6
3 T.H. Green, F.H. Bradley and Bernard Bosanquet
4 Collingwood was not *totally* isolated from his Oxford contemporaries: in *The Magdalen Metaphysicals*, 1985, James Patrick discusses affinities between Collingwood's thought and that of Clement Webb, J.A. Smith and C.S. Lewis. There are also affinities between Collingwood's work and that of Ernst Cassirer, who taught at Oxford between 1933 and 1935.

time to finish as well as I knew how, instead of leaving it in a more or less rough state.[5]

As he relates in his autobiography,[6] Collingwood objected to the view that objects are simply 'apprehended' or 'intuited', and that in this manner objects are 'known' as they 'really' are. This view, that knowledge is simply 'apprehended', was seen by realists as correlative of the claim that 'knowing in no way alters or modifies the thing known'.[7]

H.A. Prichard presents this view in the following argument.

> Knowledge unconditionally presupposes that the reality known exists independently of the knowledge of it, and that we know it as it exists in this independence. It is simply *impossible* to think that any reality depends on our knowledge of it. If there is to be knowledge, there must first *be* something to be known. In other words, knowledge is essentially discovery, or finding what already is. If a reality could only be or come to be in virtue of some activity or process on the part of the mind, that activity or process would not be 'knowing', but 'making' or 'creating', and to make and to know must in the end be admitted to be mutually exclusive.[8]

The details of Prichard's arguments against Locke's indirect realism and Kant's transcendental idealism need not concern us.[9] Collingwood himself does not mention these arguments; rather, he focuses upon the view that the external world is simply 'apprehended'. In his opinion, this view typifies the epistemological naivety of the Oxford realists.

He relates in *An Autobiography* how, during his work for the Admiralty in the First World War he had slowly moved away from the realist position of Prichard and Cook Wilson until finally in 1920 in a paper to the Oxford Philosophical Society he placed himself in direct opposition to it. He reconstructs his argument in *An Autobiography*.

> I read a paper to my colleagues, trying to convince them that Cook Wilson's central positive doctrine, 'knowing makes no difference to what is known', was meaningless. I argued that any one who claimed, as Cook Wilson did, to be sure of this, was in effect claiming to know what he was simultaneously defining as unknown. For if you know that no difference is made to a thing è by the presence or absence of a certain condition c, you know what è is like with c, and also what è is like without c, and on comparing the two find no difference. This

5   A. p.118 The genesis of E.P.M. may be traced to the introduction to Collingwood's lectures on ethics preserved among his unpublished papers in the Bodleian Library: see 1929 Introduction to Moral Philosophy lectures – Dep 10; 1932 Introduction to Moral Philosophy lectures – Dep 7.

6   A., pp.44–52

7   Prichard, H.A. *Kant's Theory of Knowledge*, 1909, p.108

8   Prichard, H.A. *Kant's Theory of Knowledge*, 1909, p.108

9   The movement to which Prichard and Cook Wilson belonged is described by Matthieu Marion in 'Oxford Realism: Knowledge and Perception' in *The British Journal for the History of Philosophy* 2000 8(2), pp.299–338 & 8(3), pp.485–519.

involves knowing what è is like without *c*; in the present case, knowing what you defined as the unknown.[10]

In other words, Collingwood points out that the argument of Cook Wilson and Prichard has two contradictory premises: that things are both known and unknown. For to claim to know that knowing makes no difference to what is known itself involves the claim that we know what is not known. Therefore, the comparison between how things appear to be and how things are in-themselves, if it is based on the above argument, is based on a false dichotomy.

In Collingwood's view, this dichotomy persists in the work of the Oxford realists in the form of a 'copy theory' of knowledge, such that holds that a belief is true if there exists a fact corresponding to it. Such a theory begs the question of how we know that a belief corresponds to a fact.

In Collingwood's view, the way out of this debate will not be found via ontological questions, but rather in further examination of conceptual questions. What Collingwood admired in the previous generation of Oxford philosophers was their comparative neglect of ontological questions in favour of conceptual, but this was not noticed by Collingwood's realist contemporaries. For example, they appeared not to have noticed that F.H. Bradley[11] repudiated the label of 'idealist'.

In particular, Collingwood was struck by the misrepresentation of Bradley's position in Cook Wilson's lectures and the misrepresentation of Berkeley in G.E. Moore's 'Refutation of Idealism'. In his *Autobiography* he relates how initially he persuaded himself that these historical errors were of secondary importance to the philosophical issues discussed by Moore and Cook Wilson. However, inspired by his experiences of archaeological excavation, in which a site yields information in relation to the acuity of the archaeologist's questions, he gradually came to the conclusion that these historical errors arose as a consequence of the realists' epistemological naivety.

Collingwood claimed that the crucial missing factor in the realists' understanding of their predecessors was the recognition that: 'Every statement that anybody ever makes is made in answer to a question'.[12] Without understanding the question to which it stands as an answer no statement can be fully understood, for only after this has been recognised can the investigator hope to understand the questions underlying other philoso-

---

10   A., p.44 Collingwood makes the same point in the unpublished 'Central Problems in Metaphysics – Lectures written April 1935, for delivery T[rinity] T[erm] 1935': '… suppose it is true that we know things as they are independently of our knowing them, how could we ever *know* this to be true? Obviously we could never do so: for if we did, we should know what a thing is at the time when *ex hypothesi* we know nothing about it. Cook Wilson's principle is in effect a claim to know that which by definition is unknown: for it is an explicit statement that we know this unknown to be in no way different from the known.' Bodleian Library Dep 20/1

11   'the greatest philosopher of Green's school' A., p.19

12   E.M. p.23 'I include questions asked him by himself.' E.M., p.23.

phies. Without this recognition, an investigator will anachronistically and inappropriately project his own *implicit* questions and answers onto the work of contemporaries and predecessors, and as a result will fail to understand any work written on the basis of different presuppositions than his own.

Furthermore, failing to recognise that 'every statement that anybody ever makes is made in answer to a question', the realist is unable to explain the co-existence of different forms of knowledge. An implication of Oxford realism is that the fields of inquiry of different disciplines are mutually exclusive. Against this idea, Collingwood argues that different forms of knowledge may co-exist since they address conceptually different questions and express equally valid ways of viewing the same objects.

This argument has far-reaching repercussions. The mind-body problem, in Collingwood's view, results from the refusal to admit that philosophical concepts may legitimately overlap, and that there may be different, but equally legitimate, ways of viewing the same objects.

This idea runs continuously through Collingwood's philosophy. In *The New Leviathan* (1942) he summarises his view of the mind-body problem, as follows.

> 2.41. 'The problem of the relation between body and mind' is a bogus problem which cannot be stated without making a false assumption.
>
> 2.42. What is assumed is that man is partly body and partly mind. On this assumption questions arise about the relations between the two parts; and these prove unanswerable.
>
> 2.43. For man's body and man's mind are not two different things. They are one and the same thing, man himself, as known in two different ways.[13]

Unless it is recognised that different means of studying the same object may be of *equal* validity philosophers will continually revert to the fruitless comparison between how things appear to be and how things are 'in themselves'. Instead, philosophers should more fruitfully devote themselves to the investigation of overlapping philosophical concepts. (This idea is first presented in *An Essay on Philosophical Method* and is then developed in *An Essay on Metaphysics*, in which it is explicitly proposed that the metaphysician's task is to discover the conceptual foundations of distinct but coexistent, and possibly overlapping, absolute presuppositions).

Collingwood argues that if this project is shunned in favour of the attempted reduction of philosophical concepts to empirical classes, natural science and history will be classed according to the imposed boundaries of non-overlapping classes. He argues that such a form of empirical (non-overlapping) classification is appropriate to the methodology of natural science but not to the methodology of philosophy.

---

13   N.L., pp.10–11

As will be seen, the critique of realism that Collingwood offers in *An Essay on Philosophical Method* (1933) makes essentially the same point as the critique of logical positivism offered in *An Essay on Metaphysics* (1940): there is no such thing as presuppositionless knowledge.

The Critique of Logical Positivism

The school of logical positivism originated in Vienna in the 1920s (the Vienna Circle[14]), with another smaller group forming slightly later in Berlin.[15] (Wittgenstein, Popper and Quine all took a sympathetic interest in the work of the Vienna Circle, although they never classed themselves as members). Logical positivism became widely known in the English-speaking world via A.J. Ayer's *Language, Truth and Logic* (1936). In this work Ayer attempted to link the work of the logical positivists to that of Bertrand Russell, and to earlier British empiricists. Thus, for example, Ayer quotes with approval Hume's conclusion to an *Enquiry Concerning Human Understanding*:

> If we take in our hand any volume; of divinity, or school metaphysics, for instance; let us ask, Does it contain any abstract reasoning concerning quality or number? No. Does it contain any experimental reasoning concerning matter of fact and existence? No. Commit it then to the flames. For it can contain nothing but sophistry and illusion.[16]

The logical positivists' hostility to any form of metaphysics extended to Kant's belief in synthetic *a priori* knowledge (knowledge that is synthetic in its logical form yet that is justified *a priori*). Shlick pointed out that Einsteinian physics had since displaced Kant's prime examples of synthetic *a priori* knowledge, our knowledge of time and space.

Scepticism was also subjected to attack, via the logical positivists' favourite anti-metaphysical weapon, the principle of verification.[17] This asserted that the meaning of a proposition is its mode of verification; that the employed mode of verification determines what a proposition means. Claims that cannot be distinguished from each other on the basis of sensory evidence must coincide. Therefore, since Descartes' real world and Descartes' dream world are indistinguishable they are also synonymous: Descartes is troubled by a metaphysical misconception rather than a real problem.

The principle of verification was also used to provide a criterion for distinguishing between the two types of non-metaphysical propositions recognised by logical positivists—analytical (or tautological) and empiri-

---

14   Members included Moritz Schlick, Rudolf Carnap, Herbert Feigl, Kurt Gödel, Hans Hahn, Karl Menger, Otto Neurath and Friedrich Waissmann.

15   Members included Hans Reichenbach and Carl Hempel.

16   Quoted by Ayer in *Language, Truth and Logic* (1936) 2001, p.40

17   See Carnap, Rudolf 'Pseudo-problems in philosophy' (1928) in *The Logical Structure of the World and Pseudo-Problems in Philosophy*, 1967, trans. R.A. George

cal. They argued that universal propositions that cannot be classed as analytical are nonsense; and that the paradigm of knowledge is provided by natural science.

However, this was as much a position aspired to as argued for. The logical positivists themselves often made criticisms of the precise formulation of the principle of verification, and even the possibility of a precise formulation. For example, Hempel pointed out that no body of evidence establishes a universal scientific claim with *complete* certainty.[18] Bergmann argued that the commitment to natural science as providing a paradigm of certain knowledge must itself presuppose some form of metaphysical theory.[19]

In *An Essay on Metaphysics* Collingwood points out that — contrary to the claims of logical positivists — the absolute presuppositions underlying various discipline of inquiry are neither verifiable nor tautological but are nonetheless still meaningful. They possess logical efficacy to the practitioners of those disciplines — even though those practitioners may themselves be unaware of their influence. An example, given by Collingwood, is the absolute presupposition of pathology — that every event has a cause.

The metaphysician does not simply apprehend these absolute presuppositions but derives them from what is commonly agreed to be good practice within different disciplines. Thus the metaphysician does not simply describe nor simply prescribe — these aspects of his work are inseparable. His work is not *directly* normative, but by working from agreed examples of good practice, and making known the absolute presuppositions of a discipline, the metaphysician's work is *indirectly* normative.

This conception of metaphysics is illustrated by the following unpublished passage from Collingwood's 1928 lecture notes.

> This science [the philosophy of history] is practical or methodological in the sense of providing guidance in the pursuit of historical knowledge, in that it studies what history everywhere and always ought to be. It is easy to object that on this showing, history always is what it ought to be, and therefore the philosophy of history can have no practical value. This would be true, were it not that people who refrain from philosophical inquiries are generally more or less at the mercy of philosophical fallacies.[20]

Sometimes the practitioners of a particular intellectual discipline may bring to light their own absolute presuppositions, but, if they do so, they

---

18 Hempel, Carl 'Problems and Changes in the Empiricist Criterion of Meaning' 1950 *Revue Internationale de Philosophie* 4, pp.41–63

19 Bergmann, G. *The Metaphysics of Logical Positivism* 1954. The criticism has also been made that the principle of verification is itself not verifiable (See, for example, White, Allan R. *Methods of Metaphysics* 1987: 109). Crispin Wright provides a thorough review of criticisms of the principle of verification in 'The Verification Principle: Another Puncture, Another Patch' *Mind* 98, 1989: 611–22.

20 I.H. p.492

do so as metaphysicians rather than as natural scientists, historians and so forth. For although the absolute presuppositions of a discipline possesses logical efficacy, and although their discovery is beneficial for the practitioners of its overlying discipline, their nature does not explicitly figure in answer to any question that will arise within that discipline.

To recap, the possibility of different though equally valid ways of studying the world is not recognised by either Oxford realism or logical positivism. However this possibility is allowed for in *An Essay on Philosophical Method* and *An Essay on Metaphysics*, in which Collingwood argues that different disciplines may view 'reality' from different, but non-conflicting, absolute presuppositions. In Collingwood's view it is the metaphysician's task to make these absolute presuppositions explicit.

Chapter IV

An Essay on Philosophical Method

The Methods and Subject of Philosophy

Collingwood states that his primary purpose in writing *An Essay on Philosophical Method* is to consider the question *'what is philosophy?'*.

He lists three means by which an answer might be approached.

1. '[T]o define the proper object of philosophical thought, and then to deduce from this the proper methods that it should follow'.[1]

2. To state what philosophy aims to achieve, and then lay down a programme to achieve it.[2]

3. To characterise philosophy not by the goals that it has achieved or hopes to achieve but as an activity.

In Collingwood's opinion both (1) and (2) are disadvantaged by their unjustified assumption that philosophy has already reached its goal, or that all philosophers aspire to reach the same goal.

Collingwood prefers the third option.[3] He argues that (3) characterises not only the approach by which an answer is obtainable but also the answer itself. For the question 'what is philosophy?' is itself part of philosophy. It is through its self-reflective nature that philosophy perpetuates itself. No other discipline is self-reflective to such a degree as philosophy; indeed it is this that distinguishes philosophy from other disciplines. Thus it is that although natural scientists and historians may reflect upon their work, insofar as they study the theory of natural science and the theory of history, they study these things in their capacity as philosophers rather than as natural scientists and historians.[4]

In presenting this argument, Collingwood has, in a rudimentary sense, already answered the question 'what is philosophy?' within the first three

---

1   E.P.M., p.2
2   E.P.M., p.3
3   In this respect Collingwood's view is similar to Wittgenstein's: '4.112 … Philosophy is not a body of doctrine but an activity …', *Tractatus Logico-Philosophicus*, p. 25.
4   E.P.M., pp.1–2

pages of his book: philosophy is self-reflective activity *par excellence*. For philosophy, unlike any other discipline, is obliged to justify its starting point.[5]

This can be done only if the arguments of philosophy, instead of having an irreversible direction from principles to conclusions, have a reversible one, the principles establishing the conclusions and the conclusions reciprocally establishing the principles.[6]

In accordance with, and in recognition of, the nature of philosophy, he states that in further descriptions of philosophy he will not attempt the impossible task of drawing a rigid dividing line between the methodology of philosophy and the subject matter of philosophy — for philosophy has no subject matter that is uniquely its own. When the philosopher studies other intellectual disciplines he studies that which is already self-reflective to some (lesser) degree. But when the philosopher studies philosophy his subject matter is the methods of philosophy, and his methods are his subject.

If the philosopher has the courage to accept this conclusion, he will be rewarded by the results that ensue when he turns to the analysis of other disciplines: for acceptance of philosophy's reversible direction is, as it were, an entry ticket that enables the philosopher to perform useful work when his gaze turns outward to the analysis of non-philosophical practices.

Collingwood states that his aim in writing *An Essay on Philosophical Method* is not to provide a history of philosophy. Although he will refer to past philosophers, his references will be selected purely on the basis of making his own arguments as clear as possible. He argues that it is this normative intent that distinguishes the philosopher from the historian of philosophy.[7] In other words, although the philosopher who wishes to ascribe a particular philosophical method may find it necessary or useful, for purposes of clarification, to refer selectively to his predecessors, he is under no obligation to expand these references into a comprehensive history of philosophical method.[8]

He states that he wishes to continue the tradition of Socrates of making implicit knowledge explicit: that is to say, to act as 'midwife to the truth'.

> This technique as he [Socrates] himself recognised, depended on a principle which is of great importance to any theory of philosophical method: the principle that in a philosophical inquiry what we are try- ing to do is not to discover something of which until now we have been ignorant, but to know better something which in some sense we knew already; not to know it better in the sense of coming to know more

---

5   E.P.M. p.159
6   E.P.M. p.160
7   E.P.M. p.4
8   E.P.M. p.10

about it, but to know it better in the sense of coming to know it in a different and better way—actually instead of potentially, or explicitly instead of implicitly, or in whatever terms the theory of knowledge chooses to express the difference: The difference has been a familiar fact ever since Socrates pointed it out.[9]

Collingwood's deliberate revival of the Socratic idea that philosophy can only make explicit that which in some confused and implicit manner we know already, can be seen as his answer to the paradox of analysis.

This paradox was later summarised by C.H. Langford as follows:

> If the verbal expression representing the analysandum has the same meaning as the verbal expression representing the analysans, the analysis states a bare identity and is trivial: but if two verbal expressions do not have the same meaning, the analysis is incorrect.[10]

Collingwood sidesteps this problem; for he claims that philosophy does not so much describe or explain a concept as explicate it. The act of exposition, or analysis, of a philosophical concept itself provides the 'definition', in that enlightenment is received not simply at the end of the exposition but *in the course of* the exposition.

An exposition is not begun from a state of absolute ignorance but with a 'dim and confused knowledge, or a knowledge definite enough in some parts but confused in others, and in others fading away to the verge of complete nescience'.[11] Some element of circularity (or question begging) is therefore unavoidable: but the analysis may nonetheless provide elucidation by exhibiting the relations that pertain between the various components of the subject of study. In other words, in Collingwood's opinion the circularity of analysis is virtuous, for *in the course of* analysis the subject of study will come to be *better* known.

Michael Beaney provides the following succinct summary of Collingwood's position:

> In effect, his position can be seen as a synthesis of the 'deductive' and the 'analytic' conception of philosophy. He agrees with the former that philosophy should be systematic, but disagrees that it should not be answerable to experience. He agrees with the latter that our starting-point is our ordinary beliefs, but disagrees that we should do nothing more than 'analyse' those beliefs.[12]

Although in some respects we do not go beyond our initial beliefs, yet our beliefs develop in the course of analysis.

This view of philosophical analysis is also expounded in the following passage from Collingwood's unpublished manuscripts.

---

9   E.P.M. p.11

10   *The Philosophy of G.E. Moore* (ed. P.A. Schilpp) 1942, p.323. See also Plato *Meno* 80.

11   E.P.M., p.96

12   Beaney, Michael 'Collingwood's Critique of Analytic Philosophy' *Collingwood and British Idealism Studies* 2001, Vol. VIII, p.114

> [T]he change is from knowing things in a dark or dim or confused way to knowing them in a clear or luminous or distinct way. I do not mean that we come to know them with any greater force or conviction. At the beginning of our philosophical inquiries we may feel as perfectly convinced as it is possible to be, but in general we do not know what it is that we are so profoundly convinced of. What we do by these inquiries is to learn our own minds, in the sense of learning what it is that we really think or really want. From this point of view it might be said that philosophical inquiry and argument cannot change people's opinions but can and does change their opinions as to what their opinions really are.[13]

Collingwood claims that Socrates' view of analysis was inspired by the ancient Greek view of mathematics. This was his model for dialectical reasoning: but the method by which one metaphysical hypothesis might be judged superior to another was unclear — mathematics could not elucidate this matter. Descartes, likewise, sought to model metaphysics (and natural science) upon mathematical principles. For example, in the second part of his *Discourse*:

> [Descartes] described the lessons he learnt there under four heads: the canons of evidence, division, order, and exhaustion. Nothing was to be assented to, unless evidently known to be true; every subject-matter was to be divided into the smallest possible parts, each to be dealt with separately; each part was to be considered in its right order, the simplest first; and no part was to be omitted in reviewing the whole.[14]

However, although these methods are profitable in the case of mathematics, in natural science Descartes' method underestimates the importance of experiment. In metaphysics it is still less sufficient. Collingwood argues that, in their attitude towards mathematics, both Socrates and Descartes make the mistake of either (1) defining the proper object of philosophical thought, or (2) stating what philosophy aims to achieve; and deducing from this the means by which philosophy should proceed.

Collingwood credits Kant (in his *Critique of Pure Reason*) with resolving the difference between philosophical and mathematical methodology. According to Collingwood's reading of him, Kant argued that the following characteristics apply to philosophy but not to mathematics.

Philosophy knows no demonstrations: its proofs are not demonstrative but acroamatic: in other words, the difference between mathematical proof and philosophical is that in the former you proceed from point to point in a chain of grounds and consequents, in the latter you must always

---

13   Lectures on Moral Philosophy, 1929 (Quoted in Connelly, J. 'Metaphysics and Method: A Necessary Unity in the Philosophy of R.G. Collingwood' in *Storia, Antropologia e Scienze del Linguaggio* 5/1-2, (ed. Bulzoni), 1990, pp.33-156)

14   E.P.M. p.17

be ready to go back and revise your premises when errors, undetected in them, reveal themselves in the conclusion.[15]

Collingwood refers here to Kant's use of transcendental, or regressive arguments, in which the premises of a philosophical argument are validated by the argument that is demonstrated to follow from them, rather than being required to demonstrate their prior reliance upon a separate argument of 'superjustification'. Giuseppina D'Oro elaborates upon this idea, as follows.

> A transcendental argument ... is one in which the premises are validated through the process of argument and have no independent justification. The distinction between a valid and a sound argument, therefore, does not apply to a transcendental argument. Transcendental arguments, unlike deductive arguments, establish certain conclusions by accepting the interdependence of beliefs and the circularity of knowledge claims. An important distinction between deductive and transcendental arguments, therefore, has to do with the fact that whereas transcendental arguments accept and possibly exploit the interdependence of belief, deductive arguments do not. This might explain why deductive arguments feature in foundationalist philosophers, whereas transcendental arguments feature in anti-foundationalist philosophers.[16]

In Collingwood's view, transcendental arguments are virtuously circular — they make use of philosophy's reversible direction — with neither the conclusion nor any premise of the argument being considered as finally immune from revision. By their use we come to know, 'in a different and better way'[17], what in some sense we know already. So although nothing follows from a transcendental argument when applied by the philosopher to philosophy itself — for philosophy has no subject matter that is uniquely its own — the same transcendental (reversible) argument as applied to the analysis of other disciplines may be informative. It may reveal the presuppositions underlying successful inquiries.

Collingwood argues that a philosophical theory that relies upon a transcendental argument can never be entirely deductive: for experience vaguely anticipates a philosopher's conclusions, and his reasoning follows. Indeed the philosopher's conclusions and the principles at work in his reasoning may be checked against our intuitions.

If this is so, the direction of the argument in respect of principles and conclusions is reversible, each being established by appeal to the other; but this is not a vicious circle, because the word established here means raised to a higher grade of knowledge: what was a mere observation is now not

---

15   E.P.M. pp.22-3
16   D'Oro, Giuseppina *Collingwood and the Metaphysics of Experience*, 2002, pp.93–4
17   E.P.M., p.161

merely observed but understood; what was a merely abstract principle is verified by appeal to facts.[18]

Philosophy therefore contains both a critical element – in its refutation of previous theories – and an analytical element – in its datum of implicit knowledge.

In his advocacy of transcendental arguments, Collingwood follows Kant. However, following Hegel, he criticises Kant as follows. He describes the *Critique of Pure Reason* as having two aims: the reform of the methodology of metaphysics; and, guided by this methodology, the provision of a substantive philosophy. However, the relation between these two projects is never made clear: 'in one sense critical philosophy was a part of metaphysics, though in another it was an introduction to it'.[19] (Kant originally described the *Critique of Pure Reason* as only a 'propaedeutic' to the system of pure reason,[20] but he later withdrew this remark[21]). In Kant's work the relation between the study of understanding and the study of the objects of understanding is never made fully clear. Although at times Kant suggests that he wishes to provide a definitive methodology, in order that 'metaphysics, reformed and reorganised, would advance with the same sure tread as mathematics and the science of nature'[22], at other times he suggests that metaphysics would expire if philosophy became sufficiently self-critical.

Whilst retaining the technique of transcendental argument, Collingwood aims to clear away this confusion by stating that philosophy has no subject that is uniquely its own, but, rather, it is an activity – that studies the external world indirectly, by studying *other* intellectual disciplines. It makes explicit their different ways of looking at the world, but it does not offer an external justification for existing conceptual schemes.

When Collingwood argues that philosophy is unique, by virtue of its 'reversible direction' he means that it is uniquely reliant upon transcendental arguments. In this it differs from 'exact' (deductive) sciences, such as geometry and mathematics, and empirical (inductive) sciences, such as geology.

Exact science relies upon certain presuppositions as a necessary condition of any inquiry. It also makes certain suppositions that, when applied to the data of that science, yield conclusions. It is because we accept scientists' suppositions that we accept their conclusions, but the reverse is not the case.

---

18   E.P.M., p.163
19   E.P.M., p.21
20   Kant, Immanuel *Critique of Pure Reason*: A11/B25
21   See Gardner, Sebastian *Kant and the Critique of Pure Reason*, 1999, p.340
22   E.P.M., p.20

This irreversibility is a necessary attribute of exact science: it can only argue forwards, from principles to conclusions, and can never turn round and argue backwards, from conclusions to principles, whether these are understood as special principles peculiar to itself and forming part of its own body, or general principles belonging to the body of logic. To guard against a misunderstanding, it may be remarked that though the argument of an exact science can never be reversible in respect of its principles, it may be and generally is reversible in respect of its data; given the axioms, which are equally necessary in both cases, we can argue that because the sides are equal the angles at the base are equal, or that because the angles at the base are equal the sides are equal.[23]

By contrast, the philosopher does not regard any part of philosophy as self-evident.

Collingwood suggests that when the metaphysician subjects the methodology of other disciplines to impartial questioning, by virtue of philosophy's reversible direction the principles of that discipline may be revealed, even though they may have been previously unknown to the practitioners of that discipline. Moreover, although philosophy does not progress from sheer ignorance to final certainty, progress in describing the conceptual foundations of other disciplines is nonetheless possible:

> To reject one account of a philosophical matter is to accept the responsibility of giving a better account of it; and hence in philosophy, whatever may be the case elsewhere, it is a rule of sound method that every negation in this special sense implies an affirmation.[24]

The means by which the metaphysician carries out this work are described in greater detail in *An Essay on Metaphysics*. But in *An Essay on Philosophical Method* it is made clear that metaphysics is ideally suited to this work — for, since it has no subject matter that is uniquely its own, it is impartial. It is also made clear that, in revealing the underlying categorical elements of different disciplines, the metaphysician is making explicit different ways of studying the world — different conceptual outlooks, that may be applied to the same objects.

Thus for example the botanist who studies a flower and the artist who studies a flower study the same 'object' but from different grounds. The metaphysician must accept this fact: he has no ground to dictate that various disciplines of inquiry should be distinguished according to the objects of their study. He can only observe the different methods of different disciplines and thence describe their different (epistemic) viewpoints.

---

23 E.P.M., p.154
24 E.P.M., p.106. Introduction to Moral Philosophy Lectures (1929) ' … philosophical inquiry and argument cannot change people's opinions, but can and do change their opinions as to what their opinions really are'. Bodleian Dep 10

Collingwood believes that, in contrast to the approach outlined above, Oxford Realism does not account for itself—it does not examine the ground upon which it stands. Indeed it sees no need to account for itself, since it maintains that knowledge is simply 'apprehended'. This approach leaves the relationship between itself and other disciplines unexamined, and so leaves open the possibility of philosophy absorbing, or being absorbed by, other forms of knowledge.

Although I am in agreement with Collingwood that philosophy is an activity, and that philosophy's reversible direction may be turned to its advantage when the philosopher turns to study other disciplines — there is room for doubt as to whether Collingwood himself *fully* accepts the idea proposed at the beginning of his argument that philosophy is an activity that 'never with any of us reaches its ultimate goal',[25] i.e. it never reaches firm ground. For, later in *An Essay on Philosophical Method*, Collingwood claims that the ontological argument (which he claims is a form of transcendental argument) demonstrates that the philosopher must presuppose that the object of his studies is 'real'.[26] I shall argue in Chapter VI that Collingwood's version of the ontological argument is vulnerable to the same criticisms that have been made against Saint Anselm's ontological argument. (Collingwood sees this argument as the foundation of his philosophy, whereas I see it as a fly in the ointment).

The Scale of Forms

According to Collingwood the philosopher is concerned with something universal, as opposed to the first order scientist, who is concerned with something individual: a philosophical concept characterises the whole of 'reality' from a particular viewpoint. He argues that to give an account of the universal is the business of logic. 'Traditional logic regards the concept as uniting a number of different things into a class'.[27] For example, 'the concept colour unites all the individual colours of all individual coloured things into a class of which they are members'[28]; generically, the concept 'also unites the specific colours red, orange, yellow, green, and so forth into a genus of which they are the species'.[29] Thus Collingwood claims that 'concepts can and should be considered from two different points of view: extension and intension'.[30]

---

25   E.P.M., p.3
26   E.P.M., p.125
27   E.P.M. p. 27
28   E.P.M. p.27
29   E.P.M. pp.27–8
30   E.P.M. *lxxxiii* (introduction by James Connelly and Giuseppina D'Oro)

The classes used by biologists, physicists and mathematicians all conform to the traditional theory of classification and division, in that they do not overlap each other, but in philosophy the class of one genus may entirely overlap another i.e. the class of one genus may be applied to the same objects as constitute the class of another genus. In fact, this is the characteristic that attracts the philosopher to his subject matter: he is interested in classifying different disciplines in such a way as to respect their different overlapping interests. Collingwood claims that overlapping, rather than mutually exclusive, classes indicate a logical structure that is peculiar to philosophical concepts: for example, in ethics, the concept of 'right' includes and makes explicit the positive element of 'expedient' but rejects the negative; likewise the concept of 'expedient' makes explicit the positive element of 'pleasant' but rejects the negative.[31]

Assuming that 'an overlap of classes is characteristic of the philosophical concept',[32] Collingwood asks what methodological consequences follow from this. His answer is that: 'No method can be used in philosophy which depends for its validity on their mutual exclusion'.[33] In other words, the classificatory aims and techniques that are appropriate to the natural sciences are inappropriate to philosophy. If these methods were to be applied to philosophy, a generic concept would be built upon the margin that is as yet unaffected by an overlap. Such a practice would fall foul of 'the fallacy of precarious margins'.[34]

> The margin unaffected by overlap 'is necessarily precarious, because once the overlap is admitted in principle there is no ground for assuming that it will stop at any particular point; and the only sound canon of method is so to conduct the inquiry that its results would stand firm however far the overlap extended.[35]

On the other hand, in avoiding this fallacy, the philosopher should not assume that because there is no difference in the extension of two concepts, there is no distinction between the concepts themselves. Collingwood terms this error 'the fallacy of identified coincidents'.[36] He suggests that realism is equally prone to both of these fallacies for it does not admit the coexistence of different but equally valid epistemic viewpoints.

In Collingwood's view, both of these fallacies originate in the principle appropriate to natural science but not to philosophy — that the instances of

---

31 E.P.M. *xvi–xxi* 'The same act may be both pleasant and right ...' 1932 Introduction to Moral Philosophy Lectures, Dep 7, Bodleian Library. In *The Principles of Art* (1938) Collingwood argues that the concept of 'art' overlaps the concept of 'craft' — P.A.: 22n.

32 E.P.M. p.45

33 E.P.M. p.46

34 E.P.M. p.48

35 E.P.M. p.48

36 E.P.M. p.49

a generic concept can be divided into mutually exclusive classes. He terms this false principle 'the fallacy of false disjunction':

> Applied positively, this yields the fallacy of precarious margins …
> Applied negatively, it yields the fallacy of identified coincidents.[37]

He argues that in philosophy, unlike natural science, it is permissible to 'speak of 'a distinction without a difference', that is, a distinction in the concepts without a difference in the instances'.[38] It may therefore be inferred that classification is not the end goal of philosophical method but a means whereby coexisting viewpoints might be distinguished.

If the hypothesis is entertained that the overlap of classes that is found in philosophy is not simply an illusion, then we must forsake two assumptions that might otherwise have been imported from natural science:

> first, that the object of which philosophy is in search will turn out to be a classificatory system; secondly, that this object will turn out to be an aggregate of parts.[39]

The latter assumption would deter the philosopher from detecting logical relations between one concept and another.

Collingwood also stresses that the detection of overlaps and of the relations that pertain between them is a principle of method that leads to necessarily revisable results, rather than final certainty.

> Thinking philosophically, whatever else it means, means constantly revising one's starting point in the light of one's conclusions and never allowing oneself to be controlled by any cast-iron rule whatever.[40]

This is consistent with the observation with which *An Essay on Philosophical Method* began — that philosophy is self-reflective to the maximum degree, since its subject matter, whatever else it may include, also includes itself.

That is not to say that there is no overlap between philosophical and non-philosophical concepts, but in such instances — when, for example, a psychologist studies 'the mind' or a physicist studies 'matter' — the non-philosophical phase of a concept will be studied. In other words, it will be studied in isolation from any other overlapping concepts.

> It appears from these instances that when a concept has a dual significance, philosophical and non-philosophical, in its non-philosophical phase it qualifies a limited part of reality, whereas in its philosophical it leaks or escapes out of these limits and invades the neighbouring regions, tending at last to colour our thought of reality as a whole. As a

---

37 E.P.M., p.49
38 E.P.M., p.50 'In general, then I suggest that the distinctions recognised within a given philosophical concept are mutually inclusive distinctions, whereas those of non-philosophical concepts are mutually exclusive.' 1932 Introduction to Moral Philosophy Lectures, Dep 7, Bodleian Library
39 E.P.M., pp.52–3
40 E.P.M., p.52

non-philosophical concept it observes the rules of classification, its instances forming a class separate from other classes; as a philosophical concept it breaks these rules, and the class of its instances overlaps those of its co-ordinate species.[41]

Thus, philosophical concepts exemplify particular ways of looking at the world that may be universally applied, but that are not mutually exclusive. In ethics, the philosopher himself formulates his concepts in response to the particular problem that has arisen; in metaphysics, the philosopher attempts to recover the philosophical concepts underlying other disciplines. Broadly speaking, *An Essay on Philosophical Method* tends to concentrate upon the former task—in that examples of overlapping concepts are drawn from ethics; whereas *An Essay on Metaphysics* tends to concentrate upon the latter.

Collingwood claims that the overlap that exists between one philosophical concept and another is not due to a difference of degree; nor is it due to a difference in kind—such as the distinctions within the genus sensation between seeing, hearing, smelling. The philosopher is ultimately uninterested in either differences in kind or differences in degree: he is interested in their coincidence.

Differences of degree coincide with differences in kind in a 'scale of forms'.[42] Thus, for example, 'pleasant' and 'expedient' are two different forms of the concept 'good' that differ from each other *both* in kind *and* in the degree to which they exemplify 'good'.

> In such a system of specifications the two sets of differences are so connected that whenever the variable, increasing or decreasing, reaches certain critical points on the scale, one specific form disappears and is replaced by another.[43]

An example of such a 'scale of forms' is to be found in Aristotle's philosophy, 'when he distinguishes the vegetable, animal and human 'souls' as three forms of life arranged on a scale so that each includes its predecessor and adds to it something new'.[44] It is this idea, relieved of applications within natural science, that Collingwood claims is of continued relevance to philosophy. Moreover, he claims that philosophy, and no other subject, is characterised by its use of this form of classification.

He argues that although there is a similarity between the philosopher's scale of forms and the natural scientist's arrangement of ice, water and steam in a scale of forms (in that both make use of the double criterion of degree and kind), this similarity is superficial. For in a non-philosophical scale of forms the essence of water, for example, is not considered to vary

---

41   E.P.M., p.35
42   James Connelly (*Metaphysics, Method and Politics* p.95) points out that a scale of forms is equivalent to what in *An Essay on Metaphysics* (p.68) is termed a *catalogue raisonné*.
43   E.P.M., p.57
44   E.P.M. p.58

according to the form taken by H_2O. In a philosophical scale of forms the essence of a concept is considered to vary according to the forms that it takes.

> The result of this identification is that every form, so far as it is low in the scale, is to that extent an imperfect or inadequate specification of the generic essence, which is realised with progressive adequacy as the scale is ascended.[45]

Thus it is that the concept of 'Good' varies — in kind *and* degree — as a philosophical scale is ascended (from 'pleasant' to 'expedient' *etcetera*), in a different manner than the concept of 'heat' or 'water' varies upon the natural scientist's scale. 'Heat' varies only in degree as a scale is ascended; 'water' varies only in 'kind' as the degree of heat is ascended: but 'Good' — as it ascends a philosophical scale of forms — varies in both degree and kind.

Collingwood claims that differences of degree of non-philosophical concepts, such as heat, can be measured (within a known degree of error), whereas differences of degree of philosophical concepts cannot be measured. The reason that differences of degree as applied to philosophical concepts cannot be measured is that they are at once *also* differences in kind. In the specification of a philosophical concept the difference in kind between the various forms in which the generic essence is embodied coincides with the difference in degree to which the various forms embody it.[46] Thus, for example, a philosophical concept such as 'bad', is opposed to good *and* is *also* distinct from good. By contrast, in the case of a non-philosophical concept such as H_2O differences in degree, for example in temperature, are related to but do not necessarily coincide with a difference in kind, between steam, water and ice. Thus to some degree water may vary in temperature without turning to steam or to ice.

In the classificatory systems of natural science distinction and opposition are two mutually exclusive kinds of relation, but in philosophy this is not the case.[47] That differences in kind and degree coincide in this manner elucidates Collingwood's earlier contention that in a philosophical scale of forms the essence of a concept is considered to vary according to the forms that it takes — whereas we do not consider that the essence of water (H_2O) varies according to the form that it takes.

> If in philosophical thought every difference of kind is also a difference of degree, the specifications of a philosophical concept are bound to form a scale; and in this scale their common essence is bound to be realised differentially in degree as well as differentially in kind.[48]

---

45   E.P.M. p.61
46   E.P.M., p.74
47   E.P.M. p.76
48   E.P.M. p. 77

Thus it is that when one example of pleasure or beauty or goodness is judged to exceed another, it is judged to do so *both* in degree *and* in kind. Moreover, Collingwood argues that through consideration of how different sorts of pleasure overlap each other on a scale of forms it becomes possible to see how it is:

> better to be Socrates dissatisfied than a fool satisfied; the pleasures of Socrates, even if inferior to the fool's by Bentham's quantitative tests, are superior in quality, so that they deserve the name of pleasure in a sense in which the fool's do not.[49]

He argues that utilitarian philosophers tend to recognise only differences in degree or only differences in kind rather than their conjunction.[50] The former of these errors he terms 'the fallacy of calculation'[51] — the fallacy that philosophical concepts are susceptible of measurement. The latter of these errors he terms 'the fallacy of indifference' — the fallacy that all pleasures are equally pleasant; all good acts are equally good, and so forth.

The ethical consequences of the scale of forms, in which the concepts of good and bad overlap in degree and in kind, are as follows. Collingwood first describes the overlap of good over bad.

> There is no crime or vice which does not appear to the person who embraces it as good — good within its own limits and in the special way in which at the moment goodness appeals to him; no error so double-dyed that the person who falls into it does not for the time being think it true; no work of art so exquisitely false in taste that it may not be thought beautiful. The people who accept and admire these things are deceived, but not purely and simply deceived; we can see for ourselves, if we put ourselves at their point of view, that a person satisfied with so low a degree and kind of goodness, truth, or beauty is in these cases really getting what he asks, and is deceived only in thinking that goodness truth, or beauty contains no more than that. The vice really does achieve something good: relief from pain, good fellowship, or a sense of emancipation. The error really does enshrine some truth, the bad work of art does contain some beauty.[52]

On the other hand, bad can also be seen as overlapping good.

> The lowest case in the scale, when compared with the next above it, not only loses its own intrinsic goodness and acquires the character of badness, but it actually becomes identical with evil in general; in it the abstract idea of evil finds a concrete embodiment, and at this point in the scale the achievement of goodness simply means the negation of

---

49   E.P.M., pp.79–80

50   The Oxford ethicist William David Ross may perhaps have had some influence in the development of these ideas. In *The Right and the Good* (1930) Ross criticises utilitarianism on the grounds that it recognises only one type of moral duty. Ross argues that different kinds of good should be arranged in a scale of forms. In *An Essay on Philosophical Method*, p.78, in one of his very few *direct* references to his contemporaries, Collingwood mentions in particular chapter vi of *The Right and the Good*.

51   E.P.M., p.80

52   E.P.M., p.83

this one thing. Examples are common and familiar. Every particular way of being good involves a struggle against some specific form of evil, some besetting sin; and in such a situation this besetting sin appears not as one alternative form of wrongdoing but as wrongdoing itself.[53]

Thus the philosophical scale of forms is a relation at once of distinction and of opposition. Perhaps the most obvious advantage of this scale of forms is that it accounts for and legitimates our use of such terms as 'good' and 'bad' as *both* relative *and* absolute terms. Each member of the scale is good in itself but bad in relation to the one above. This advantage is made clear as follows.

Each term in the scale, therefore, sums up the whole scale to that point. Whenever we stand in the scale, we stand at a culmination. Infinity as well as zero can thus be struck out of the scale, not because we never reach a real embodiment of the generic concept, but because the specific form at which we stand is the generic concept itself, so far as our thought yet conceives it. The proximate form, next below where we stand, is from this point of view at once the alternative possible way of specifying this concept, and the wrong way of specifying it; opposite to the way which we think the right way, and therefore opposite to the concept itself.[54]

Within a foundationalist philosophy the last sentence might be considered to beg the question of what *is* the right way to think of a concept. But, according to Collingwood, philosophy can only inform us of that which in some sense we already know. If this is accepted, the scale of forms provides us with, at least, an apparatus whereby disputants might resolve their differences.

He argues that in the derivation and application of a philosophical scale of forms the philosopher does not work from a single fixed and known point, but he must nonetheless grant that we are not completely in error. It is for this reason that he suggests that moral philosophy, in common with the rest of philosophy, makes use of transcendental arguments — 'giving an account of how people think they ought to behave'.[55] In making this explicit the moral philosopher performs simultaneously a descriptive and a normative act. Likewise in metaphysics, the philosopher plays a similar role (both normative and descriptive) in making clear how the practitioners of different intellectual disciplines view the world.

A philosopher deals in hypotheticals only to the extent that the affirmation of one theory 'must be supported by considering what the conse-

---

53 E.P.M., p.84. 1929 Introduction to Moral Philosophy Lectures — Good and Bad 'co-exist dialectically' Bodleian Library, Dep 10

54 E.P.M., p.89

55 E.P.M., p.132

quences would have been, had any of the alternative theories been true'.[56] But the hypothetical element in a philosophical theory will always be subsidiary to the categorical (the descriptive and normative element).

Collingwood notes that a complete theory of knowledge would have to examine relations between science, in which propositions are hypothetical, and philosophy, in which propositions are categorical. This subject is pursued in *An Essay on Metaphysics* (1940). He argues that an overlap between hypothetical and categorical propositions also exists in science, in that 'the purely hypothetical propositions forming the body of science involve certain categorical elements which are necessary to their being but form no part of their essence *qua* science'.[57] These categorical elements – explored further in *An Essay on Metaphysics* in the form of absolute presuppositions – are the means by which philosophy and science are related, in that philosophy makes these categorical elements explicit, and explores the relationship between one categorical element and another.

In the next chapter I shall examine Collingwood's view as to how the philosopher might make these categorical elements explicit. However, it should first be noted that there is perhaps an unjustified tendency in *An Essay on Philosophical Method* to assume that what applies in ethics applies *mutatis mutandis* to every other branch of philosophy, for there is a difference between ethics and other branches of philosophy that Collingwood tends to overlook: the philosopher himself encounters ethical dilemmas, at first hand, whether or not this is his special field. This suggests that the arrangement of moral concepts upon a scale of forms may ultimately be a response to the immediate need to choose between one course of action and another.[58] Elsewhere, although there is a prescriptive element to his work, there is no obvious immediate need for the philosopher to choose between the categorical elements of history and natural science, and so there is perhaps no obvious need to relate these categorical elements upon a scale of forms. That is to say, although the foundations of history and natural science may be, in Collingwood's vocabulary, 'consupponible'[59] – they may overlap without logical conflict – it need not be assumed that the foundations of history are in some way superior or more fundamental than those of natural science, or *vice versa*.

---

56   E.P.M., p.133

57   E.P.M., p.135

58   Collingwood touches in passing upon the immediacy of ethical problems in 'The Theory of Historical Cycles' *Antiquity*, December 1927, p.435, remarking: 'There is no sense in using terms like good or bad except of persons or things, that come into practical relations with one's own will.'

59   E.M., p.66

Chapter V

An Essay on Metaphysics

By the time Collingwood came to write *An Essay on Metaphysics* in 1939 a new 'enemy' had appeared in his sights — logical positivism. *An Essay on Metaphysics* was written partly in deliberate opposition to the logical positivists' dismissal of metaphysics; and partly to develop and clarify an idea first mentioned in *An Essay on Philosophical Method*, namely that 'the purely hypothetical propositions forming the body of science involve certain categorical elements which are necessary to their essence *qua* science'.[1] These two aims complement each other in Collingwood's 'theory of presupposition'. The vocabulary employed in the presentation of this theory, and its manner of presentation, were chosen so that its implications would be clear to logical positivists.

Collingwood opposed the logical positivists' argument that metaphysical claims, being neither analytical nor verifiable, are neither true nor false but nonsense. He characterised their position as follows:

> Any proposition which cannot be verified by appeal to observed facts is a pseudo-proposition. Metaphysical propositions cannot be verified by appeal to observed facts. Therefore metaphysical propositions are pseudo-propositions, and therefore nonsense.[2]

This characterisation approximates to Ayer's position in *Language, Truth and Logic*:

> I require of an empirical hypothesis, not indeed that it should be conclusively verifiable, but that some possible sense-experience should be relevant to the determination of its truth or falsehood. If a putative proposition fails to satisfy this principle, and is not a tautology, then I hold that it is metaphysical, and that, being metaphysical, it is neither true nor false but literally senseless.[3]

---

1   E.P.M., p.135 In *An Autobiography* (p.42) Collingwood claims that the germ of this idea was worked out as early as 1917 in *Truth and Contradiction*. 'This claim can be neither confirmed nor denied in detail as only chapter two of the book is extant; but it can be said that chapter two is both in line with his other early writings and also not incompatible with any later writings'. Connelly, James *Metaphysics, Method and Politics* 2003, p.10

2   E.M., pp.162–3

3   Ayer, A.J. *Language, Truth and Logic* (1st ed. 1936) 2001, p. 9

Against this position, Collingwood argues that, although neither the scientist nor the metaphysician is interested in determining their truth or falsehood, 'certain categorical elements'[4] are nonetheless meaningful, in the sense that they determine the characteristics of the sciences that presuppose them.

In *An Essay on Metaphysics* Collingwood terms these categorical elements 'absolute presuppositions'. These are roughly equivalent to those elements that, in *An Essay on Philosophical Method,* are referred to as 'philosophical concepts': in *An Essay on Philosophical Method* Collingwood relates how a philosophical concept characterises the whole of 'reality' from a particular viewpoint. However, the term 'absolute presupposition' is more precise than 'philosophical concept' in that Collingwood details how absolute presuppositions are to be discovered. It is to the process of their discovery that he applies the name 'metaphysics'.

Although *An Essay on Philosophical Method* was written in opposition to the Oxford realists, no one of them is singled out for disapproval by name. Collingwood gives the impression in this work that his greatest influences were Plato, Aristotle, Anselm, Kant and Hegel. By contrast in *An Essay on Metaphysics* Collingwood seems more keen to make clear his position in relation to his contemporaries. Although ultimately dismissive of logical positivism, it is evident that Collingwood found their arguments a great spur to the development of his own views.[5]

James Connelly also notes the possible influence of Michael Foster.[6] Michael Foster wrote an article that appeared in two parts, in *Mind* 1935 and 1936, entitled 'Christian Theology and Modern Science of Nature'. (As Connelly notes, the second part of this article coincided with the publication in *Mind* of A.J. Ayer's 'The Principle of Verification'). Foster's article opens with the following declaration:

> Every science of nature must depend upon presuppositions about nature which cannot be established by the methods of the science itself. Thus it is the method of the inductive natural sciences, described by Mill, to proceed from experience of particular natural phenomena to a conclusion about all natural phenomena of the same kind. The procedure depends upon the presupposition that nature is 'uniform' in

---

4   E.P.M., p.126

5   His respect for Ayer, in particular, is confirmed by the following anecdote from Ayer's autobiography. 'Gilbert Ryle told me that on a visit to Blackwell's he had overheard Prichard and Joseph saying that it was scandalous that the book [*Language, Truth and Logic*] had found a publisher. This does not imply that they had read it. Collingwood, who happened to be in the shop turned to them and said, 'Gentlemen, this book will be read when your names are forgotten.' I suspect that this was less a tribute to me than an expression of his contempt for them.' *Part Of My Life,* 1972, p.166

6   James Connelly makes this point in an unpublished paper 'New Metaphysics for Old'.

Mill's sense of the word; but the uniformity of nature is incapable of being established by the methods of inductive science.[7]

An Essay on Metaphysics opens with the assertion that metaphysics is a science, 'science' being taken to mean 'a body of systematic or orderly thinking about a determinate subject matter'.[8] Contrary to popular belief, metaphysics does not study God, for this would be impossible – since God is that which is 'the logical ground of everything else'.[9] God is studied by theology (although *how* theology studies God is a subject that *An Essay on Metaphysics* does not explore).

Collingwood argues that there are two alternative meanings of metaphysics that are both implicitly present, though confused, within the philosophy of Aristotle:

1. Metaphysics is the science of pure being.
2. Metaphysics is the science which deals with the presuppositions underlying ordinary science.[10]

He denies the first of these meanings, claiming that it is a contradiction in terms: for predicating the existence of an object does not alter its concept; it does not imply that the object should be studied in any particular way. Therefore, 'the science of pure being would have a subject-matter entirely devoid of peculiarities; a subject-matter, therefore, containing nothing to differentiate it from anything else, or from nothing at all'.[11] For this reason, 'there can be no science nor even a quasi-science or pseudo-science of pure being'.[12] (This is why Kant claims that 'being is not a predicate' – it contains no definite subject matter.[13] To the error of pursuing metaphysics as a science of pure being he gives the name 'ontology'. He declares that, ignoring the first of the above meanings, he intends to provide a 'metaphysics without ontology'.[14] (Whether this ambition is jeopardised by Collingwood's acceptance of the ontological argument is a question that will be explored in Chapter VI).

But although metaphysics is unable to study pure being, Collingwood does not believe that it should therefore be abandoned. For, whereas Ayer recognises fundamentally only one science, split into different departments through 'the unnecessary multiplication of current scientific termi-

---

7   Foster, M.B. 'Christian Theology and Modern Science of Nature' (I) *Mind* Vol. XLIV 1935, p.439
    The influence of Michael Oakeshott's *Experience and its Modes* (1933) should also be noted.

8   E.M. p.4

9   E.M. p.10

10 E.M. p.11

11 E.M., p.14

12 E.M., p.17

13 E.M., p.15

14 E.M., pp.17–20

nologies',[15] Collingwood believes that these different terminologies rest upon different 'absolute presuppositions', that the metaphysician alone is able to reveal.[16]

In this respect Collingwood's conception of metaphysics is related to Kant's. Kant argues that the pursuit of metaphysics in sense 1 is futile, for the science of pure being ignores the manner in which knowledge is dependent upon experience. In Kant's view, rather than strive to be independent of experience metaphysics should study different forms of experience so as to be able to specify the conditions whereby these experiences are possible. Collingwood argues that metaphysics can do this most efficiently and accurately not at 'first hand' but via study of the methods of different disciplines, with the aim of discovering their underlying presuppositions.

According to Collingwood, metaphysics in sense 2 acknowledges that each distinct intellectual discipline is reliant upon 'absolute presuppositions' — the truth or falsity of which does not arise in the course of that discipline's practice. To debate the truth of such 'absolute presuppositions' is in his view not a characteristic of metaphysics but of 'pseudo-metaphysics'.[17]

He claims that Ayer and the logical positivists confuse presuppositions with propositions. He does not necessarily doubt that the truth or falsity of propositions must be debated with reference to their manner of verification but he disputes that the same holds for absolute presuppositions.

In Collingwood's view, the logical positivists, having correctly perceived that propositions do not form the entire subject matter of metaphysics, erroneously infer that the aim of metaphysics is to superimpose superstition upon natural science: but this is a misconceived notion of metaphysics.[18]

If the logical positivists' attack upon metaphysics is based not on the misinterpretation of presuppositions but as an attack upon all presuppositions per se this may be interpreted as a direct attack upon natural science itself: for the natural scientist is himself aware that in asking certain questions he is also making certain presuppositions. On the other hand, the logical positivists are committing the same error as the Oxford realists if they assume that knowledge is attained simply by 'apprehension'.

The danger in the assumption that knowledge is acquired through 'apprehension' is that this ignorance will lead to the imposition of one's own

---

15 Ayer, A.J. *Language, Truth and Logic* (1936) 2001, p.167

16 The term 'absolute presupposition' was first used by F.H. Bradley in 'The Presuppositions of Critical History' [1876] in *Collected Essays*, 1976, p.22. The influence upon Collingwood of F.H. Bradley and R.H. Lotze are discussed in Chapter 1 of Chinatsu Kobayashi's unpublished PhD thesis, 'Collingwood on Re-Enactment: Understanding in History and Interpretation in Art', University of Ottawa, 2003.

17 E.M., p.163

18 E.M., p.169

unexamined standpoint. In explicit contrast to this approach, Collingwood proposes that: *'Every statement that anybody ever makes is made in answer to a question'*.[19]

> In proportion as a man is thinking scientifically when he makes a statement, he knows that his statement is the answer to a question and knows what that question is. In proportion as he is thinking unscientifically he does not know these things.[20]

Collingwood argues that it is the task of philosophy to examine these questions so as to make explicit the presuppositions upon which they are based. For, every question is in turn based upon a prior presupposition.[21] He gives the following example:

> [W]hen I am trying to decipher a worn and damaged inscription I know very well that before I begin answering the question 'What does that mark mean?' I must first assure myself that the mark is not accidental but is part of the inscription; that is to say, I must first answer the question 'Does it mean anything?' An affirmative answer, i.e. the statement 'That mark means something', causes the question to arise, 'What does it mean?'.[22]

In other words, that the mark means something is a presupposition logically prior to the question 'what does it mean?'.

He argues that the logical efficacy of the presuppositions upon which questions are grounded is not diminished if we are unaware of them. However insofar as thinking *is* to any extent orderly or scientific we will be aware of the presuppositions that underlie our questions.

> Here lies the difference between the desultory and casual thinking of our unscientific consciousness and the orderly and systematic thinking we call science. In unscientific thinking our thoughts are coagulated into knots and tangles; we fish up a thought out of our minds like an anchor foul of its own cable, hanging upside-down and draped in seaweed with shellfish sticking to it, and dump the whole thing on deck quite pleased with ourselves for having got it up at all. Thinking scientifically means disentangling all this mess, and reducing a knot of thoughts in which everything sticks together anyhow to a system of thoughts in which thinking the thoughts is at the same time thinking the connections between them.[23]

Because logical positivism ignores the logical efficacy possessed by implicit presuppositions it also overlooks the role that metaphysics can play in disentangling these implicit presuppositions and arranging them in a logical order.

---

19   E.M., p.23
20   E.M., p.24
21   E.M., p.25
22   E.M., pp.26–27
23   E.M., pp.22–23

In order to demonstrate the continued usefulness of metaphysics, in *An Essay on Metaphysics* Collingwood proposes a 'theory of presupposition' whereby the unquestioned absolute presuppositions of different disciplines of inquiry might be isolated. The outlines of this I have reproduced below.[24] I shall argue that, despite some modification that needs to be made to this theory, the core of Collingwood's conception of metaphysics still stands.

'PROP. 1 *Every statement that anybody ever makes is made in answer to a question*'[25] Collingwood includes in the terms of this proposition statements made silently to oneself, and the questions to which they are answers. He maintains that insofar as a statement (public or private) makes sense the question to which it is an answer is also still in mind.[26]

Statements can be analysed so as to reveal the questions that they attempt to answer: that the question may not have been consciously articulated even at the time of asking makes no difference to its logical priority. This applies to both scientific and non-scientific statements. However:

> When thinking is scientifically ordered, this logical priority is accompanied by a temporal priority: one formulates the question first, and only when it is formulated begins trying to answer it. This is a special kind of temporal priority, in which the event or activity that is prior does not stop when that which is posterior begins. The act of asking the question begins and takes a definite shape as the asking of a determinate question before the act of answering it begins; but it continues for the whole duration of this latter.[27]

The above proposition may be clarified by the following restatement from Collingwood's *Autobiography*:

> [Y]ou cannot find out what a man means by simply studying his spoken or written statements, even though he has spoken or written with perfect command of language and perfectly truthful intention. In order to find out his meaning you must know what the question was (a question in his own mind, and presumed by him to be in yours) to which the thing he has said or written was meant as an answer.[28]

It is this fact that, in Collingwood's view, is ignored by logical positivists and realists, and which is likely to lead to their misunderstanding of any philosophers, past or present, with different views than their own. The unexamined presupposition underpinning their position is that other philosophers' answers were made in response to the same questions as their

---

24   E.M., p.23

25   E.M., p.23

26   There is an overlap, or coincidence, here between what in *An Autobiography* is termed 'a logic of question and answer'. Unfortunately, as will be seen in Chapter XIV, Collingwood's sketch of the logic of question and answer is extremely brief, and tends to raise more questions than it solves. I prefer to speak of the *method* of question and answer.

27   E.M., p.24

28   A., p.31

own. This presupposition is made when our own and other people's pre-suppositions are unexamined — when only 'answers' are attended to, in isolation from the questions that they are intended to answer.

In opposition to this position, Collingwood sees himself as reviving the view of Descartes and Francis Bacon that 'knowledge' means 'both the activity of knowing and what is known'.[29]

'PROP. 2 *Every question involves a presupposition*'.[30] It is likely that most questions involve many presuppositions. However, when a question is made *directly* on the basis of a single presupposition it is said to 'arise'. The damaged inscription may again be taken as an example: '"That mark means something", allows the question to arise, "What does it mean?"'.[31] In other words, 'That mark means something' is the presupposition that allows the question to arise, 'what does it mean?'.

'*The fact that something causes a question to arise I call the "logical efficacy" of that thing*'.[32] Collingwood notes that the thought that 'this mark means something' need not have been consciously proposed for it to have prompted the question 'what does it mean?' The logical efficacy of the thought would have been the same had it been (as is more likely) presupposed — it would still have caused the question to arise. A presup-position, assumption or proposition may all possess, in equal measure, 'logical efficacy'.

'PROP. 3 *The logical efficacy of a supposition does not depend upon the truth of what is supposed, or even on its being thought true, but only on its being sup-posed*'.[33] For example, in a *reductio ad absurdum* in order to eliminate a par-ticular line of inquiry a natural scientist or an historian might assume the premise of a particular argument in order to derive a valid but false con-clusion from it. We rightly accord suppositions (including assumptions) logical efficacy while yet distinguishing them from propositions. Collingwood illustrates this as follows.

> A man (or at any rate an intelligent man) does not regard himself as insulted if some one who has paid him a sum of money asks him for a receipt, or if the family of a lady whom he is about to marry proposes that a marriage settlement should be drawn up. He knows that the

---

29   A., p.30 Many philosophers and historians of philosophy would judge the attribution of this view to Bacon and Descartes to be somewhat eccentric. G.H. Von Wright's view of the history of philosophy is in this regard more generally accepted. Von Wright places Collingwood within the hermeneutic tradition (together with Croce, Gentile, Dilthey, Simmel, Weber, Gadamer, Kant, Vico, Aristotle, Fichte, Schelling and Herder): as opposed to the other major tradition in western philosophy, which sees the natural sciences as providing the ideal paradigm of knowledge. Within the latter tradition Von Wright places Galileo, Bacon, logical positivism, Cook Wilson and Samuel Alexander — see Von Wright, G.H. *Explanation and Understanding*, 1971, pp.1–33.

30   E.M., p.25

31   E.M., pp.26–27

32   E.M., p.27

33   E.M., p.28

request or proposal is based on the assumption that he is capable, or will one day become capable, of acting dishonourably; but though he knows people assume this he does not necessarily think they believe it. He finds no difficulty in distinguishing between their supposing him a rascal and their believing him one, and he does not regard the former as evidence of the latter.[34]

Again, in Collingwood's opinion the logical positivists overlooked the logical efficacy that we grant to presuppositions.

'PROP. 4 *A presupposition is either relative or absolute ... By a relative presupposition I mean one which stands relatively to one question as its presupposition and relatively to another question as its answer*'.[35] In Collingwood' example, the accuracy of a tape measure is a *relative* presupposition that a surveyor might make. It is a relative presupposition since its truth or falsity can be verified — either, within an acceptable parameter, the tape is accurate or it is not. That it might not occur to a surveyor to check the accuracy of his tape is irrelevant in a *logical* inquiry — we know that the tape's accuracy can be verified. That the tape's accuracy *can* be verified is an indication that the surveyor's presupposition is relative rather than absolute.

Although the nature of a relative presupposition is different to that of an absolute presupposition, the method of its discovery — the method of question and answer — is the same in both cases.[36]

'*An absolute presupposition is one which stands, relatively to all questions to which it is related, as a presupposition, never as an answer*'.[37] Metaphysics, as 'the science of absolute presuppositions',[38] has the task of making explicit, via the theory of presupposition, the absolute presuppositions of different intellectual disciplines. For whereas different relative presuppositions may co-exist within the same mode of inquiry, each set of absolute presuppositions underpins a different discipline. However, 'when I speak of finding out what they are I do not mean finding out what it is to be an absolute presupposition, which is the work of the logician; I mean finding out what absolute presuppositions are in fact made'.[39] Nor does metaphysics judge that one absolute presupposition is 'right' and another is 'wrong': for an absolute presupposition is not itself true or false.

The different absolute presuppositions possessed by a person 'are not like a set of carpenter's tools, of which the carpenter uses one at a time; they are all suppositions, each must be *consupponible* with all others; that is, it must be logically possible for a person who supposes any one of them

34   E.M., pp.28–9
35   E.M., p.29
36   E.M., p.42
37   E.M., p.31
38   E.M., p.53
39   E.M., p.54

to suppose concurrently all the rest'.[40] Thus a man may be described as an historical novelist and an archaeologist — without the implication that when digging he ceases to be an historical novelist.[41]

In the case of the archaeologist's examination of the damaged inscription 'That mark means something' is a *relative* presupposition that allows the question to arise, 'what does it mean?'. In *The Idea of History* (1946) and *The Principles of History* (1999) Collingwood asks 'what are the *absolute* presuppositions of history?'. (His pursuit of an answer to this question is the subject of the second part of this book).

The methods that will be used in this inquiry are already laid down in *An Essay on Metaphysics* in the theory of presuppositions. The relative presupposition 'that mark means something' is, as we saw, itself an answer to the question 'does it mean anything?'. But what presupposition is involved in *this* question? This theory of presuppositions, upon which the method of question and answer relies, will, in Collingwood's view, end at the absolute presuppositions of history.

'PROP. 5 *Absolute presuppositions are not propositions*'.[42] Having studied a discipline via the theory of presuppositions, the metaphysician is able to make previously implicit absolute presuppositions explicit, by showing that they are necessary to the pursuit of that particular discipline. The inquiry by which this discovery or revelation is made 'has a normative element because in uncovering a presupposition the metaphysician detects what one ought to believe as a matter of logic, i.e. to presuppose, rather than what one believes as a matter of psychological or historical fact'.[43] In other words, the metaphysician is not just interested in what people believe but in what they presuppose.

However, the metaphysician does not himself propound an absolute presupposition, rather, he propounds the proposition that 'this or that one of them is presupposed'.[44] He thereby hopes to contribute both to metaphysics and to whatever discipline he has studied.

The crucial point that Collingwood makes against logical positivism is that a presupposition may have logical efficacy even though it is not known. Logical positivism cannot accommodate this acknowledgement. Once the validity of this point is admitted the way is left open for the return of metaphysics.

---

40 E.M., p.66
41 Gilbert Ryle expresses a similar idea in *The Concept of Mind*, 1949, p.113: 'When a cow is said to be a ruminant, or a man is said to be a cigarette-smoker, it is not being said that the cow is ruminating now or that the man is smoking a cigarette now. To be a ruminant is to tend to ruminate from time to time, and to be a cigarette-smoker is to be in the habit of smoking cigarettes'.
42 E.M., p.32
43 D'Oro, Giuseppina, *Collingwood and the Metaphysics of Experience*, 2002, p.97
44 E.M., p.33

However, in the above argument the doubtfulness of Collingwood's first proposition – that '[e]*very statement that anybody ever makes is made in answer to a question*'[45] somewhat obscures this point.[46] It is not obvious, for example, that any question underlies the mathematical fiat 'let AB = BC'.

Collingwood's argument may be run to the same conclusion if his first proposition is replaced by:

> PROP.1 *In dealing with statements whose full meaning is not immediately apparent it is useful to ask 'what question was this statement intended to answer?'.*

The caution should also be given that asking 'what question was this statement intended to answer?' does not guarantee an answer that is immune to revision: for, as previously mentioned, the metaphysician cannot eradicate an element of circularity from his inquiries, since he begins his work from commonly agreed examples of good practice. The latter point suggests an alternative and less controversial second proposition:

> PROP.2 *The metaphysician must himself make presuppositions.*[47]

Collingwood's Allies

Although *An Essay on Philosophical Method* and *An Essay on Metaphysics* attracted attention upon their publication – and although together they form one of the very few thorough investigations of the twentieth century into the task and nature of metaphysics – these works did not immediately attract followers. Admittedly, the influence of *An Essay on Philosophical Method* may be detected in an essay by Collingwood's pupil, Isaiah Berlin, 'The Purpose of Philosophy', in which Berlin argues that the subject matter and purpose of philosophy is different to that of all other disciplines, in that the philosopher does not rely purely upon observation or upon calculation, but instead surveys 'the permanent or semi-permanent categories in terms of which experience is conceived and classified'[48]; with the goal of increasing our self-understanding.[49] But, despite his popularity as a lec-

---

45 E.M., p.23

46 Michael Beaney makes this criticism in 'Collingwood's Conception of Analysis' *Collingwood and British Idealism Studies*, 2005, Vol. 11, no.2, pp.41–114.

47 Collingwood readily admits this point – see E.M., p.63

48 Berlin, Isaiah 'The Purpose of Philosophy' in *Concepts and Categories* (ed. H. Hardy) 1982, p.9. Collingwood's influence is also noticeable in Berlin's 'The Concept of Scientific History' *History and Theory* vol. 1, no.1, 1960, pp.1–31 – although, curiously, Collingwood is not named in this essay. Berlin attended Collingwood's lectures on the philosophy of history in 1931. According to Berlin's biographer: 'If there was any single source for Berlin's later interest in the philosophy of history, in philosophical pioneers like the eighteenth-century Neapolitan Giambattista Vico, and in his evolving conviction that thinking historically was the best way to do philosophy, it was Collingwood. The two never became close – Collingwood gently rebuffing one of Belin's invitations to join a seminar – but the influence was important.' Ignatieff, Michael *Isaiah Berlin: A Life*, 1998, p.58

49 I am grateful to Guido Vanheeswijk for pointing out this influence.

turer[50] and writer,[51] Collingwood did not found a distinctive 'school' of philosophy: as a result, *An Essay on Philosophical Method* and *An Essay on Metaphysics* remain comparatively neglected works.

In recent years, since the formation of the Collingwood Society in 1994, there has been a resurgence of interest in Collingwood's work, but his metaphysics has yet to fully reconnect to the mainstream of contemporary philosophical debate.

To this end, James Connelly has attempted to establish common ground with Wittgenstein's supporters. He points out that, although it is very doubtful that Collingwood and Wittgenstein directly influenced each other's work, many of Wittgenstein's propositions in *On Certainty* are sympathetic to Collingwood's arguments in *An Essay on Metaphysics*.[52] Perhaps the most striking are the following:

> All testing, all confirmation and disconfirmation of a hypothesis takes place already within a system. And this system is not a more or less arbitrary and doubtful point of departure for all our arguments: no, it belongs to the essence of what we call an argument. The system is not so much the point of departure, as the element in which arguments have their life.[53]

> That is to say, the *questions* that we raise and our *doubts* depend on the fact that some propositions are exempt from doubt, are as it were like hinges on which those turn.[54]

> That is to say, it belongs to the logic of our scientific investigations that certain things are *in deed* not doubted.[55]

Connelly notes that the parallels between the philosophies of Collingwood and the later Wittgenstein have been obscured by a difference in vocabulary:

> Collingwood ... wished to retain the term metaphysics while Wittgenstein was happy to let it go. Hence, what, for Wittgenstein, is metaphysics is, for Collingwood, pseudo-metaphysics; and what Collingwood described as metaphysics might be described by Wittgenstein as simply 'philosophical investigations'.[56]

Thus, although it remains a significant difference that Collingwood did not seek to hasten the end of philosophy, if Wittgenstein's supporters were to make allowance for the difference of vocabulary between Wittgenstein

---

50   'As a lecturer he was a spell-binder.' Emmet, Dorothy *Philosophers and Friends: Reminiscences of Seventy Years in Philosophy*, 1996, p. 9

51   In *Philosophy in the Twentieth Century*, 1982, p.193, A.J. Ayer describes *An Essay in Philosophical Method* as 'a contribution to *belles-lettres* rather than philosophy'.

52   I am grateful to James Connelly for allowing me to make use of an unpublished essay on this subject: 'New Metaphysics for Old'.

53   Wittgenstein, Ludwig *On Certainty* (ed. G.E.M. Anscombe), 1972, §105

54   Wittgenstein, Ludwig *On Certainty* (ed. G.E.M. Anscombe), 1972, §341

55   Wittgenstein, Ludwig *On Certainty* (ed. G.E.M. Anscombe), 1972, §342

56   Connelly, James 'New Metaphysics for Old', unpublished, p.11

and Collingwood they might perhaps profitably read *An Essay on Meta-physics* as a systematic defence of certain of the later Wittgenstein's gnomic sayings, particular in *On Certainty*. (Although supporters of Wittgenstein and Collingwood are not necessarily aware of their similarities, it is notice-able that Donald Davidson, in 'Actions, Reasons and Causes' (1963) attacks both groups without distinction. Davidson's criticisms are exam-ined in Chapter XII, in which Collingwood's conceptual approach to the mind–body problem is contrasted to Donald Davidson's).

Common ground can also be established with those sympathetic to A.N. Whitehead's approach to metaphysics. Guido Vanheeswijck points out that Whitehead's principal metaphysical intention was:

> to bring philosophy once again in touch with the sciences of his era (quantum mechanics, relativity theory, non-mechanical biology) and to elaborate a cosmological-metaphysical theory on the basis of the analysis of their presuppositions.[57]

In *An Autobiography* Collingwood is careful to distinguish Whitehead's form of realism from that of the logical positivists':[58] qualified admiration for Whitehead is expressed both in *The Idea of Nature* and in correspon-dence with Samuel Alexander (13/2/35).[59] Concerning the relationship between philosophy and other forms of inquiry, Collingwood would have agreed with the following passage from Whitehead's *The Function of Reason* (1929):

> The claim of science that it can produce an understanding of its proce-dures within the limits of its own categories, or that those categories themselves are understandable without reference to their status within the wider categories under exploration by the speculative Reason – that claim is entirely unfounded. Insofar as philosophers have failed, scien-tists do not know what they are talking about when they pursue their own methods; and insofar as philosophers have succeeded, to that extent scientists can attain an understanding of science.[60]

Collingwood's absolute presuppositions are sometimes described as 'syn-thetic *a priori*'.[61] However, this description may give the impression that they are necessary existential claims concerning the essential nature of 're-ality'. As has been seen, the more modest claim presented in the theory of presupposition is that the metaphysician presents the *proposition* that this

57   Vanheeswijck, Guido 'R.G. Collingwood on Metaphysics, History and Cosmology' *Process Studies* pp.215-36 vol. 27 no.3-4, fall-winter 1998, p.230

58   A., pp.45–6

59   Vanheeswijck, Guido, 1998, p.226

60   Whitehead, Alfred North *The Function of Reason*, 1929, pp.47–8

61   D'Oro, G. *The Metaphysics of Experience*, 2002, pp.33. As will be seen in the next chapter, in a letter to Gilbert Ryle Collingwood himself refers to absolute presuppositions as synthetic *a priori*.

or that absolute presupposition is present, in this or that discipline.[62] It is this avoidance of ontological problems that, I believe, warrants contemporary interest in Collingwood's metaphilosophy.

In its avoidance of ontological problems, Collingwood's 'metaphysics without ontology' is comparable to Nicholas Rescher's 'conceptual idealism'. Those of Rescher's works that Collingwood's supporters may find of particular interest are his early papers on historical explanation[63] and his 'Pragmatic Idealism' trilogy consisting of *Conceptual Idealism* (1973), *The Primacy of Practice* (1973) and *Methodological Pragmatism* (1977). Also of interest, by way of comparison to *An Essay on Philosophical Method*, is *Philosophical Reasoning: A Study in the Methodology of Philosophising* (2001).

In *Conceptual Idealism* Rescher proposes that transcendental arguments may be used to a subtly different end to that envisaged by Kant. Whereas Kant uses transcendental arguments with the aim of deducing the primary features of the world from the mind's innate *a priori* organising principles, Rescher (like Collingwood) aims to use transcendental arguments to reveal 'the conceptual schemata that we in fact deploy in the rational structure of our experience'.[64] He argues that this analysis can, and should, be carried out without reference to ontological or causal terms:

> [C]onceptual idealism — unlike phenomenalism — is *not* a theory as to the structural nature of reality (this is left altogether to science), but addresses itself solely to the nature of the framework of concepts in terms of which this conception of the real is articulated.[65]

In both *Conceptual Idealism* and *The Primacy of Practice* Rescher's pronouncements upon the aims of conceptual analysis accord with the aims of Collingwood's 'metaphysics without ontology'. For example, Collingwood would agree wholeheartedly that:

> A proper practice of conceptual analysis can surely clarify how our concepts do in fact work and — when appropriate — render explicit their dependency upon facets of our view of the world. This calls for an endeavour to study concepts *in situ* with a view also to the empirical commitment that underwrites their use. The resulting study would heed the functional ecology of concepts, concerning itself not with

---

62 E.M.: 33

63 'The Problem of Uniqueness in History' Joynt, Carey B. and Rescher, N. in *History and Theory* vol. 1 1961, pp.150–62; 'On Explanation in History' Joynt, Carey B. and Rescher, N. in Mind vol. 68, July 1959, pp.383–88; 'Evidence in History and in the Law' Joynt, Carey B. and Rescher, N. in *Journal of Philosophy* vol. 56, June 1959, pp.561–77. Rescher argues that historians' explanations are of a different character to natural scientists', due to the historian's presumption of the historical agent's rationality. He argues that although this presumption provides an economic means by which the historian proceeds it remains defeasible — it holds 'until proven otherwise'.

64 Rescher, Nicholas *Conceptual Idealism*, 1973, p.93

65 Rescher, Nicholas *Conceptual Idealism*, 1973, p.166

semantics alone, but with the factual views operative within the common habitat of their standard employment.[66]

However, although Rescher agrees with Collingwood that '[p]hilosophy has no distinctive information sources of its own'[67], he infers from this that 'it also does not have any altogether distinctive method'.[68] By contrast, Collingwood argues that although philosophy has no subject matter that is uniquely its own, when the philosopher turns to study other disciplines (when he is engaged in metaphysics) he is equipped with a distinctive method — that suggested by the theory of presupposition.

In Rescher's philosophy the example of successfully practiced science provides philosophy with its criteria and methodology — of cohesion and pragmatic usefulness. He cautions that his *methodological pragmatism* should not be confused with what he terms *thesis pragmatism* — the idea that if a thesis ultimately prevails, then it must be true. He maintains that:

> [W]ith respect to methodology at any rate, the pragmatists were surely right: there can be no more natural way of justifying a *method* than by establishing that 'it works' with respect to the specific tasks in view.[69]

Although Collingwood for the most part ignores the arguments of pragmatism, the term 'methodological pragmatism' would not be wholly inappropriate as applied to his metaphysics. For Collingwood's metaphysics aims to examine the most well established claims of different sciences and the methods that were used in making those claims and to establish what presuppositions were made in the course of establishing those claims.

Another ally, whose interest in Collingwood has hitherto attracted almost no attention, is Bernard Williams. Williams' knowledge of Collingwood's philosophy is evident from his first published paper 'Tertullian's Paradox' in which he refers to Collingwood's view of the 'ontological proof' as 'the presupposition of any religious statement'.[70] In his final years and in his posthumous publications Williams paid Collingwood one compliment after another. In *Truth and Truthfulness* (2002), in the year before his death, he described Collingwood as:

> the most unjustly neglected of twentieth-century British philosophers.[71]

His admiration is further manifested in the article on Collingwood that he co-authored (with Stefan Collini) for the *Dictionary of National Biography* in which Collingwood is credited with having:

---

66 Rescher, Nicholas *The Primacy of Practical Reason*, 1973, p.122
67 Rescher, Nicholas *Philosophical Reasoning: A Study in the Methodology of Philosophising* 2001, p.4
68 Rescher, Nicholas *Philosophical Reasoning: A Study in the Methodology of Philosophising* 2001, p.4
69 Rescher, Nicholas *The Primacy of Practical Reason*, 1973, pp.2–3
70 Williams, Bernard 'Tertullian's Paradox' [1955] reprinted in *Philosophy as a Humanistic Discipline* (ed. A.W. Moore) 2006, p.7
71 Williams, Bernard *Truth and Truthfulness*, 2002, p.237

almost single handed kept alive an anti-positivist understanding of history through a dark period largely dominated by the narrow sympathies of analytic philosophers and the brisk empiricism of political historians.[72]

In the posthumously published collection of essays *In the Beginning was the Deed* (2005) Collingwood is described as 'consistently'[73] and 'grossly underestimated';[74] and in posthumously published 'Essay on Collingwood' in *The Sense of the Past* (2006) he is described as:

> offering philosophical writing which in twentieth-century British philosophy is unrivalled in its brilliance.[75]

However, in the same essay Williams is dismissive towards *An Essay on Philosophical Method*, perhaps seeing it as an instance of his chief philosophical bugbear, metaphysical system-building — but, regrettably, no detailed criticism is given. Yet, he agrees with Collingwood that the method of question and answer can be used to reconstruct the original meaning of a statement[76] and he is in agreement with Collingwood on the logical structure of action explanation[77] (discussed in the second part of this book).

An 'Essay on Collingwood' concludes with the suggestion that Collingwood's philosophy has strengths in areas where Wittgenstein's is weak. His specific criticisms of Wittgenstein are that:

> Wittgenstein did not spend much time on considering how reflective descriptions of practice might be related to practice itself.[78]

And:

> Wittgensteinian accounts of social understanding have, notoriously, tended to favour a static picture of a fully functioning and coherent system.[79]

Williams refers to these weaknesses in Wittgenstein's philosophy in a number of other essays. He complains that 'no Wittgensteinian argument tells us who, in any given connection is meant by *we*';[80] and that it is unclear in Wittgenstein's philosophy how one 'we' might come to recognise what was believed by another 'we'.[81] In this respect, Williams

---

72   Collini, Stefan and Bernard Williams 'R.G. Collingwood' *The Dictionary of National Biography*, 2004, p.681

73   Williams, Bernard *In the Beginning was the Deed*, 2005, p.53

74   Williams, Bernard *In the Beginning was the Deed*, 2005, p.67

75   Williams, Bernard *The Sense of the Past*, 2006, p.358

76   Williams, Bernard *The Sense of the Past*, 2006, p.344

77   Williams, Bernard 'Internal and External Reasons' [1980] in *Moral Luck*, 1981, pp.101–13

78   Williams, Bernard *The Sense of the Past*, 2006, p.357

79   Williams, Bernard *The Sense of the Past*, 2006, p.357

80   Williams, Bernard *In the Beginning was the Deed*, 2005, p.24

81   Williams, Bernard *Moral Luck*, 1981, p.156

suggests that Wittgenstein's 'use of Gestaltist illumination can stun, rather than assist, further and more systematic explanation'.[82]

Williams argues that when Wittgenstein mentions 'we' he is ultimately using the word in its royal sense. He is above all interested in exploring his own world view — he is not greatly interested in other groups of people. Williams points out that this is not a criticism that can be made of Collingwood and he suggests that Collingwood's theory of presupposition might be used to recover the beliefs of other communities.

But though he admires the importance and originality of the theory of presupposition he is reluctant to admit that it may be used not only in the history of ideas but also in metaphysics. One of his reservations is as follows:

> Since metaphysics is identified as the study of absolute presuppositions, it seems to be assimilated to the history of ideas. Collingwood was prepared, in a sense, to accept this both because the study of remoter systems of thought itself involved having those thoughts, and because he saw the present as in effect always 'the recent past'. Reflection on the presuppositions of inquiry in the past, and on our own in the present, equally involves the aim, which can never be completely realised, of making an inchoate set of presuppositions coherent. The questions of relativism that have been much discussed by Collingwood's commentators in this connection are perhaps best directed to the issue of how far criteria of coherence are themselves historically variable.[83]

Williams' exposition of Collingwood's ideas has here gone slightly astray. In Collingwood's view metaphysics is not primarily the study of absolute presuppositions but the attempt to discover them, via the study of other disciplines — it is an activity. As such, problems involving the criteria of coherence (or correspondence) do not arise. (In this instance, Williams' interpretation of 'metaphysics without ontology' may have been unduly affected by his own inclination in favour of the permanency of philosophical problems).

Nonetheless, despite Williams reluctance to see the theory of presupposition as part of metaphysics, Williams' preoccupation with Collingwood's philosophy, and his own preoccupation with the relation between philosophy and history, suggests that this is one of the most interesting (and least explored) of Collingwood's possible alliances.

Williams tended to flit from one problem to another (or at least he liked to give that impression), whereas Collingwood tended more towards a preoccupation with one specific concern at a time: first, Oxford realism; then, logical positivism; and finally, fascism. But this does not necessarily

---

82   Williams, Bernard *Moral Luck*, 1981, p.159
83   Collini, Stefan and Bernard Williams 'R.G. Collingwood' *Dictionary of National Biography*, 2004, p.680

reflect a philosophical difference. *Philosophically*, Williams makes clear his wholehearted agreement with Collingwood that:

> Every piece of philosophical writing is primarily addressed by the writer to himself. Its purpose is not to select from among his thoughts those of which he is certain and to express those, but the very opposite: to fasten upon the difficulties and obscurities in which he finds himself involved, and try, if not to solve or remove them, at least to understand them better.[84]

In furtherance of introducing Collingwood's analysis of historical explanation and encouraging Collingwood's metaphysics towards the mainstream of contemporary philosophy, this chapter completes my exposition of what I see as the valid core of 'metaphysics without ontology.' However, before proceeding to explore Collingwood's analysis of historical explanation, it should be noted that there are occasions when Collingwood himself forsakes his stated ambition of pursuing metaphysics without ontology. The prime example is his espousal of the ontological argument — the subject of the next chapter.

---

84   E.P.M., p.209 — quoted by Williams in *The Sense of the Past*, 2006, p.343

Chapter VI

The Ontological Argument

In this chapter I intend to provide an account of Collingwood's ontological argument. My underlying concern is that readers who might otherwise be sympathetic to the arguments of Collingwood's *Essay on Philosophical Method* and *An Essay on Metaphysics* may believe that the arguments of these works are invalidated by Collingwood's commitment to the ontological 'proof'. This may indeed have been Gilbert Ryle's attitude to *An Essay on Philosophical Method*: Ryle discusses the ontological argument but no other aspect of this work.

After describing the response that Collingwood's ontological argument elicited from Gilbert Ryle, I examine the original ontological argument proposed by Saint Anselm with which Ryle associates Collingwood's position. I also examine the correspondence that ensued between Collingwood and Ryle; and argue that Collingwood's position is insufficiently different from Saint Anselm's as to avoid criticisms made by Ryle and Kant. However, despite siding with Ryle on this issue, I argue that Collingwood's metaphysics can stand unsupported by any form of the ontological argument. Moreover, when the ontological argument is set to one side it is noticeable that there are a number of similarities between the philosophies of Collingwood and Ryle that were overlooked at the time of their correspondence.

In the final section of this chapter ('Intuition') I speculate that whereas the ontological argument would have it that faith and reason are compatible, this relationship might more accurately be described as consupponible — logically non-conflicting.

Collingwood's Ontological Argument

In Collingwood's opinion the ontological argument applies to any object of philosophical study, in that *the philosopher must be committed to the existence of that which he studies*: 'in the special case of metaphysical thinking the distinction between conceiving something to exist and thinking it to exist is a distinction without a difference'.[1]

Thus logic, in Collingwood's opinion, provides an example of how, in its pursuit of categorical propositions, philosophy stands committed to the ontological 'proof'. In Collingwood's opinion, the subject matter of logic, as studied by the philosopher, must be conceived as existing, rather than being hypothetical.

> [L]ogic cannot be in substance merely hypothetical. Geometry can afford to be indifferent to the existence of its subject-matter; so long as it is free to suppose it, that is enough. But logic cannot share this indifference, because, by existing it constitutes an actually existing subject-matter to itself. Thus, when we say 'all squares have their diagonals equal', we need not be either explicitly or implicitly asserting that any squares exist; but when we say 'all universal propositions distribute their subject', we are not only discussing universal propositions, we are also enunciating a universal proposition; we are producing an actual instance of the thing under discussion, and cannot discuss it without doing so. Consequently no such discussion can be indifferent to the existence of its own subject-matter; in other words, the propositions which constitute the body of logic cannot ever be in substance hypothetical. A logician who lays it down that all universal propositions are merely hypothetical is showing a true insight into the nature of science, but he is undermining the very possibility of logic; for his assertion cannot be true consistently with the fact of his maintaining it ... Logic, therefore, stands committed to the principle of the Ontological Proof. Its subject-matter, namely thought, affords an instance of something which cannot be conceived except as actual, something whose essence involves existence.[2]

The above account outlines the role that the ontological argument plays in Collingwood's metaphilosophy. It is this understanding of the ontological argument that Collingwood has in mind when, after tracing the history of the argument from Saint Anselm (via Descartes' *Discourse on Method*,[3] Spinoza's *Ethics* and Leibniz's *Monadology*) he claims:

> With Hegel's rejection of subjective idealism, the Ontological Proof took its place once more among the accepted principles of modern philosophy, and it has never again been seriously criticised.[4]

Ryle's Response

Collingwood's description of the ontological argument as 'among the accepted principles of modern philosophy' prompted the following response from Gilbert Ryle:

---

1   E.P.M., p.125
2   E.P.M., p.130
3   Collingwood claims that the *Cogito* was not viewed by Descartes as a self-evident truth from which deductions might be made, but as a necessary condition of inquiry.
4   E.P.M.: 126

> To my mind this dictum almost merits tears. One of the biggest advances in logic that has been made since Aristotle, namely Hume's and Kant's discovery that particular matters of fact cannot be the implicates of general propositions, and so cannot be demonstrated from *a priori* premises, is written off as a backsliding into an epistemological or psychological mistake, and all's to do again.[5]

Ryle denies that a predicate can exist of such a form that from it there can be deduced the existence of a particular object. He argues that this is what an ontological argument amounts to. He asks Collingwood: 'How can "something is an A" follow from the proposition "anything that is an A, is B-ish"? How can a particular matter of fact be deduced from *a priori* or non-empirical premises?'.[6]

Ryle makes clear that he is prepared to admit that there are cases 'where we can say that being of such and such a sort involves having such and such a property'[7] but these cases are cases of analytic truths. Ryle is prepared to admit only empirical (existential) and analytic (hypothetical) propositions, but not 'categorical' (*necessary and existential*) propositions. He argues that subject and predicate are necessarily related only in analytic propositions — for example, in the case of a bicycle necessarily having two wheels. However, analytic statements, being hypothetical, have no existential import.

> There is ... no way of arguing validly to the existence of something of a certain description from non-empirical premises, namely from premises about the characters the combination of which is symbolised by the description. There is no way of demonstrating *a priori* particular matters of fact. Inferences to the existence of something, if there are any, must be causal inferences and inferences from the existence of something else. Nor are there any 'demands of reason' which can make us accept as proofs of existence combinations of propositions which contain an overt fallacy.[8]

Ryle denies the argument that the subject-matter of logic — thought — affords an instance of something which cannot be conceived except as actual, something whose essence involves existence. He argues that hypothetical propositions 'do not *deny* the existence of their subjects, they only do not affirm or imply their existence'.[9] The logician's proposition might

5   Ryle, Gilbert 'Mr. Collingwood and the Ontological Argument' *Mind* vol. XLIV, 1935: 137–51, p.142

6   Ryle, Gilbert 'Mr. Collingwood and the Ontological Argument' *Mind* vol. XLIV, 1935: 137–51, p.142

7   Ryle, Gilbert 'Mr. Collingwood and the Ontological Argument' *Mind* vol. XLIV, 1935: 137–51, p.143

8   Ryle, Gilbert 'Mr. Collingwood and the Ontological Argument' *Mind* vol. XLIV, 1935: 137–51, p.146

9   Ryle, Gilbert 'Mr. Collingwood and the Ontological Argument' *Mind* vol. XLIV, 1935: 137–51, p.148

incidentally apply to itself but it does not on that count imply its own existence.

He denies the implication of Collingwood's argument that there is any contradiction in asserting that someone is a 'bad logician'.

Saint Anselm's Ontological Argument

When Ryle argues, against Collingwood, that 'there is no way of demonstrating *a priori* particular matters of fact'[10] he is suggesting that Collingwood's ontological argument falls foul of the same logical error as the original ontological argument, as proposed by Saint Anselm.

In its original form — as an argument by Saint Anselm against the Fool who 'hath said in his heart, *There is* no God'[11] — the ontological argument runs as follows.

> So even the fool must admit that something than which nothing greater can be thought exists at least in his understanding, since he understands this when he hears it, and whatever is understood exists in the understanding. And surely that than which a greater cannot be thought cannot exist only in the understanding. For if it exists only in the understanding, it can be thought to exist in reality as well, which is greater. So if that than which a greater cannot be thought exists only in the understanding, then that than which a greater *cannot* be thought is that than which a greater *can* be thought. But that is clearly impossible. Therefore, there is no doubt that something than which a greater cannot be thought exists both in the understanding and in reality.[12]

The logical structure of this argument is as follows.

(1)   The Fool understands the concept of God ('something than which nothing greater can be thought').

(2)   That which is understood exists in the understanding.

(3)   Hence, God ('something than which nothing greater can be thought') exists in the Fool's understanding.

(4)   If God ('something than which nothing greater can be thought') exists in understanding but not in reality, then a greater being can be conceived: one that exists in reality.

(5)   But, it is contradictory to claim that 'something than which nothing greater can be thought' is greater than 'something than which nothing greater can be thought'.

(6)   God exists not just in the Fool's understanding, but in reality.[13]

---

10   Ryle, Gilbert 'Mr. Collingwood and the Ontological Argument' *Mind* vol. XLIV, 1935: 137–51, p.146

11   Psalm 14, verse 1

12   *Proslogion* (trans. Thomas Williams), 1995, p.7

13   This reconstruction, and the following discussion of Anselm's argument, has been influenced by Graham Oppy's *Ontological Arguments and Belief in God*, 1995. Oppy provides a thorough survey of debates centred on the ontological argument in reply to Alvin Platinga's contention

The above argument provoked the following parody from Anselm's contemporary, Gaunilo.

> For example, there are those who say that somewhere in the ocean is an island, which, because of the difficulty — or rather, impossibility — of finding what does not exist, some call 'the Lost Island'. This island (so the story goes) is more plentifully endowed than even the Isles of the Blessed with an indescribable abundance of all sorts of riches and delights. And because it has neither owner nor inhabitant, it is every-where superior in its abundant riches to all the other lands that human beings inhabit. Suppose that someone tells me all this. The story is eas-ily told and involves no difficulty, and so I understand it. But if this person went on to draw a conclusion, and say, 'You cannot any longer doubt that this island, more excellent than all others on earth, truly exists somewhere in reality. For you do not doubt that this island exists in your understanding, and since it is more excellent to exist not merely in the understanding, but also in reality, this island must also exist in reality. For if it did not, any land that exists in reality would be greater than it. And so this more excellent thing that you have under-stood would not in fact be more excellent.' - If, I say, he should try to convince me by this argument that I should no longer doubt whether the island truly exists, either I would think he was joking, or I would not know whom I ought to think more foolish: myself, if I grant him his conclusion, or him, if he thinks he can establish the existence of that island with any degree of certainty, without first showing that its excellence exists in my understanding as a thing that truly and undoubtedly exists and not in any way like something false or uncer-tain.[14]

In his reply to Gaunilo, Anselm contests the validity of the island anal-ogy, arguing that the notion of the greatest island does not make sense. For, like the notion of the largest integer, we can always conceive of a larger. This is true of whatever criteria we use — size, number of trees *etcet-era*. But, according to Anselm, this is not true of God — for of 'something than which nothing greater can be thought' it *is* possible to claim maxi-mum omniscience, omnipotence and perfect goodness.

The first criticism of Anselm's argument to gain widespread con-sent — and still the most widely known criticism — was made by Kant. It is as follows:

> '*Being*' is obviously not a real predicate; that is, it is not a concept of a something that could be added to the concept of a thing. It is merely

---

that there is no conclusive refutation of the argument: Platinga, Alvin 'The Ontological Argument' in *God, Freedom, and Evil* 1974, p.86

14 Quoted in Hick, J. and McGill, A. (eds.) *The Many-Faced Argument: Recent Studies on the Ontological Argument for the Existence of God* 1967, pp.22–3 Following Gaunilo's example, Schopenhauer terms the ontological argument a 'charming joke'. (He prefers to ascribe aseity to 'the Will').

the positing of a thing, or of certain determinations, as existing in themselves. Logically, it is merely the copula of a judgment.[15]

Kant's point is that although anything that has any property has existence — existence *per se* is not itself an identifiable property: recognition of an object's 'being' or 'existence' follows *a posteriori* from the recognition that an object possesses a certain property. Therefore, although we may debate whether an object falls under a concept (for example, we can debate whether an object exists), we cannot legitimately argue from the existence of a concept ('something than which nothing greater can be thought') to the existence of its referent object.[16]

Saint Anselm's argument would amount to the claim that there is an existential proposition that is analytically true: but this claim would contravene the manner in which all other existential propositions are judged true or false.

Nathan Salmon makes the point (closely related to Kant's objection) that predication always precedes the attribution of existence. A hypothetical concept is proposed, but it is always a further question as to whether something exists to instantiate the concept. For example, although no dinosaurs presently exist, they all presently have the property of being extinct:[17] their past existence is inferred *a posteriori* from present evidence. In Anselm's argument this process is reversed: God's existence is inferred *a priori* from the evidence of the fool's 'understanding'.

Anselm's argument gains a spurious credibility by trading on an ambiguity in its second premise. The second premise of the argument — that which is understood exists in the understanding — may be mistakenly granted owing to its resemblance to the tautology that that which is understood is understood. But in fact Anselm is making a different claim: the second premise of his argument introduces an ontological distinction between 'understanding' and 'reality' that does not follow from the first premise.[18]

---

15 Kant, Immanuel *Critique of Pure Reason* (1781) trans. Norman Kemp Smith, 1933, p.504. Kant had in mind Descartes' ontological argument, but his objection applies equally well to Anselm's argument.

16 Most recent philosophers agree with Kant's criticism of the ontological argument, although they disagree as to the ramifications of this criticism. Recent supporters of the ontological argument form a small minority: they include Charles Hartshorne, Norman Malcolm, Alvin Platinga and Nicholas Rescher — see Oppy, Graham *Ontological Arguments and Belief in God*, 1995.

17 Salmon, N. 1987 'Existence' in J.Tomberlin (ed.) *Philosophical Perspectives* Vol.1 *Metaphysics*, p.97

18 In defence of Saint Anselm, Thomas Williams points out in his introduction to the *Proslogion* (1995), that the original title of the *Proslogion* (*fides quarens intellectum*, faith seeking understanding) suggests not that Anselm wishes to replace faith with understanding but rather that he intends to illustrate how understanding can augment and extend a pre-existing faith. According to this interpretation, *fides quarens intellectum* may be interpreted as 'an active love of God seeking a deeper knowledge of God.' This interpretation is further backed by

Returning to Ryle's criticisms, Ryle believes that, in supporting the ontological argument, Collingwood has fallen victim to the same logical error as Saint Anselm: that he is inferring actual existence from the existence of a concept.

The Ryle-Collingwood Correspondence

Ryle's article in *Mind* prompted a reply by E.E. Harris, entitled 'Mr Ryle and the Ontological Argument', in which he defends Collingwood and Anselm by means of the Kantian argument that 'the deduction of 'matters of fact' rests on the systematic character of the experienced world'.[19] In other words, examination of our experience of the world allows us to deduce necessary existential propositions (synthetic *a priori*). Ryle replies that he doubts the existence of synthetic *a priori* propositions, *on the same ground* that he doubts the ontological argument: 'existence propositions are synthetic, and are never logically necessary'[20]; they are established by induction and their denial would contain no contradiction.[21] He is prepared to defend the existence only of existential and analytical propositions. He suggests that when Kant proposed the existence of synthetic *a priori* propositions he ignored his own criticisms of the ontological argument.

Ryle invited Collingwood to publish an answer in response to his criticisms in *Mind*. Collingwood declined: instead he wrote a letter, 'twice the length of the paper itself, and ... a document which no editor of a journal would dream of publishing'. A total of three letters passed between Ryle and Collingwood upon the subject of the ontological argument: the first, from Collingwood to Ryle, dated 9 May 1935; the second, from Ryle to Collingwood, dated 21 May 1935; and the third, from Collingwood to Ryle, dated 6 June 1935. The most noticeable feature of this correspondence is the failure of both Ryle and Collingwood to understand the other's position. As Charlotte Vrijen points out:

> In the course of their correspondence, Ryle and Collingwood failed to convince each other on any point whatsoever. Moreover, they did not even understand each other's position. And yet Ryle and Collingwood asked each other questions, begged for clarification, and revealed their

---

Anselm's quotation of Augustine's translation of Isaiah 7:9: 'I do not seek to understand in order to believe; I believe in order to understand.' However, although this makes Anselm's argument more intelligible, in that it helps us understand that Anselm did not intend to entertain any viewpoint other than his own, it does not make his argument any more acceptable.

19   Harris, E.E. 'Mr Ryle and the Ontological Argument' *Mind* vol.XLV, Oct.1936: 474–80, p.476

20   Ryle, Gilbert 'Back to the Ontological Argument' *Mind* vol.XLVI, 1937: 53–57, p.55

21   Ryle, Gilbert 'Back to the Ontological Argument' *Mind* vol.XLVI, 1937: 53–57, p.56

definitions. How could all this have failed to contribute to mutual understanding of each other's position?[22]

Part of the reason is that Ryle believes Collingwood to be engaged in a 'traditional' metaphysical inquiry — observing the world at 'first hand'. The revelation in the third letter (6 June 1935) that Collingwood takes synthetic *a priori* propositions to exist would probably have confirmed Ryle's impression that there is no significant difference between Collingwood's position and Kant's — other than that Collingwood makes the *additional* mistake of 'falling for' the ontological argument. Collingwood's commitment to the ontological argument prevents Ryle from realising that Collingwood's aims are primarily epistemological and conceptual. Neither Harris nor Collingwood himself succeed in communicating to Ryle the nature of this project.

In his letter of 9 May 1935 Collingwood protests that Ryle, in his article in *Mind*, ascribes to him a doctrine that he does not hold. He states his agreement with Ryle that philosophical propositions do not establish *particular* matters of fact; and that 'hypothetical propositions do not *deny* the existence of their subjects, they only do not affirm or imply their existence'.[23] However, his (Collingwood's) claim is that philosophical propositions are neither hypothetical nor empirical.

To Ryle's claim that a logician's proposition might incidentally apply to itself, but that it does not on that count imply its own existence — Collingwood replies: 'If I ask you outright, *can* a logician expound satisfactorily a satisfactory theory of inference, without in the course of his exposition using inferences and thus showing that he believes inferences to exist? I feel fairly confident that you will answer, No'.[24]

Collingwood believes the onus falls upon Ryle to demonstrate that there is no contradiction in asserting that someone is a 'bad logician'. 'When you say that 'there is no contradiction in asserting that someone is a bad logician' it makes me at once wonder whether or not you have considered the very obvious reasons for saying the opposite, and what your reply would be'.[25]

In his reply of 21 May 1935, it is clear that Ryle believes he has not made himself sufficiently clear. He restates his position as follows: 'I don't mind how much the ontological argument is restated. If on any revision it involves the principle that the Essence of So and So involves that there

22　Vrijen, Charlotte 'Ryle and Collingwood: Their Correspondence and its Philosophical Context' *British Journal for the History of Philosophy* vol.14 no.1, Feb. 2006: 96

23　E.P.M., p.268 (9. 5. 35)

24　E.P.M., p.272 (9. 5. 35)

25　E.P.M., p.290 (9. 5. 35)

exists a so and so (or the so and so), then, I am maintaining, it contains a fallacy'.[26]

> [T]he only way of demonstrating a synthetic proposition is by the use of premises of which at least one must also be synthetic ... Without *any a posteriori* premises no existence propositions can be demonstrated; ... matters of fact cannot be the implicates of *a priori* propositions.[27]

Accepting Collingwood's invitation, Ryle also returns to the case of the 'bad logician': 'though we can know what a good logician *would be*, this knowledge can't tell us whether there is one or not'.[28] According to Ryle:

> Even, i.e., if it was part of the essence of the enquiry, called Logic, that *if* anyone takes part in that enquiry, he must be exemplifying the implications which he is exploring in the procedure of his enquiry, what is entailed by the nature of the enquiry and its subject matter is not the *fact* that someone does so proceed but only the hypothetical truth that *unless* someone does so proceed he won't be doing logic properly ... I'll grant (again for the sake of argument) that the enquiry called logic *can't* be done properly save in arguments which exemplify the forms of implication to be studied — and *still* I say that this is no case of Essence involving Existence — it is only a case of a big hypothetical proposition implying a smaller hypothetical proposition. We are saying 'the Essence of Implication involves that *any* logical enquiry into it *would* have such and such a character' which is exactly parallel to the Essence of *triangularity* involves that the internal angles of a triangle are equal to two right angles.[29]

In other words, what is termed the 'essence' of implication and the 'essence' of triangularity should more accurately be termed the analytic truth that implication is of such and such a character, and the analytic truth that triangularity is of such and such a character.

In the final letter of the series, that from Collingwood to Ryle, dated 6 June 1935, there is no sign that Collingwood and Ryle are approaching any nearer to a resolution of their differences. Collingwood states his belief in the existence of synthetic *a priori* propositions; and asks of Ryle: 'could you show that it is a pure verbal tautology that any triangle has its internal angles equal to two right angles?'.[30]

At this point the correspondence breaks off. In the case of the 'bad logician' both continue to believe the onus of justification is upon the other.

Metaphysics without Ontology

As outlined above, Ryle's replies to Collingwood are perhaps not conducive to the resolution of their differences. He fails to make the point that he

---

26   E.P.M. p.298 (21. 5. 35)
27   E.P.M. p.300 (21. 5. 35)
28   E.P.M. p.315 (21. 5. 35)
29   E.P.M., p.311–12 (21. 5. 35)
30   E.P.M., p.326 (6. 6. 35)

is not obliged to demonstrate that, for example, the geometrical properties of a triangle are hypothetical: if judgement is reserved concerning such questions, it remains the case that the ontological argument is invalid.

However, in his first letter to Ryle, Collingwood claims to have attempted a *revision* of Anselm's argument. This is apparent from the following passage:

> My own view of the Ontological Proof is that there is 'something *in* it', as we say but that its defect, in its traditional form, is that this something is left vague, and that the term God (as anyone might indeed guess, who is familiar with the general drift of neo-Platonic and early medieval thought) has to be taken as standing for 'that which we are thinking about when we are thinking philosophically.' When this is made clear, it is to me also clear that the traditional Ontological Proof will have to be revised and restated to bring it, so to speak, up to date; and this is what I have tried to do ... .[31]

This raises the question as to whether Collingwood's 'revised' version of the ontological argument is sufficiently different as to avoid the criticisms of Anselm's argument that have been raised above.

According to *An Essay on Metaphysics*: 'What it [the ontological argument] proves is not that because our idea of God is an idea of *id quo maius cogitari nequit* [that without which nothing follows] therefore God exists, but that because our idea of God is an idea of *id quo maius cogitari nequit* we stand committed to belief in God's existence'.[32] This suggests that Collingwood wishes to posit the existence of God as an absolute presupposition rather than as a proposition. That this is indeed how Collingwood sees the ontological argument is confirmed by his 1919 'Lectures on the Ontological Proof of the Existence of God' in which the idea is taken from Clement Webb's *Problems in the Relations of God and Man* (1911) that the ontological argument supports a prior system of metaphysics by telling us that our metaphysical concepts constitute a description of actual existence. It makes explicit the previously presupposed principle that our thought is thought of reality.[33] As such, according to Collingwood, the ontological argument—as opposed to scepticism or dogmatism—provides the only tolerable answer to the question: 'How can we ever be sure that we ever transcend the merely subjective world and get into touch with the objective?'.[34]

But, although an absolute presupposition possesses logical efficacy, it is as a series of propositions that an argument must stand or fall. Collingwood's faith may have been built upon the absolute presupposition that 'because our idea of God is an idea of *id quo maius cogitari nequit*

---

31   E.P.M., p.257 (9. 5. 35)

32   E.M., p.190

33   1919 'Lectures on the Ontological Proof of the Existence of God', p.92 (Bodleian)

34   1919 'Lectures on the Ontological Proof of the Existence of God', p.92

we stand committed to belief in God's existence'[35]; but this statement, whether taken as an absolute presupposition or as a proposition, does not add weight to the idea that God exists, or to the idea that we stand committed to belief in God's existence.

However, it is important to note that the failure of both Anselm's and Collingwood's version of the ontological argument does not invalidate Collingwood's epistemological and conceptual project. For, as Collingwood himself writes, at the conclusion of his theory of presupposition: 'The metaphysician's business ... is not to propound them [absolute presuppositions] but to propound the proposition that this or that one of them is presupposed'.[36] Questions of ontology are irrelevant to conceptual inquiries that begin with commonly agreed examples of good practice within a particular discipline of inquiry and end with the proposition that that discipline is reliant upon this or that absolute presupposition.

In view of the fact that Collingwood's project is not necessarily dependent upon the ontological argument, it is regrettable that Collingwood and Ryle did not discuss any other aspect of *An Essay on Philosophical Method*: for Collingwood's commitment to the ontological argument does not in any way invalidate his theory of presuppositions or his theory concerning the overlap of classes. However, in fairness to Ryle, at the time of their correspondence Collingwood had in *An Essay on Philosophical Method* (1933) only hinted at the role that he envisaged metaphysics might play in making absolute presuppositions explicit. This role was not made fully clear until *An Essay on Metaphysics* (1940).

By 1945 Ryle seems to have read more of Collingwood's work, for his inauguration address upon his succession to Collingwood's professorship at that date indicates a change in his attitude towards Collingwood's project, and a greater understanding of it.

> Professor Collingwood saw more clearly, I think, than did his most eminent predecessors in the philosophy of history that the appearance of a feud or antithesis between Nature and Spirit, that is to say, between the objectives of the natural sciences and those of the human sciences, is an illusion. These branches of inquiry are not giving rival answers to the same questions about the same world; nor are they giving separate answers to the same questions about rival worlds; they are giving their own answers to different questions about the same world.[37]

Commentators on Collingwood's work have subsequently noted a number of similarities between the philosophies of Ryle and Collingwood

---

35 E.M., p.190

36 E.M., p.33

37 Quoted by Charlotte Vrijen in 'Ryle and Collingwood: Their Correspondence and its Philosophical Context' *British Journal for the History of Philosophy* vol.14 no.1, Feb. 2006, p.125

— particularly with regard to the mind-body problem.[38] For example, in a similar manner to Collingwood, Ryle dismisses the mind-body problem as resting upon a 'category mistake'. He illustrates the meaning of this term, and his view of the mind-body problem, with the following well-known story.

> A foreigner visiting Oxford or Cambridge for the first time is shown a number of colleges, libraries, playing fields, museums, scientific departments and administrative offices. He then asks 'But where is the University? I have seen where the members of the Colleges live, where the Registrar works, where the scientists experiment and the rest. But I have not yet seen the University in which reside and work the members of your University.' It has then to be explained to him that the University is not another collateral institution, some ulterior counterpart to the colleges, laboratories and offices which he has seen. The University is just the way in which all that he has already seen is organised. When they are seen and when their coordination is understood, the University has been seen ... He was mistakenly allocating the University to the same category as that to which the other institutions belong.[39]

As illustrated by this story, the university is not a different entity than the colleges, libraries, playing fields *etcetera*, but a different category. Likewise, the mind is not a different category than the brain but a different category. Collingwood's project might be described *in Ryle's terms* as making manifest the absolute presuppositions that support different *categories* of understanding.

Intuition

For Collingwood, the ontological argument describes the relationship between faith and reason. 'Reason', according to Collingwood 'is Faith Cultivating Itself'.[40] That is to say (in the words of Lionel Rubinoff): 'Not only is faith the ground and source of reason, but reason itself, according to Collingwood, is no more than the development of faith into an articulated system'.[41]

But if the ontological argument is to be abandoned, does this leave reason as our sole means of understanding? Not entirely: there remains the act of intuiting whereby when we would seek an intuitive answer to a particular question we must purposely quiet our reason's interminable concern with the attainment of immediate practical objectives. Concentration and receptivity, but not passivity, are crucial to this process. In this respect

38 Dray, W. 'R.G. Collingwood and the Acquaintance Theory of Knowledge' *Revue Internationale de Philosophia* 1957 11: 427 – 8, p.431; Donagan, A. *The Later Philosophy of R.G. Collingwood* (1962) 1985, p.292; Van der Dussen, W.J. *History as a Science* 1981, p.367

39 Ryle, Gilbert *The Concept of Mind*, 1990, pp.17–18

40 Collingwood, R.G. 'Reason is Faith Cultivating Itself' in the *Hibbert Journal* XXVI (1927) reprinted in *Faith and Reason* (ed. Lionel Rubinoff), 1967, pp.108–21

41 Collingwood, R.G. *Faith and Reason* (ed. Lionel Rubinoff), 1967, pp.99–100

there is a similarity between the act of intuiting and the mystic's act of contemplation. Of course, if the believer would gain wider assent to the belief thus attained, he is obliged to provide reasonable answers to reasonable questions; and, in the course of this process, he may well find that his original belief is altered or overturned. However, it is worth noting that, in the reverse direction, the process whereby the conclusion of a reasoned argument is altered or overturned is often begun by an act of intuiting. This would seem to suggest that not only may we talk of reason as intuition cultivating itself, but we may also talk of intuition as reason cultivating itself; and that the act of intuiting and the act of reasoning are indeed, as Collingwood believes, compatible philosophical concepts, or (in Ryle's vocabulary) compatible categories of understanding.

But, strictly speaking, the act of intuiting and the act of reasoning should not be seen as compatible but as consupponible — logically non-conflicting — philosophical concepts. This may be illustrated by means of the following two examples of intuitively attained convictions.

She's a Pretty Girl.

It would be possible to provide a *reasonable* justification of this conviction but — to paraphrase Collingwood[42] — a pretty girl regarded in *this* way, ceases to be a pretty girl at all. Likewise:

The World Exists.

Assuming that the concern of reason is, in the first instance, with practical affairs — with problems arising from the practical necessity of choice — it is little wonder that reasonable justification entangles itself upon this conviction. In the case of this conviction, since I have never needed to persuade anyone of its truth, it would seem that an 'uncultivated' act of intuiting (or 'act of faith') is all that I require.

---

42   A., p.93

Chapter VII

Coda

In summary, in the preceding chapters I have attempted to provide an account of Collingwood's conception of philosophy and metaphysics without ontology. I have interpreted the latter as a means by which to answer the question of how we know what we know. In Collingwood's view the metaphysician is able to answer this question by recovering the absolute presuppositions of different disciplines of inquiry. In the face of the logical positivists' criticism of metaphysics, Collingwood points out that although absolute presuppositions are not encountered in an explicit form within the disciplines that they support, they nonetheless possess logical efficacy within those disciplines. In the previous chapter I have argued, against Collingwood, that the recovery of absolute presuppositions might be achieved without commitment to the ontological argument.

I have also attempted to demonstrate possible influences upon, and parallels to, Collingwood's philosophy, whilst yet not losing sight of his originality. This is not always easy, since Collingwood himself makes comparatively few references to his contemporaries, and is generally reluctant to categorise his philosophy in relation others. Nonetheless, since Collingwood makes plain his opposition to 'realism' the question naturally arises as to what sort of idealist he is. Indeed, it is sometimes remarked by Collingwood scholars that no informative study of his philosophy can avoid this question. Some scholars stress his affinity to Kant,[1] whilst others stress his affinity to Hegel.[2]

As was seen in the previous chapter, his commitment to the ontological argument is influenced by Hegel. So too is the criticism of Kant found in *An Essay on Philosophical Method*.

> If the methodology of philosophy (Kritik) is a propaedeutic to philosophy itself (Metaphysik), the name of philosophical science (Wissenschaft) cannot belong to them both; and we get the result, either that this name must be denied to the Critique of Pure Reason itself, a paradox rightly rejected by Kant's followers, or that it belongs

1   D'Oro, Giuseppina *Collingwood and the Metaphysics of Experience*, 2002
2   Browning, Gary K. *Rethinking R.G. Collingwood: Philosophy, Politics and the Unity of Theory and Practice*, 2004

exclusively to the propaedeutic and must be denied to substantive philosophy, which was from Kant's own point of view still more paradoxical. But on the other alternative, if methodology is a part of philosophy, Kant's programme collapses; for we can no longer hope to settle the methodological problems once for all and then go on with the substantive philosophy, because any advance in that will react upon and reopen the problems of methodology.[3]

On the other hand his claim, made in correspondence with Ryle,[4] that propositions concerning absolute presuppositions are 'synthetic *a priori*' suggests an affinity with Kantian metaphysics.

However, Collingwood himself, in his correspondence with Ryle (9 May 1935), disowns the label of 'idealist' completely. He asks:

why presume me an Idealist? I have nowhere in this essay or any other publication or lecture so described myself, and I do not see why you should attach the label to me without giving some reason.[5]

He also disowns the term 'idealist' in his autobiography. Yet, in 'Central Problems in Metaphysics' he admits to the positive influence of Hegel's 'objective idealism':

His system [Hegel's], imposing as it is and forming one of the most impressive monuments of philosophical thought, perhaps the most impressive since the close of the Middle Ages, contains a great deal of jerry-building and could not possibly be accepted even by his warmest admirers now, a hundred years after his death. But the main metaphysical idea which inspired it, the conception of objective idealism, is the most promising of the metaphysical ideas current today, and in my judgement the only one which is likely to prove fertile in the metaphysical work to be done in the near future.[6]

Earlier in this document Collingwood summarises 'objective idealism' somewhat cryptically as follows:

The view which I have been putting before you is that the world which we perceive does really and truly exist as we perceive it, but that it exists *as* we perceive it only *because* we perceive it.[7]

This sentence might be interpreted to mean 'knowledge is necessarily of what is the case', but it is difficult to know how to interpret '*because*'. Elsewhere, in the 'Central Problems of Metaphysics', Collingwood seems to follow Hegel in arguing that an immanent 'Idea' underlies and logically necessitates the existence of the material world, an Idea made manifest in

---

3   E.P.M., p.21 See Hegel's criticisms of Kant's 'subjective idealism' in *Hegel's Logic*, 1975, p.73

4   E.P.M., p.318 (6 . 6. 35)

5   E.P.M., p.256

6   'Central Problems in Metaphysics — Lectures written April 1935, for delivery [T]rinity [T]erm 1935' Bodleian Library, Dep.1, p.69.

7   'Central Problems in Metaphysics — Lectures written April 1935, for delivery [T]rinity [T]erm 1935' Bodleian Library, Dep.1, p.37 Confusingly, Hegel refers to his own form of idealism not as 'objective idealism' but as 'absolute idealism' — *Hegel's Logic*, 1975, p.73

the mind's self-awareness. However in *The New Leviathan* Collingwood criticises this form of Hegelian argument:

> 33. 85. Hegel thought that a dialectical world is a world where everything *argued itself into existence*.
>
> 33. 86. He thought that a Platonic 'dialectic in words' set the standard of a dialectical pattern to which the 'dialectic of things' must conform.
>
> 33. 87. This was theology, and anthropomorphic theology of a quite low type. 'In the beginning was the word, and the word was with God, and the word was God'.
>
> 33. 88. Hegel says outright that his dialectical logic is an exposition of the nature of God; and that the transition from God to Nature in his *Encyclopaedia* is an exposition of the process whereby God creates Nature.
>
> 33. 89. The mistake is the Fallacy of the Misplaced Argument. Hegel aims at building up the concrete out of abstractions; not realising that, unless the concrete is given from the start, the abstractions out of which it is built up are not forthcoming'.[8]

It is difficult to know how Collingwood can praise 'objective idealism' as he does in the light of these criticisms of Hegel.

But it is important that these exegetical problems concerning Collingwood's relations to Kant and Hegel do not obscure the fact that Collingwood's goal of discovering the absolute presuppositions of various disciplines of inquiry is essentially a conceptual project: it aims to discover the logical conditions of knowledge.

As such Collingwood's philosophy is sometimes seen as a form of conceptual or transcendental idealism. However, this categorisation may also be misleading. Bearing in mind that his philosophy has no aspirations to answer ontological questions, it is perhaps misleading to characterise it as any form of 'idealism' or 'realism'. It may be wiser to follow Collingwood's lead and to restrict ourselves — in name and practice — to 'metaphysics without ontology'.

---

8   N.L., p.278

PART TWO

Chapter VIII

History

Its Subject Matter and Absolute Presuppositions

As previously mentioned, *The Principles of History*—the book that was intended as the definitive presentation of history's absolute presentation—remained unfinished at the time of Collingwood's death in 1943. (It was published in its unfinished form in 1999.) Moreover *The Idea of History*, Collingwood's most widely read work in the philosophy of history, exists in a form unenvisaged by its author, its first four parts being works of historiography, and only its latter fifth part (the 'Epilegomena', compiled by Knox, after Collingwood's death) being a work of philosophy. Consequently, although Collingwood wrote extensively on the philosophy of history there is no single definitive text in which he reveals the absolute presuppositions of history by working, via the theory of presupposition and the method of question and answer, through the historian's relative presuppositions to the historian's unquestioned but logically essential absolute presuppositions. Nonetheless he makes plain his view that: 'all history is the history of thought'[1]; and that this, in his view, is an absolute presupposition of history.

In making this claim, Collingwood intends to convey the idea that all history worthy of the name is the history of thought. He fully admits that there are many histories that are *not* histories of thought: but he claims that these are histories by default, in that we have no other name for them.[2]

Collingwood dismisses these histories as 'unscientific.' It is only history that attends to the thought of historical agents that he praises as 'scientific'. These acts of praise and dismissal are logically simultaneous: Collingwood consciously aims to work from what are commonly agreed to be the best examples of historians' practice—so as to arrive at the absolute presuppo-

---

1   A., p.110; I.H., pp.215, 317; P.H., pp.67, 98, 100
2   P.H., p.12; I.H., p.257

sitions that the historian does and should rely upon. He aims to examine what a discipline is 'like' before pronouncing what it is 'about'.[3]

Collingwood claims that history is a science in that it is organised according to the nature of its subject matter; and in such a manner as to be able to justify its conclusions concerning that subject matter. He uses the word 'science' in the Latin sense of *scientia* meaning an organised body of knowledge[4] — that must justify its claims to knowledge by exhibiting the grounds upon which it is based.[5]

> History has this in common with every other science: that the historian is not allowed to claim any single piece of knowledge, except where he can justify his claim by exhibiting to himself in the first place, and secondly to anyone else who is both able and willing to follow his demonstration, the grounds upon which it is based.[6]

However, before proceeding to describe the special characteristics of historical inference, Collingwood first describes several forms of history that *cannot* justify their claims to knowledge.

Scissors-and-Paste History

Collingwood uses the term 'scissors-and-paste' history to describe a form of history that is unscientific, in that it accepts the accuracy of an authority 'on trust': any inferences that are subsequently drawn by the historian are ultimately reliant upon this assumption of trust. It is therefore completely dependent upon the testimony of authorities.

'Scissors-and-paste' history (such as predominated in classical and medieval Europe) consists not in consciously asking specific questions but in simply deciding what one wants to know about and searching for the relevant statements made by the eyewitnesses of particular events — omitting the most unbelievable accounts, either because they contradict other more believable accounts, or because they were thought to be incredible by the standards of the historian's own age. No attempt is made to understand the motives behind incredible statements or to understand the context in which they were made. That is to say no attempt is made to understand the questions that these statements attempt to answer, and the presuppositions upon which these questions were based.

Collingwood describes the methods of the scissors-and-paste historian as follows.

> As a rule, where he has many statements to draw upon, he will find that one of them tells him what another does not; so both or all of them will be incorporated. Sometimes he will find that one of them contra-

---

3   P.H., pp.39–40
4   P.H., p.3; I.H., p.249
5   P.H., p.7; I.H., p.252
6   P.H., p.7; I.H., p.252

dicts another; then, unless he can find a way of reconciling them, he must decide to leave one out; and this, if he is conscientious, will involve him in a critical consideration of the contradictory authorities' relative degree of trustworthiness. And sometimes one of them, or possibly even all of them, will tell him a story which he simply cannot believe, a story characteristic, perhaps, of the superstitions or prejudices of the author's time or the circle in which he lived, but not credible to a more enlightened age, and therefore to be omitted.[7]

This crude form of scissors-and-paste history was displaced in the seventeenth century when it was realised that the credibility of any statement is dependent upon what might be gathered as to the circumstances of its origin. Collingwood terms history written in the light of this realisation 'critical history'.

Critical History

Critical history still consists of a straightforward process of rejection and acceptance of *sources* (as opposed to the historian's previous reliance upon *authorities*); and the 'pasting' of these sources together so as to form a narrative. In this respect it is still a form of scissors-and-paste history, albeit a more sophisticated form than that found in the classical and medieval periods. According to Collingwood:

> As soon as it became understood that a given statement, made by a given author, must never be accepted for historical truth until the credibility of the author in general and of this statement in particular had been systematically inquired into, the word 'authority' disappeared from the vocabulary of historical method, except as an archaistic survival; for the man who makes the statement came henceforth to be regarded not as someone whose word must be taken for the truth of what he says, which is what was meant by calling him an authority, but as someone who has voluntarily placed himself in the witness-box for cross-examination. The document hitherto called an authority now acquired a new status, properly described by calling it a 'source', a word indicating simply that it contains the statement, without any implications as to its value. That is *sub judice*; and it is the historian who judges.[8]

The Common-sense Theory of History

In *The Idea of History* Collingwood also mentions 'the common-sense theory of history', according to which:

> the essential things in history are memory and authority. If an event or a state of things is to be historically known, first of all some one must be acquainted with it; then he must remember it; then he must state his recollection of it in terms intelligible to another; and finally that other must accept the statement as true. History is thus the believing some

---

7   P.H., p.13; I.H., p.257
8   P.H., p.14; I.H., pp.258–9

one else when he says that he remembers something. The believer is the historian; the person believed is called his authority.[9]

Due to the editing of *The Idea of History*, the relationship between this theory and scissors-and-paste history is not made explicit. (The common-sense theory of history was the subject of Collingwood's inaugural lecture as Waynflete Professor of Metaphysical Philosophy (1935) – which Knox incorporated into the Epilegomena of The Idea of History under the heading of 'The Historical Imagination'[10]). However, it is safe to infer that it is this theory that underlies scissors-and-paste history.

Collingwood argues that the influence of this theory is still to be seen, when historians attempt to defend history by attempting to minimize or downplay the extent to which selection, construction and criticism take place.

> In general, when we [as historians] reflect on our own work, we seem to accept what I have called the common-sense theory, while claiming our own rights of selection, construction and criticism. No doubt these rights are inconsistent with the theory; but we attempt to soften the contradiction by minimizing the extent to which they are exercised, thinking of them as emergency measures, a kind of revolt into which the historian may be driven at times by the exceptional incompetence of his authorities, but which does not fundamentally disturb the normal peaceful regime in which he placidly believes what he is told because he is told to believe it.[11]

Precursors of Scientific History

In *The Idea of History* Collingwood relates how critical history thrived in Germany during the late eighteenth and early nineteenth centuries, and how to its detriment it ignored the criticisms that Vico had made of scissors-and-paste history at the beginning of the eighteenth century. In *Scienza nuova* (first published in 1725) Vico had argued that if a statement could not be accepted as literally true it should not on that account be rejected as entirely worthless, for we cannot imbue the actions of earlier periods with the influence of contemporary modes of thought. Instead, the historian's explanation should begin by describing the point at which its subject begins to take shape.

> Now, anyone who had read Vico, or even a second-hand version of some of his ideas, must have known that the important question about any statement contained in a source is not whether it is true or false, but what it means. And to ask what it means is to step right outside the world of scissors-and-paste history into a world where history is not

---

9   I.H., pp.234–5
10   Boucher, D. 'The Significance of Collingwood's *Principles of History*' *Journal of the History of Ideas*, 1997, 58, p.312
11   I.H., pp.235–6

written by copying out the testimony of the best sources, but by coming to your own conclusions.[12]

Collingwood argues that this insight was not fully realized even in the late eighteenth and early nineteenth centuries: and that it is only in the twentieth century that the value of Vico's insight has come to be realized by historians, though not by philosophers.[13]

Vico's approach is contrasted to that of Descartes, who is preoccupied with skeptical problems of a type that do not occur in 'history'. (Vico had argued that Descartes' principle of universal doubt was inapplicable to historical research).

> Descartes, starting his researches into the method of natural science from the sceptical point of view which then prevailed in France, had to begin by assuring himself that there really was such a thing as the material world. For history as conceived by Vico no such problem could exist. The sceptical point of view is impossible. History, for Vico, is not concerned with the past as past. It is concerned, in the first instance, with the actual structure of the society in which we live; the manners and customs which we share with the people around us. In order to study these we need not ask whether they really exist. The question has no meaning. Descartes, looking at the fire, asked himself whether in addition to his own idea of a fire there was also a real fire. For Vico, looking at such a thing as the Italian language of his own day, no parallel question could arise. The distinction between the idea of such an historical reality and the reality itself would be meaningless.[14]

In the nineteenth century, F.H. Bradley anticipated the means whereby the historian justifies his claims: Collingwood relates how in 'The Presuppositions of Critical History' Bradley rightly argued that in weighing his evidence the historian relies on his own experience as a criterion by which to judge its accuracy. However, in Collingwood's opinion, Bradley misconceives the means by which the historian's experience is brought into play. Bradley conceives of the historian's own experience as remaining the same during the process of interpretation. He also overestimates the similarities between history and natural science.

> He [Bradley] regards the historian's scientific knowledge as giving him the means of distinguishing between what can and what cannot happen; and this scientific knowledge he conceives in the positivistic manner, as based on induction ... Bradley rightly saw that the historian's criterion is something which he brings with him to the study of the evidence, and that this something is simply himself; but it is himself not *qua* scientist, as Bradley thought, but *qua* historian. It is only by practising historical thought that he learns to think historically. His

---

12 P.H., p.15; I.H., p.260

13 Vico presented his ideas in a somewhat garbled fashion. They were relatively neglected until their translation into French by the historian Jules Michelet in the early nineteenth century. No English translation existed until 1968: *The New Science of Giambattista Vico*, trans. Thomas G. Bergin and Max H. Fisch, Ithaca: Cornell University Press.

14 I.H., pp.65–6

criterion is therefore never ready-made; the experience from which it is derived is his experience of historical thinking, and it grows with every growth in his historical knowledge. History is its own criterion; it does not depend for its validity on something outside itself, it is an autonomous form of thought with its own principles and its own methods.[15]

Thus Bradley is a precursor of scientific history in that he realizes the faults of scissors-and-paste history, but he does not fully grasp the remedy.

Scientific History

Collingwood argues that since the scientific historian deals with potentially unlimited evidence (that may include both written and unwritten sources) it is incumbent that he asks the right questions in the right order. A good historian asks only questions that he sees some way of answering.[16] For — although the historian hopes to discover the questions and the presuppositions behind the agent's 'answers' — in a piece of historical evidence, he can not expect to read this answer as a *direct* answer to his own initial questions, in the manner suggested by Bradley. He must understand the agent's statements as 'answers' to questions *asked by the agent*.

> Confronted with a ready-made statement about the subject he is studying, the scientific historian never asks himself: 'Is this statement true or false?', in other words 'Shall I incorporate it in my history of that subject or not?' The question he asks himself is: 'What does this statement mean?' And this is not equivalent to the question 'What did the person who made it mean by it?', although that is doubtless a question that the historian must ask, and must be able to answer. It is equivalent, rather, to the question 'What light is thrown on the subject in which I am interested by the fact that this person made this statement, meaning by it what he did mean.[17]

In other words, the historian must ask himself: 'what question does the agent's statement attempt to answer and what presupposition underlies this question?' It is by the use of these methods the historian should be able to defend his own assertions, rather than by taking another authority 'on trust'.

In order to understand an agent's action, the historian must first understand previous historians' interpretations of that action — what questions these historians asked and what presuppositions prompted these questions. This involves asking the right questions in the right order, so as to view the agent's action with as few preconceptions as possible. The agent's

---

15   I.H., pp.139–40

16   'A sensible question (the only kind of question that a scientifically competent man will ask) is a question which you think you have or are going to have evidence for answering.' P.H., p.36; I.H., p.281

17   P.H., p.30; I.H., p.275

action may then itself be viewed as the answer to a particular question asked by the agent, e.g. 'what should I do in this situation?' It is thus that the historian eventually arrives at the presuppositions underlying – and explaining – the actions of the historical agent.

Underlying this process of discovery is the absolute presupposition 'all history is the history of thought':[18] by this Collingwood is not claiming that all history is the history of ideas, but that in granting the capacity to reason to the historical agent, the historian is able to understand beliefs that may differ from his own. He is able to forestall the unfounded imposition of his own contemporary values, such as occurs in scissors-and-paste history. This is illustrated in the following well-known passage.

> If the reason why it is hard for a man to cross the mountains is because he is frightened of the devils in them, it is folly for the historian, preaching at him across a gulf of centuries, to say 'This is sheer superstition. There are no devils at all. Face facts, and realize that there are no dangers in the mountains except rocks and water and snow, wolves perhaps, and bad men perhaps, but no devils.' The historian says these are the facts because that is the way he has been taught to think. But the devil-fearer says that the presence of devils is a fact, because that is the way in which he has been taught to think. The historian thinks it a wrong way; but wrong ways of thinking are just as much historical facts as right ones, and, no less than they, determine the situation (always a thought-situation) in which the man who shares them is placed. The hardness of the fact consists in the man's inability to think of his situation otherwise. The compulsion which the devil-haunted mountains exercise on the man who would cross them consists in the fact that he cannot help believing in the devils. Sheer superstition, no doubt: but this superstition is a fact, and the crucial fact in the situation we are considering. The man who suffers from it when he tries to cross the mountains is not suffering merely for the sins of his fathers who taught him to believe in devils, if that is a sin; he is suffering because he has accepted the belief, because he has shared the sin. If the modern historian believes that there are no devils in the mountains, that too is only a belief he has accepted in precisely the same way.
>
> The discovery that the men whose actions he studies are in this sense free is a discovery which every historian makes as soon as he arrives at a scientific mastery of his own subject.[19]

Collingwood's point is that the attribution of reason and choice of action to the historical agent maximizes the lines of interpretation and inquiry that are open to the historian. The historian does not impose his own criterion of rationality upon the devil-fearers, and thereby dub them 'mad'. He allows for the fact that the reasoning underlying their actions may be valid, although predicated upon a premise that he (the historian) might not share. The fact that the historian gives priority to understanding of the historical agent's reason allows for the possibility of the agent's premises

---

18 A., p.110; I.H., pp.215, 317; P.H., pp.67, 98, 100
19 P.H., pp.100–1; I.H., pp.317–18

being different from the historian's. He attempts to reconstruct the questions that past agents attempted to answer, and the presuppositions implicit within those questions. He is alert to the existence of alien *rationales*.

It is the historian's interest in, and reliance upon, the reconstruction of reason that distinguishes his work from, for example, the work of the psychologist:

> Thus the historian is not interested in the fact that men eat, sleep and make love and thus satisfy their natural appetites; but he is interested in the social customs which they create by their thought as a framework within which these appetites find satisfaction in ways sanctioned by convention and morality.[20]

Reason may study the irrational forces upon which reason itself is built, but in so doing (within the discipline of psychology) reason is not studying itself:

> By learning to know them, it finds out how it can help them to live in health, so that they can feed and support it while it pursues its own proper task, the self-conscious creation of its own historical life.[21]

The historian, as opposed to the psychologist and the natural scientist, is primarily interested in past acts of *thought*. His interest is not primarily in how geographical and climactic conditions dictate the course of human lives. This is not to imply that he minimizes the effect that these factors have upon human lives, but rather that he determines their effects by analysing agents' *awareness* of these factors, as expressed in the evidence of their *thought*.

> To be sure, there is an intimate relation between any culture and its natural environment; but what determines its character is not the facts of that environment, in themselves, but what man is able to get out of them; and that depends on what kind of man he is.[22]

Objections

Jan van der Dussen summarises objections to Collingwood's conception of history under three headings: 'a) the irrational aspects of human action are not taken into account; b) social and economic history fall outside its sphere; and c) it is only relevant for individual actions, but not for group or mass-behaviour'.[23] Two other possible objections may be added to this list: d) that Collingwood's view would limit the study of history to the study of written evidence; and that e) Collingwood limits history to the study of human beings, assigning humanity a privileged place in the universe.

---

20   I.H., p.216
21   I.H., p.231
22   I.H. p.79
23   Van der Dussen, W.J. *History as a Science: The Philosophy of R.G. Collingwood*, 1981, p.83

In response to these objections, a broad agreement has been achieved between Collingwood's defenders: Collingwood is not advocating a particular methodological precept that *guarantees* understanding. He is attempting to provide an analysis of the logical nature of historians' explanations. Admittedly, Collingwood does advocate that the historian, whenever possible, should nurture empathy with his subject matter; but his primary concern is not with historical methodology but with historical understanding:

> When Collingwood says that historical understanding consists of penetrating to the thought-side of actions — discovering the thought and nothing further — the temptation to interpret this in the methodological way is understandably strong. But there is another way in which the doctrine can be formulated: 'Only by putting yourself in the agent's position can you *understand* why he did what he did'. The point of the 'projection' metaphor is, in this case, more plausibly interpreted as a logical one. Its function is not to remind us of *how we come to know* certain facts, but to formulate, however tentatively, certain *conditions which must be satisfied* before a historian is prepared to say: 'Now I have the explanation'.[24]

I shall now examine exactly how Collingwood might be defended against each of the five objections listed above — saving, in my view, the most serious charge (that Collingwood fails to account for the irrational aspects of human action) until last.

(i) Social and Economic History

Collingwood claims that economic activity has a history for the reason that:

> A man who builds a factory or starts a bank is acting on a purpose which we can understand; so are the men who accepts wages from him, buy his goods or his shares, or make deposits and withdrawals. If we are told that there was a strike at the factory or a run on the bank, we can reconstruct in our own minds the purposes of the people whose collective action took those forms.[25]

In short, economic activity may be subject matter for the historian because it embodies reflective purposive thought that, by its nature, is capable of transcending its immediate context.

> In order ... that any particular act of thought should become subject-matter for history, it must be an act not only of thought but of reflective thought, that is, one which is performed in the consciousness that it is being performed, and is constituted what it is by that consciousness.[26]

---

24   Dray, W.H. *Laws and Explanation in History*, 1957b, p.128

25   I.H., p.310

26   I.H., p.308

It is true that an economic condition is non-reflective, but reactions to an economic condition should be understood whenever possible *via* the agent's reflective nature of thought. Dray argues that once this is understood it may then be admitted that one might know an agent's thought better than he knew it himself.[27] But, what the historian cannot do is to determine *a priori* that he knows the agent's thought better than he knew it himself, and thereby over-ride the possibility of the reconstruction of the agent's reasoning, for it is this potential rationality subject that distinguishes the historian's subject matter. Collingwood claims that any action that embodies this reflective and purposive character may become a subject of history.

> An act is more than a mere unique individual; it is something having a universal character; and in the case of a reflective or deliberate act (an act which we not only do, but intend to do before doing it) this universal character is the plan or idea of the act which we conceive in our thought before doing the act itself, and the criterion by reference to which, when we have done it, we know that we have done what we meant to do.[28]

Even art, as a 'reflective or deliberate act (an act which we not only do, but intend to do before doing it)', may be a subject of history, though the artist may not know the exact form of the solution to the 'problem' he works on until the moment of that work's completion.[29]

Conversely, *unscientific* history is that in which the historian does not allow for the possibility of reconstructing the agent's thought. This is the point that Collingwood is making in the following well-known passage:

> It makes no difference to the historian, as an historian, that there should be no food in a poor man's house; though it may and must make a difference to him as a man with feelings for his fellow creatures; and though as an historian he may be intensely concerned with the shifts by which other men have contrived to bring about this state of things in order that they should be rich and the men who take wages from them poor; and equally concerned with the action to which the poor man may be led not by the fact of his children's unsatisfied hunger, the fact, the physiological fact, of empty bellies and wizened limbs, but by his thought of that fact.[30]

In unscientific history the poor man's *thought* of 'his children's unsatisfied hunger' is ignored so as to concentrate upon 'the physiological fact'. Collingwood argues that the latter may illuminate the former, but it should not be understood as replacing it, even though the former may rarely be expressed. An understanding of the physiological fact may be

27 Dray, W. 'R.G. Collingwood and the Acquaintance Theory of Knowledge' *Revue Internationale de Philosophie* 11 1957a, p.426

28 I.H., p.309

29 I.H., p.314

30 P.H., pp.98–99; I.H., pp.315–16

gained via theories from geography, sociology and economics, but the historian must remember that these theories are tools used in pursuit of his primary *historical* aim. If this is forgotten the historian is likely to impose his own preconceptions upon his data. The historian may prove himself adept at the detection of patterns within his data, but, if the detection of patterns and laws is considered to be his primary aim, he is likely to miss clues that might illuminate reasoning different from his own.

Collingwood terms this 'pigeon-holing.' As seen in the following passage, his views on 'pigeon-holing' are similar to Popper's views on 'historicism'[31]:

> all those schemes and patterns into which history has again and again, with surprising docility, allowed itself to be forced by such men as Vico, with his pattern of historical cycles based on Greco-Roman speculations; Kant, with his proposal for a 'universal history from a cosmopolitan point of view'; Hegel, who followed Kant in conceiving universal history as the progressive realization of human freedom; Comte and Marx, two very great men who followed Hegel's lead each in his own way, and so on down to Flinders Petrie, Oswald Spengler, and Arnold Toynbee in our own time, whose affinities are less with Hegel, than with Vico.[32]

According to both Collingwood and Popper 'grand narrative' accounts of history directed towards a particular end are prone to make the mistake of—in Collingwood's example—ignoring the poor man's *thought*. This occurs when history is 'anthropogenetic'—when it aspires to display the process by which humanity comes to its full self-realisation; and when, to this end, the historian grants himself *carte blanche* to arrange events so as to lead to this event. Popper points out that even if there is an 'end' in history we could not know it since we could have no evidence that we have reached the end of history. Likewise, Collingwood points out:

> History terminates not in the future but in the present. The historian's task is to show how the present has come into existence; he cannot show how the future will have come into existence, for he does not know what the future will be.[33]

According to Popper, historicists 'feel bound to avoid any selective point of view; but since this is impossible, they usually adopt points of view without being aware of them. This must defeat their efforts to be objective, for one cannot possibly be critical of one's own point of view, and conscious of its limitations, without being aware of it'.[34] The historicist's own unexamined viewpoint provides the fulcrum upon

31   In this work I use the term 'historicism' solely in Popper's sense of the word.

32   P.H., p.19; I.H., p.264

33   I.H., p.104

34   Popper, Karl *The Poverty of Historicism*, 1957, p.152

which his 'laws' are constructed, between the objects of his study and his predictions concerning the future. In particular:

> The belief ... that it is the task of social science to lay bare the *law of evolution of society* in order to foretell its future ... might perhaps be described as the central historicist doctrine.[35]

Popper argues that since the fulfilment of these laws is predicted to occur in the future, they can never be falsified. He suggests that, to the extent that there is empirical evidence for these 'laws', they should more accurately be termed 'trends'.

Both Popper and Collingwood are concerned lest consideration of economic and social factors overwhelm the ambition of understanding the peculiarly unique situations of past historical agents. Both:

> ... are deeply committed to the view that there is one and only one common human rationality, and that the presuppositions of alien people, past or present, are always in principle intelligible, given sufficient, patience and goodwill.[36]

Collingwood believes that although economic and social considerations are in many cases extremely important they should not be allowed to overwhelm that which is conceptually distinctive about history – the reconstruction of an agent's reasons.

In summary, Collingwood's view of 'scientific history' attempts to account for the role played by economic and social trends in history whilst yet still according *logical* priority to the reconstruction of the agent's reasoning. This logical priority stands as a conceptual barrier against the consideration of economic and social factors overwhelming the distinctively historical ambition of reconstructing past reasoning.

(ii) Group Behaviour

The charge that Collingwood's conception of history takes no account of group or mass behavior presupposes that Collingwood is an advocate of methodological individualism. However, this label, as applied to Collingwood, is misleading. He does not subscribe to Thomas Carlyle's belief, that:

> Universal History, the history of what man has accomplished in this world, is at bottom the History of the Great Men who have worked here.[37]

Nor does he subscribe to John Stuart Mill's belief that laws that apply to society as a whole must be deduced from laws that apply to society's constituents (i.e. from psychological laws). The latter view is traceable to

---

35   Popper, Karl *The Poverty of Historicism*, 1957, pp.105–06
36   Skagestad, Peter *Making Sense of* History, 1975, p.19
37   Carlyle, Thomas 'On Heroes, Hero-Worship, and the Heroic in History' (1840) in *The Varieties of History* (ed. Fritz Stern), 1956, p.101

Hobbes; and is advocated by Popper and Von Hayek. According to Von Hayek:

> There is no other way towards an understanding of social phenomena but through our understanding of individual actions directed towards other people and guided by their expected behaviour.[38]

This view is often contrasted to 'methodological holism' — the view, of sociologists such as Emile Durkheim, that the subject matter of the social sciences is the entire structure of society, which need not be studied via its constituent parts.

Collingwood does not view the issue as a straightforward choice between methodological individualism and methodological holism: indeed, he does not face this choice. His argument is simply that the historian must reconstruct the agent's *reasoning*.

He should not be interpreted as advocating the expulsion from history of insights derived from economics, geography, sociology and anthropology. Nor should he be interpreted as disapproving of historians themselves formulating laws concerning 'group behaviour'. Indeed there are examples from Collingwood's own work in archaeology that demonstrate his willingness to make use of general laws. For example, in an article on the prehistory of Cumbria, Collingwood quotes with approval the following generalization by Sir Cyril Fox:

> In the lowlands of Britain new cultures of continental origin tend to be *imposed*. In the highland, on the other hand, these tend to be *absorbed*. In the *lowlands* you get replacement, in the highlands *fusion*.

Collingwood adds: 'I shall venture to refer to this principle as "Fox's law"'.[39] There is also the example from 'Town and Country in Roman Britain'[40] in which Collingwood provides an estimate of the total population of Roman Britain. According to Collingwood:

> The reason why it is worth while to ascertain the total population of a given country, at a given time, is that a necessary relation exists between the density of a population and the way it lives ... a figure, expressing the number of inhabitants to the square mile is a valuable index of the economic condition of the country.[41]

Collingwood is eager to make use of insights from geography and economics, whilst yet retaining the conceptual independence of history.

However, his attitude to anthropology is different to his attitude to geography and economics: he regards at least a part of anthropology as a

---

38 Von Hayek, Friedrich *Individualism and Economic Order*, 1949, p.6

39 Collingwood, R.G. 'An Introduction to the Prehistory of Cumberland, Westmorland and Lancashire north of the Sands' p. 171 *Transactions of the Cumberland and Westmorland Antiquarian and Archaeological Society* 33 (1933), pp.163–200

40 Collingwood, R.G. 'Town and Country in Roman Britain' *Antiquity* 3 (1929), pp.261–76. See also A., pp.135–7.

41 Collingwood, R.G. 'Town and Country in Roman Britain' *Antiquity* 3 (1929), pp.262–3.

'historical science'. In the introduction to *The Philosophy of Enchantment*
Wendy James locates Collingwood's views within the context of contemporaneous anthropology and demonstrates that he was fully conversant
with recent work in that field: she views Collingwood's position as sympathetic to that of the anthropologist Evans-Pritchard[42] and critical of the
position of Radcliffe-Brown. Radcliffe-Brown sees anthropology as a
branch of natural science; Evans-Pritchard disagrees — he stresses the need
for sympathy with the people under study. In Collingwood's view:

> In anthropological science man is trying to understand man; and to
> man his fellow-man is never a mere external object, something to be
> observed and described, but something to be sympathized with, to be
> studied by penetrating into his thoughts and re-enacting those
> thoughts for oneself. Anthropology — I refer to cultural, not physical,
> anthropology — is an historical science, where by calling it historical as
> opposed to naturalistic I mean that its true method is thus to get inside
> its object or recreate its object inside itself.[43]

Collingwood does not imply that man can never be studied as something
external to a writer's own interests, but that the anthropologist who does
not attempt 'to recreate in his own mind the experiences whose outward
expression he is studying'[44] will not achieve the fullest understanding of
his subject matter.

(iii) Unwritten Evidence

As is evident from the following passage Collingwood's attitude to
unwritten evidence of intentional action is essentially the same as that
which he takes towards written evidence.

> For a rational animal, in so far as he is rational (and in the case of man, I
> repeat, that is never very far), every action has the character of lan-
> guage: every action is an expression of thought. Every trace of his
> action left upon the world he inhabits has the character of writing:
> every such trace is evidence, to a person who can read it, of what his
> thought was. A man climbing a snow-covered mountain is putting
> into practice his plan for getting to the top; and if he sticks to his plan,
> his movements during the ascent make up a continuous piece of lan-
> guage, from which an understanding watcher can make out, with as
> much precision as if he were listening to a running commentary given
> by the climber in words, what the plan is. And because he leaves tracks
> in the snow, which as long as they remain legible preserve a tolerably
> complete notation of his movements, it remains possible to read his

---

42   Evans-Pritchard favourably reviewed the second edition of Collingwood's *Roman Britain* in
     Man 32 (1932), pp.220–21. Collingwood quotes Evans-Pritchard's *Witchcraft, Oracles and Magic
     among the Azande*, 1937 in P.A., p. 8 f.n..

43   P.E., pp.153–4

44   P.E., p.153 This is the kernel of Collingwood's criticism of James Frazer's *The Golden Bough*
     (1913). Wittgenstein makes similar criticisms : see *Philosophical Occasions 1912–51*, 1993,
     pp.115–55.

movement-language after he has ceased to utter it, and reconstruct the history of his ascent from the evidence of his footprints.[45]

This suggests that there is no conceptual difference between explanations in history and explanations in 'prehistory' — both contain accounts of rational actions.[46]

For Collingwood, '[w]ords are historical and social facts'.[47] This suggests that certain fundamental questions asked of written evidence will be the same as that concerning unwritten evidence — for example, questions concerning the provenance of the historian's evidence.

He dismisses the idea that archaeology is the 'handmaid of history',[48] useful only in cases where there is no written evidence, and suggests instead that archaeology should be seen as 'the methodology of history'.[49]

(iv) Human Chauvinism[50]

As is perhaps clearer in *The Principles of History* than in *The Idea of History*, Collingwood does not simply define human beings as rational and on that ground conclude that the subject matter of history is human beings. As he indicates in the following passage, his argument is not that the subject matter of history is human beings but that it is rational thought.

> *Res Gestae* are not the actions, in the widest sense of that word, which are done by animals of the species called human; they are actions in another sense of the same word, equally familiar but narrower, actions done by reasonable agents in pursuit of ends determined by their reason.
>
> These include — is it necessary to add? — acts done by an unreasonable agent in pursuit of ends (or in the adoption of means) determined by his unreason; for what is meant by unreason, in a context of this kind, is not the absence of reasons but the presence of bad ones; and a bad reason is still a reason.[51]

According to Collingwood, it is simply a contingent fact that humans have displayed the most evidence of reasonable chains of thought. The issue of 'species chauvinism' has risen in prominence since Collingwood's death, with the realization that in the past our species lived alongside neanderthals and homo floresiensis: both of which displayed characteris-

---

45   P.H., p.49

46   In this he follows the example of that 'bold revolutionary' David George Hogarth (A., p.82). See also P.H., p.49; P.A., p.50; N.L., p.40

47   Unpublished 'Central Problems in Metaphysics — Lectures written April 1935, for delivery T[rinity] T[erm] 1933' Dep 20/1, Bodleian Library.

48   Bruce, J. Collingwood 'The Practical Advantages Accruing from the Study of Archaeology' *Archaeological Journal* 14 (March 1857), p.7

49   I.H., p.491

50   I have adopted this term from Val Plumwood and Richard Routley 'Against the Inevitability of Human Chauvinism' in E. Goodpaster and K.E. Sayre (eds.) *Ethical Problems of the Twenty First Century* (1979).

51   P.H., pp.46-47

tics previously thought to be the exclusive preserve of homo sapiens. He appears to anticipate and deflect the charge of 'species chauvinism' by arguing that it is impossible to draw a rigid dividing line between rational and non-rational animals.

> As an example of what I mean, the American writer Ernest Thompson Seton, some years ago, published a series of books in which he professed to reconstruct, from such evidence as that of their tracks, the processes of reason which had determined the actions of various wild animals. If genuine, these were real history of *Res Gestae*. But many readers must have doubted whether they were not sentimentalized portraits falsified by a desire to find in the wild animals he loved a resemblance to human beings closer than actually exists. However that may be, this is clear, that the question whether history of non-human deeds is possible is to be answered not by arguing, but by trying to write it.[52]

Untouched by human chauvinism, the archaeologist Robert Heizer classes the search for radio signals from extraterrestrial civilizations as a form of archaeology.[53] There is nothing in Collingwood's philosophy that would rule out this classification.

(v) Irrationality

The criticism that Collingwood's absolute presupposition ('all history is the history of thought'[54]) is inadequate in the face of irrationality might proceed along the lines that, since historians (in their work) are unfazed by their many encounters with characters of dubious morality and sanity, this absolute presupposition cannot be essential to their inquiries.

On behalf of Collingwood the reply might be given that the historian allows for the possibility of valid reasons by reading back from the agent's answers the questions that the agent asked. This allows the historian to suggest what premises *the agent* (not the historian) may have considered to be sound.[55] In other words, it is the historian's practice to grant validity to the reasoning underlying *apparently* irrational actions in order to recreate the premises from which those actions ensued. So long as the historian is able to attribute validity to the action of a historical agent, he will be able to suggest a premise for that action, although that premise *might*, in fact or in the historian's opinion, be unsound.

Nonetheless, against Collingwood, to argue that, for example, Nero is not an historical agent since his thoughts are irrational and irrecoverable is

---

52   P.H., p.47

53   Heizer, Robert F. *Man's Discovery of his Past*, (1962) 1980, p.3

54   A., p.110; I.H., pp.215, 317; P.H., pp.67, 98, 100

55   'A person may act hastily, for example, or he may act for foolish goals. In neither case is rational understanding, as Collingwood conceives it, ruled out for we can still follow the agent's practical deliberations from the stand point of what he *did* take into account.' Dray, W.H. *Philosophy of History*, 1964: 13

to ignore historians' practices: all historians regard Nero as an historical agent.

A more constructive reply would be to recast Collingwood's famous absolute presupposition ('all history is the history of thought'[56]) in favour of the slightly less sweeping 'the agent's reasoning should be recovered whenever possible'; and perhaps to admit that there is more to history than action explanation. This possibility is explored in Chapter XV. But for now it should be noted that Collingwood himself argues that any piece of thinking is likely to rely upon more than one absolute presupposition; moreover, none of the above objections casts doubt upon Collingwood's account of action explanation.

Collingwood expatiates further upon this form of explanation via the provocative claims that, for the historian, the cause of an event is 'the inside of the event itself'[57], and that the historian re-enacts in his own mind the experience of the historical agent.[58] These claims are the respective subjects of the next two chapters.

---

56   A., p.110; I.H., pp.215, 317; P.H., pp.67, 98, 100
57   I.H., p.215
58   I.H. p.282

Chapter IX

The Inside-Outside Distinction

Having established that history dealing with written and non-written evidence rests upon the same conceptual footing, Collingwood asks whether the historian's field of study is restrained only by the current imperfections of his techniques? Since archaeology has already extended the scope of historian's investigations:

> Might not a similar but even more revolutionary extension sweep into the historian's net the entire world of nature? In other words, are not natural processes really historical processes, and is not the being of nature an historical being?[1]

Collingwood rejects this suggestion: he contends that it is the *rational* nature of the historian's subject matter that demands a different methodology. This difference in methodology is ultimately derived from a difference in the subject matter of the historian compared to that of the natural scientist.

> The historian's 'special technique, depending as it does on the interpretation of documents in which human beings of the past have expressed or betrayed their thoughts, cannot be applied just as it stands to the study of natural processes; and the more this technique is elaborated in its details, the farther it is from being so applicable. There is a certain analogy between the archaeologist's interpretation of a stratified site and the geologist's interpretation of rock-horizons with their associated fossils; but the difference is no less clear than the similarity. The archaeologist's use of his stratified relics depends on his conceiving them as artefacts serving human purposes and thus expressing a particular way in which men have thought about their own life; and from his point of view the palaeontologist, arranging his fossils in a time-series, is not working as an historian, but only as a scientist thinking in a way which can at most be described as quasi-historical.[2]

---

1   I.H., p.210
2   I.H., p.212

Such passages have attracted controversy, for, at least in isolation from the rest of his philosophy, it appears that Collingwood simply defines human beings as rational and on that ground concludes that the subject matter of history is human beings. This impression may be *in some measure* due to Knox's editing of *The Idea of History*, for, as was seen in the last chapter, in *The Principles of History* he claims:

> the question whether history of non-human deeds is possible is to be answered not by arguing, but by trying to write it.[3]

Certain wilfully provocative passages in *The Idea of History*, compounded by the effects of Knox's editing, might also give the impression that Collingwood's philosophy is reliant upon the Cartesian dichotomy of mind and body. For example:

> For science, the event is discovered by perceiving it, and the further search for its cause is conducted by assigning it to its class and determining the relation between that class and others. For history, the object to be discovered is not the mere event, but the thought expressed in it. To discover that thought is already to understand it. After the historian has ascertained the facts, there is no further process of inquiring into their causes. When he knows what happened, he already knows why it happened.[4]

Collingwood then goes on to claim:

> When an historian asks 'Why did Brutus stab Caesar?' he means 'What did Brutus think, which made him decide to stab Caesar?' The cause of the event, for him, means the thought in the mind of the person by whose agency the event came about: and this is not something other than the event, it is the inside of the event itself.[5]

In claiming that history, unlike natural science, is concerned with 'the inside of an event', he is not claiming to possess knowledge of an unchangeable and eternal 'inner' spirit or substance: indeed he warns against confusing references to the 'inner' side of his subject matter with the 'category of substance', as described by Graeco-Roman historians.[6] He claims only to have observed that, unlike natural scientists, historians conduct their investigations with reference to the *rationale* of historical agents.

The historian's explanation takes the form of Aristotle's practical syllogism: the *causa quod* (the efficient cause – 'a situation or state of things known or believed by the agent in question to exist'[7] being the major premise; and the *causa ut* (the final cause – the agent's intention to act in a

---

3   P.H., p.47
4   I.H., p.214
5   I.H., pp.214–15
6   I.H., p.42 See also the 1934 conclusion to I.N.:'[T]o speak of human nature at all is only a way of referring to the summed results of human history down to the present time.' P.H., p.352
7   E.M., p.292

certain way[8]) being the minor premise. (According to Collingwood, in the case of historian's explanations: 'Neither of these could be a cause if the other were absent'[9]). Thus, by the 'inside of the event' Collingwood refers to the rational connection between, on the one hand, the *causa quod* and the *causa ut* and, on the other hand, the action (the conclusion of the practical syllogism). (As Heikki Saari points out, in the above passage the *causa ut* is the intention to contribute to the aims of the conspiracy by killing Caesar; the *causa quod* is what Brutus believed he knew about the political situation of his time[10]).

By the provocative claim that—'When he [the historian] knows what happened, he already knows why it happened'[11]—Collingwood suggests that, as opposed to explanations in natural science, in history an explanation is uninformative, unless it incorporates an understanding of *why*. For example, I may describe someone opening a window[12] but unless I can describe such an action with some reference to the sense of the agent's motive I will not understand it. I will not know whether he is letting air into the room or letting a fly out. It is the sense of the agent's intention that is the 'inside' of the inside-outside distinction and that the historian must understand and communicate in his explanations. It is this sense that, according to Collingwood, is absent from the explanations of natural science.

In order to make this distinction clear, Dray suggests that the events studied by the historian, as opposed to the natural scientist, should more properly be termed 'actions' rather than 'events'. In Dray's terminology, an 'action' is a happening that may be made sense of via reference to its 'inside' (its *rationale*); by contrast, an 'event' is a happening that can not be made sense of in this way but which may be made sense of via reference to its relationship with other non-purposive events. The former characteristic is to be found, for example, not only in the historian's explanation of the

---

8   E.M. p.292

9   E.M. p.292 According to Aristotle there are four kinds of cause or explanatory factor: (1) *causa materialis* (the material cause) the materials out of which something is made; (2) *causa formalis* (the formal cause) that in virtue of which something is what it is; (3) *causa efficiens* or *causa quod* (the efficient cause) that which brings about a change in something; *causa finalis* or *causa ut* (the final cause)the purpose for which a change in something is brought about. In the case of a bronze statue: the *causa materialis* is the bronze; the *causa formalis* is that which the statue represents, its shape; the *causa efficiens* or *causa quod* is the sculptor; the *causa finalis* or *causa ut* is the purpose for which the statue was made. *Physics* ii.3.194b 23–4 *Metaphysics* i.3.983a 26-33 and v.1.1013a

10 According to Heikki Saari: 'if we put Collingwood's view of historical explanation in von Wright's terms, he means that the historian has explained the agent's action, if he has been able to show that his deed followed as a practical inference from the epistemic and motivational premises of his action.' *Re-enactment: A Study in R.G. Collingwood's Philosophy of History*, 1984, p.28. (G.H. von Wright terms this an 'Intentional Explanation Model').

11 I.H., p.214

12 This example is discussed by Giuseppina D'Oro in 'Collingwood, Psychologism and Internalism' *European Journal of Philosophy* 12:2 2004, p.172.

actions of a man who is afraid of crossing devil-haunted mountains but also in an explanation of Nelson's actions at Trafalgar.

By arguing that the historian must account for an action's *rationale* Collingwood is not intending to claim that an action that possesses this 'inside' possesses a mysterious inner dimension, but rather that the historian's subject matter may best be made sense of with reference to the agent's reasoning. As the following passage illustrates, by the outside of an event Collingwood refers to an event's occurrence and by the inside of an event Collingwood refers to the reasoning that accounts for, and that led to, an event's occurrence.

> The historian, investigating any event in the past, makes a distinction between what may be called the outside and the inside of an event. By the outside of the event I mean everything belonging to it which can be described in terms of bodies and their movements: the passage of Caesar, accompanied by certain men, across a river called the Rubicon at one date, or the spilling of his blood on the floor of the senate-house at another. By the inside of the event I mean that in it which can only be described in terms of thought: Caesar's defiance of Republican law, or the clash of constitutional policy between himself and his assassins. The historian is never concerned with either of these to the exclusion of the other. He is investigating not mere events (where by a mere event I mean one which has only an outside and no inside) but actions, and an action is the unity of the outside and inside of an event.[13]

In summary, in referring to the 'inside' of an event Collingwood intends to make clear a conceptual distinction between history and the natural sciences as different forms of inquiry.

Privileged Access

Gilbert Ryle interprets Collingwood's references to the 'inside' and 'outside' of an event to imply adherence to some form of privileged access theory. This may be inferred from the many scattered allusions to *The Idea of History* found throughout *The Concept of Mind*.[14]

In *The Concept of Mind* Ryle famously rails against 'Descartes' myth' — the idea that we discover the content of our minds by different means than those by which we discover the content of the physical world. On the one hand we know our own minds with certainty, though in private (privileged access); on the other hand, the external world, including our own bodies, although seen to be subject to mechanical laws, is invariably known with less certainty. Hence, an antithesis is created between 'inner' and 'outer' worlds.

> Underlying this partly metaphorical representation of the bifurcation of a person's two lives there is a seemingly more profound and philo-

---

13   I.H., p.213
14   See, in particular, pp.55–6

sophical assumption. It is assumed that there are two different kinds of existence or status. What exists or happens may have the status of physical existence, or it may have the status of mental existence – What has physical existence is composed of matter, or else is a function of matter, what has mental existence consists of consciousness, or else is a function of consciousness.[15]

Ryle argues that the idea that there are two different kinds of existence is unjustified. For when we attribute particular thoughts to a subject, those thoughts – insofar as they can be meaningfully discussed – are invariably accompanied by attributions of 'behavioural dispositions':

When we characterise people by mental predicates, we are not making untestable inferences to any ghostly processes occurring in streams of consciousness which we are debarred from visiting; we are describing the ways in which those people conduct parts of their predominantly public behaviour.[16]

Ryle denies that our reliability concerning our own thoughts provides sufficient evidence to posit the existence of an 'inner' world that is different from, and mysteriously unconnected to, the 'outer' world. He argues that even though there are sensations of which the subject alone can give a first hand account this does not merit the idea of two different worlds.[17] Awareness of one's own state of mind is by no means always certain. In summary:

The superiority of the speaker's knowledge of what he is doing over that of the listener does not indicate that he has Privileged Access to the facts of a type inevitably inaccessible to the listener, but only that he is in a very good position to know what the listener is often in a very poor position to know.[18]

Ryle is correct to suggest that many philosophers who have argued that there exists a fundamental difference between social science and natural science have based this view upon a privileged access theory. For example, Wilhelm Dilthey is, in this respect, typical of the Cartesian philosophers whom Ryle criticizes, in that he believes we experience two different worlds: an 'inner' world, the subject of the social sciences (*Geisteswissenschaften*), known via understanding (*verstehen*); and the external 'outer' world, the subject of the natural sciences (*Naturwissenschaften*), known via explanation (*erklaren*).[19] Dilthey writes of *verstehen*, as follows:

---

15   Ryle, Gilbert *The Concept of* Mind, 1990, pp.14–5
16   Ryle, Gilbert *The Concept of Mind*, 1990, p.50
17   Ryle, Gilbert *The Concept of Mind*, 1990, p.199
18   Ryle, Gilbert *The Concept of Mind*, 1990, p.171
19   Dilthey makes this claim in his *Introduction to the Human Sciences* (1883) in *Selected Works* Volume I, 1996.

> We ... call understanding that process by which we recognise, behind signs given to our senses, that psychic reality of which they are the expression.[20]

According to Dilthey, the inner 'lived experience' (*erlebnis*) of the social scientist's study is the 'inner' conscious side of an agent's actions, the contents of which are experienced by the social scientist (including the historian) when those experiences are 're-experienced' (*nacherlebt*).

In response to the problem of how the social scientist re-experiences 'lived experiences' other than his own, philosophers such as Croce and Georg Simmel emphasise the role of intuition. Dilthey's response is to suggest that 'lived experiences' might be recreated with the aid of psychology. However, this has the effect of subjugating all the *Geisteswissenschaften* – including, according to Dilthey, history, philology and philosophy – to the dictates of psychology.

Collingwood admits to have been inspired by predecessors and contemporaries, such as Dilthey and Croce, who have compared and contrasted *Geisteswissenschaften* to *Naturwissenschaften*. For example, he hails Dilthey as a 'lonely and neglected genius'.[21] But he objects Dilthey's subjection of history, philology and philosophy to the dictates of psychology, as follows.

> The differences between different philosophies are thus reduced to mere resultants of differences in psychological structure or disposition. But this way of treating the subject makes nonsense of it. The only question that matters about a philosophy is whether it is right or wrong. If a given philosopher thinks as he does because, being that kind of man, he cannot help thinking like that, this question does not arise. Philosophy handled from this psychological point of view ceases to be philosophy at all.[22]

Collingwood need not have recourse to Dilthey's measures; since, contrary to Ryle's interpretation, he is not beset by the problem of two different worlds. Despite his references to the 'inside' and 'outside' of events, Collingwood does not subscribe to any form of privileged access theory. He believes that we gain access to our own past reasoning by the same means that we gain access to the actions of any historical agent, i.e. by rationalizing them. For, however rash or ill-considered a past action may have been, it is only by granting validity to the thoughts underlying that action that we may revive the idea behind it.[23] This applies equally to understanding our own past actions and to understanding the actions of

---

20 Dilthey, Wilhelm *Hermeneutics and the Study of History* in *Selected Works* Volume IV, 1996
21 I.H., p.171
22 I.H., p.173
23 'If I strike a man in a fit of passion my action is certainly not deliberate; but it would be idle to deny that there was, as we say, an idea behind it.' Walsh, W.H. *An Introduction to the Philosophy of History*, 1951, pp.53–4

others. It is the idea of rational reconstruction rather than empathy that characterises historical understanding.

It is also this feature—explored further in the next chapter—that, in Collingwood's view, distinguishes *the logical structure* of the historian's explanation from the natural scientist's.[24]

24 I am grateful to chapter 3 of Chinatsu Kobayashi's unpublished PhD thesis for helping to elucidate some of the differences between the philosophies of Collingwood, Dilthey and Ryle: 'Collingwood on Re-Enactment: Understanding in History and Interpretation in Art', University of Ottawa, 2003.

Chapter X

Re-Enactment

In one of the most compactly reasoned sections of *The Idea of History*, 'History as Re-Enactment of Past Experience', Collingwood argues that historical understanding consists of the re-enactment of the historical agent's reasoning.

Unfortunately his use of the term 're-enactment' has commonly led to his argument being misinterpreted as a claim that the agent's thoughts are somehow mystically intuited. As I shall try to show in this chapter this was certainly not Collingwood's intention.

In Collingwood's view that which is re-enacted is the fit between, on the one hand, the *causa quod* and the *causa ut* and, on the other hand, the agent's action. In this context the *causa quod* and the *causa ut* form the premises of a practical syllogism and the agent's action forms its conclusion. As was seen in the last chapter, although Collingwood refers metaphorically to the rational connection between the premises of the practical syllogism and its conclusion as the 'inside of the event'[1] this does not imply the endorsement of any form of privileged access theory. With the removal of this frequent source of misunderstanding the path towards understanding 're-enactment', although still difficult, becomes somewhat clearer.

Collingwood argues that the re-enactment of a practical syllogism does not require the historian to make an exact copy of the agent's internal dialogue; nor does it require the historian to have access to the agent's psychology; or for the agent to have been fully conscious of his own motives. These are not requirements of historical understanding. It should be remembered that Collingwood's primary aim is not to provide a comprehensive method for recovering past thoughts but to show what historical understanding is—what logical form it takes. The term 're-enactment' possibly distracts from this point, suggesting the work of intuition and empathic identification. In *The Principles of History* this vocabulary is not used, although his discussion of historical explanation is consistent with

---

1   I.H., p.215

that found in *The Idea of History*.[2] Leon Pompa makes the point that a slightly different terminology would suffice in place of 're-enactment':

> What is correct about the claim is better expressed not in terms of re-thinking or re-enacting the same acts of thought but of *reconstructing* a material argument that enables us to understand an agent's action in virtue of conforming to a schema for the structure of action, i.e., a schema which is proper to action as such and therefore, common to both the agent's and the historian's understanding of something as an action.[3]

That Collingwood's aim is primarily conceptual is made clear in the following passage:

> In its immediacy, as an actual experience of his own, Plato's argument must undoubtedly have grown up out of a discussion of some sort, though I do not know what it was, and been closely connected with such a discussion. Yet if I not only read his argument but understand it, follow it in my own mind by re-arguing it with and for myself, the process of argument which I go through is not a process resembling Plato's, it actually is Plato's, *so far as I understand him rightly* [my italics].[4]

Re-enactment should not be seen as a way to gain an exact copy of an agent's internal dialogue; it is rather — that which the historian means when he speaks of understanding an agent — the rationalization of an action.

Collingwood argues that the traditional dichotomy of 'subjective' and 'objective' thought is bound up with the copy theory of knowledge. He argues that this distinction should be replaced by the less misleading distinction between thought in its 'immediacy' and thought in its 'mediacy' (or 'mediation'). In a nutshell, thought in its immediacy can not be re-enacted; thought in its mediacy (or mediation) can. In more detail: by thought in its immediacy Collingwood means experience without awareness; by thought in its mediacy he means the propositional content and logical structure of thought — thought that is to some degree self-aware. The immediacy of thought:

> consists not only in its context of emotions (together, of course, with sensations, like the buoyancy of Archimedes' body in the bath) but in its context of other thoughts.[5]

The mediacy of thought consists of:

> the knowledge of oneself as living in these activities.[6]

---

2   P.H., *lxvi* editors' introduction by W.H. Dray and W.J. van der Dussen. (The idea of re-enactment is anticipated in R.P., pp.97–101, S.M., pp.301–2 and *Libellus de Generatione*)

3   Pompa, Leon 'Some Problems of Re-Enactment' *Collingwood Studies*, 2002, 9, pp.42–3

4   I.H., p.301

5   I.H., p.298

6   I.H. p.297

Thought in its immediacy is never wholly devoid of its mediacy; thought in its mediacy is never wholly devoid of its immediacy. Thus, feelings are never experienced without some rudimentary awareness, or if they are then it is impossible to have reliable recollections of them. It is this rudimentary awareness that is preserved in the form of a recollection, or in the form of evidence that enables recollection. Hence, what the historian or the autobiographer recollects, or 're-enacts', is not a past feeling but the thought or idea of that feeling.[7]

The historian, but not the natural scientist, is primarily interested in the self-reflective 'mediacy' (or 'mediation') of an agent's thought.[8] This aspect of thought transcends its context of immediate thoughts, so that, for example, it is unnecessary to have a bath in order to re-enact the chain of reasoning that leads to an understanding of Archimedes' principle.

> This double character of thought provides the solution of a logical puzzle that has a close connection with the theory of history. If I now re-think a thought of Plato's, is my act of thought identical with Plato's or different from it? Unless it is identical, my alleged knowledge of Plato's philosophy is sheer error. But unless it is different, my knowledge of Plato's philosophy implies oblivion of my own. What is required, if I am to know Plato's philosophy, is both to re-think it in my own mind and also to think other things in the light of which I can judge it.[9]

In the case of Archimedes' principle, the immediate Eureka-moment of its original discovery will never reoccur, but the principle, in its mediacy, can yet be rediscovered in different contexts of immediate thoughts, simply by reading a physics textbook. Thus when we understand the principle we may claim to have re-enacted Archimedes' thoughts (in their mediacy): for there are no grounds to distinguish between our understanding of the principle and Archimedes'. Collingwood suggests that it is part of the historian's job to create a suitable context in which the agent's thought might be revived.

In summary, although there is no criterion of understanding external to the historian's explanation of the agent's thought whereby the historian might demonstrate that understanding has occurred — if the historian shows that an action is the result of a practical inference from certain

---

7   That thought in its mediacy (or mediation) is shareable is an idea that is also found in *The Principles of Art* (p.158): 'A hundred people in the street may all feel cold, but each person's feeling is private to himself. But if they all think that the thermometer reads 22 Fahrenheit, they are all thinking the same thought: this thought is public to them all.'

8   This idea also appears in *The Principles of Art* (171 f.n.): 'Thus a science of feeling must be 'empirical' (i.e. devoted to ascertaining and classifying 'facts' or things susceptible of observation), but a science of thought must be 'normative', or (as I prefer to call it) 'criteriological', i.e. concerned not only with the 'facts' of thought but also with the 'criteria' or standards which thought imposes on itself.'

9   I.H., pp.300–01

epistemic and motivational premises then he has revived, not the entirety of the agent's thought, but the agent's thought in its mediacy.

Patrick Gardiner and Karl Popper

Collingwood's underlying aim in this section of *The Idea of History* is to make explicit the logical conditions under which the writing of history is possible. This project has methodological repercussions for the historian, but Collingwood's aim is not simply to provide a prescriptive methodology. This point seems not to have been fully appreciated by certain critics of 're-enactment' — such as Patrick Gardiner and Karl Popper.

According to Patrick Gardiner:

> 'When in doubt as to why a person did something, put yourself in his position' may be a useful methodological percept, but it is far from always being reliable. People differ. From the fact that, if I did *x*, it would be because I wanted *y*, i.e. would have been satisfied if *y* occurred, would have given *y* as my aim if asked, Ac., it does not follow that when a medieval baron did *x* he wanted *y*.[10]

In reply, the point should be made that Collingwood does not argue that, by imagining himself in the agent's position, the historian will inevitably understand the agent's actions. His argument is that, insofar as the historian claims to have understood the baron's actions, he will claim to have understood how a state of things believed by the baron to exist prompted him to act in a certain way.

Karl Popper, like Gardiner, also tends to interpret Collingwood as promoting re-enactment as primarily a methodological tool. Popper claims that the historian who is not able to fully and imaginatively 're-enact', for example, particular acts of cruelty or heroism may yet make interesting historical discoveries: in such cases, he argues, 're-enactment' will often be impossible. But, he argues, even if the re-enactment of such actions were possible, it would be superfluous: for once a *situation* has been analysed it may then become obvious that the action of the agent was adequate to that situation, 'in a trivial and ordinary way'.[11] For example, we can understand Galileo's failure to reply to Kepler's letters on the grounds that Galileo was dismissive of Kepler's belief that the moon influences the tides. The *complete* re-enactment of the workings of Galileo's mind (including his exact opinion of Kepler's theory) is not a necessary condition of the historian understanding this situation.[12]

Popper assumes that Collingwood would disagree with these comments, but this is not the case. For example, Collingwood might well agree

---

10 Gardiner, Patrick *The Nature of Historical Explanation*, 1952: 129–30.

11 Popper, Karl *Objective Knowledge*, 1972: 173; *Conjectures and Refutations* 1963: 38, f.n. 4

12 Popper, Karl 'A Pluralist Approach to the Philosophy of History' (1967) reprinted in *Roads to Freedom: Essays in Honour of Friedrich A. von Hayek* 1969, pp.198–200

that in Popper's example the workings of Galileo's mind are re-enacted 'in a trivial and ordinary way', for no other more interesting questions hinge on this matter. Collingwood does not claim that the historian re-enacts *all* of the agent's reasonings; nor does he claim that the historian exercises empathy for cruelty or heroism.

Popper believes that 'the question — 'what were the important or operative elements in the situation?' — is the central question which the historian tries to solve. To the extent that he solves it, he has *understood* the historical situation, and that piece of history which he tries to recapture'.[13] But, again, it need not be assumed that Collingwood would disagree with this statement. As Van der Dussen points out[14], it is consistent with Collingwood's philosophy that in his work as a historian he re-enacts Caesar's reasoning only to the extent that he is able to postulate answers to the questions he asks concerning Caesar's motives.

Popper argues that the historian investigates 'real but unnoticed' contemporaneous influences upon historical agents. But, as previously seen, in anticipation of this criticism, Collingwood writes that even in a history of economics the historian must assume that 'a man who builds a factory or starts a bank is acting on a purpose that we can understand'.[15]

Misleading Comparisons

(i) Simulation Theory

Martin Davies and Tony Stone have recently cited Collingwood's ideas on re-enactment as antecedents of simulation theory in the philosophy of psychology.[16]

Simulation theory is not a single theory but is the name of a theory of several different interwoven strands that date from two independently written papers published in 1986 by Robert Gordon[17] and Jane Heal.[18] In general terms, its subscribers aver to the idea that our understanding of other people's thoughts and actions is carried out by the same means as our understanding of ourselves. They argue that we do not understand other people by means of an innate theory of how the actions of other people instantiate particular psychological processes. Rather, we learn of others' states by projecting ourselves into others' situations. According to the simulation theorist, the mental activities of others are 'represented' by

13   Popper, Karl 'A Pluralist Approach to the Philosophy of History' (1967) reprinted in *Roads to Freedom: Essays in Honour of Friedrich A. von Hayek* 1969, p.198

14   Van der Dussen, W.J. *History as a Science: The Philosophy of R.G. Collingwood*, 1981, p.347

15   I.H., p.310

16   Davies, Martin and Stone, Tony 'Simulation Theory' in *The Routledge Encyclopaedia of Philosophy* (2000) (ed. E. Craig)

17   Gordon, Robert 'From Folk Psychology to Cognitive Science' *Mind and Language*, 1986, 1, pp.158–71

18   Heal, Jane 'Replication and Functionalism' in *Language, Mind and Logic*, 1986

'pretend' inputs, which the investigator entertains 'off-line'. No meta-theory concerning mental functioning is required. That is not to say that simulation theorists spurn all psychological theories, but they maintain that an antecedent theoretical knowledge of psychological processes is not a pre-requisite of our understanding of the actions of other agents.

By contrast, theory theory (the stalking horse of simulation theory), inspired by Noam Chomsky, and proposed by Stephen Stich in 1983,[19] posits a tacit or innate folk theory of mind by which we predict and explain the actions of other people.

Whilst Collingwood would agree with simulation theorists that knowledge of psychological theories is not a prerequisite for understanding the actions of other agents, his metaphysics is primarily concerned with the discovery of the absolute presuppositions of historical understanding. By contrast, simulation theorists are primarily concerned with the development of an efficient methodology. Overlooking this difference, Davies and Stone misinterpret Collingwood's intentions.

(ii) The Principle of Charity
Simon Blackburn suggests that when Collingwood argues that you cannot tell whether propositions contradict each other until you know that they are answers to the same question, he is 'in effect ... highlighting a version of what later became called the principle of charity'.[20]

The principle of charity was made famous by Quine—in a thought experiment termed 'radical translation'.[21] Quine considers the case of an English-speaking linguist who attempts to understand the language of an isolated and hitherto unvisited tribe. The tribe speaks 'Jungle', a language completely unknown to the visiting linguist.

Quine describes how, upon the appearance of a rabbit, a Jungle-speaker points towards it and utters 'gavegai'. The linguist translates this as 'here-is-a-rabbit'. Quine argues that, although 'gavegai' and 'here-is-a-rabbit' may be stimulus synonymous, there is no evidence that is sufficient to *guarantee* that the linguist has correctly translated 'gavegai'. Thus, in this example, 'gavegai' might also be translated as 'this-is-rabbithood' or 'there-are-rabbit-ears'. The Jungle-speaker's meaning cannot be empirically determined. In this situation two conflicting translations may describe the same physical state equally well—there is no way to say which is correct, for there is no 'fact of the matter' by which we may distinguish one translation from another. Quine terms this thesis the 'indeterminacy of translation'. (He stresses that this thesis is proposed as a plausible

19   Stich, Stephen *From Folk Psychology to Cognitive Science*, 1983
20   Blackburn, Simon (1998) 'Collingwood, Robin George' in E. Craig (ed.) *Routledge Encyclopedia of Philosophy*.
21   Quine, W.V. *Word and Object*, 1960, chapter 2

conjecture rather than as a deductive argument). He summarises it as follows:

> These reflections leave us little reason to expect that two radical trans-
> lators, working independently on Jungle, would come out with inter-
> translatable manuals. The manuals might be indistinguishable in
> terms of any native behavior that they give reason to expect, and yet
> each manual might prescribe some translations that the other transla-
> tor would reject. Such is the thesis of indeterminacy of translation.[22]

Quine argues that in the light of the indeterminacy of translation we adopt the principle of charity: where different interpretations of an action are available we choose the interpretation that would render the action as reasonable as possible. The agent's implicit arguments are considered *ceteris paribus* to be strong. This involves the translator presupposing, or assuming, that the agent has the same *true* beliefs as himself. By the use of this principle the translator is able to use his own beliefs as a guide to the alien speaker's meaning — he is able to attribute beliefs, and modify and adjust these attributed beliefs in the light of subsequently observed behaviour, and so on.

In suggesting that Collingwood anticipates the principle of charity, Simon Blackburn overlooks the fact that the idea of the truth does not play a heuristic role in re-enactment.[23] Thus, for example, when the historian re-enacts the views of those who fear devils in the mountains his own view as to whether or not there are devils in the mountains is irrelevant. Validity is granted to the argument underlying an agent's actions in order to reconstruct a propositional attitude not necessarily shared by the historian: this is different to Quine's principle of charity.

The naïve form of history-writing that Collingwood terms 'scissors-and-paste' might be described as *exclusively* reliant upon the principle of charity, in that the historian has no other means of understanding historical agents aside from assuming that the protagonists in question hold the same true beliefs as himself. In scissors-and-paste history the protagonists in question are characterized according to the way that they are seen to ignore or uphold the historian's own beliefs. According to Collingwood, historical inquiry remains unscientific when it is committed to the idea that historical knowledge is ultimately reliant upon the ascription of true belief.[24]

As will be seen in the next chapter, another distinguishing feature of historians' explanations is their use of a particular sense of 'cause'.

---

22   Quine, W.V. *Pursuit of Truth*, 1992, pp.47–8

23   Giuseppina D'Oro makes this point in contrasting re-enactment to the role Donald Davidson grants to the principle of charity: see 'Re-Enactment and Radical Interpretation' *History and Theory* 43, 2004b, pp.198–208. See also Davidson, Donald 'Radical Interpretation' *Dialectica* 27, 1973, pp.313–28; reprinted in *Inquiries into Truth and Interpretation*, 1984, pp.125–40.

24   However, although Collingwood demonstrates that the historian is not solely reliant upon the ascription of true belief, that is not to say that the historian's inquiries are *never* moved forward by the ascription of true belief.

Chapter XI

Causation

Philosophical discussions of causation are vast, and made more complicated by the fact that they are found within (and straddling) the philosophy of history, the philosophy of science, the philosophy of mind, and the philosophy of action. With this in mind, in order to avoid unnecessary diversions, my primary aims in this chapter are restricted to providing and locating this view in relation to more recent discussions.

Collingwood describes three different senses of the word 'cause', as follows.

> It ['cause'] has three senses; possibly more; but at any rate three.
> Sense I. Here that which is 'caused' is the free and deliberate act of a conscious and responsible agent, and 'causing' him to do it means affording him a motive for doing it.
> Sense II. Here that which is 'caused' is an event in nature, and its 'cause' is an event or state of things by producing or preventing which we can produce or prevent that whose cause it is said to be.
> Sense III. Here that which is 'caused' is an event or state of things, and its 'cause' is another event or state of things standing to it in a one-one relation of causal priority: i.e. a relation of such a kind that (a) if the cause happens or exists the effect also must happen or exist, even if no further conditions are fulfilled, (b) the effect cannot happen or exist unless the cause happens or exists, (c) in some sense which remains to be defined, the cause is prior to the effect; for without such priority there would be no telling which is which.[1]

He claims that each of these senses of the word 'cause' is typically found within a distinctive discipline of inquiry.

Sense I

According to Collingwood, Sense I is the *'historical* sense' of the word cause, in which both cause and effect are human activities.

---

[1] E.M., pp.285-86 Collingwood lifts much of his argument on causation in *An Essay on Metaphysics* from his earlier article 'On the So-called Idea of Causation', *Proceedings of the Aristotelian Society*, 38 (1937–8), pp.85–112. The unpublished manuscripts in the Bodleian Library (Dep. 19) reveal his extensive reading on the subject.

A cause in this sense consists of a '*causa quod* or efficient cause and a *causa ut* or final cause'.[2] The *causa quod* is a situation or state of things 'known or believed by the agent in question to exist'.[3] Likewise, 'the *causa ut* is a purpose or state of things to be brought about. Neither of these could be a cause if the other were absent'.[4]

One agent can cause another agent to perform a certain act either through persuading him as to the nature of a certain situation (*causa quod*) and/or through persuading him of the benefits of forming a certain intention (*causa ut*). In either case the historian may talk of one agent affording another agent a motive. (The process is essentially the same if the agent affords himself a motive, by both envisaging a situation and forming an intention.) In all of these cases the historian re-enacts the agent's argument (the 'inside' of the event) by reconstructing the logical inference between the premises of the agent's argument (the *causa quod* and the *causa ut*) and the agent's action.

Sense II

Sense II is that used in the practical sciences of nature, such as engineering and car mechanics, in which specific aims must be achieved with finite means, and in which the cause is immediately under human control but the effect is only indirectly (via the cause) under human control. The word 'cause' in this sense refers to the 'handle' by which human beings manipulate an event in nature. In this sense:

> A cause is an event or state of things which it is in our power to produce or prevent, and by producing or preventing which we can produce or prevent that whose cause it is said to be.[5]

The example Collingwood gives is of turning on a light switch.[6] Sense II predominates in practical science, 'or in Aristotle's terminology, "what admits of being otherwise"'.[7]

This sense of the word 'cause' invariably relates to 'something conceived as capable of being produced or prevented by human agency'.[8]

> A cause in sense II is never able by itself to produce the corresponding effect. The switch ... only works the light subject to certain indispensable conditions. Among these are the existence of an appropriate current and its maintenance by insulation and contacts. These are called *conditiones sine quibus non*. Their existence, over and above the cause,

---

2   E.M., p.292
3   E.M., p.292
4   E.M., p.292
5   E.M., pp.296–97
6   Donald Davidson discusses the same example in 'Actions, Reasons and Causes' *Journal of Philosophy* 60 (1963)
7   E.M., p.297
8   E.M., p.299

constitutes one of the differences between sense II and sense III of the word 'cause'.[9]

Collingwood credits John Stuart Mill with having recognised that there commonly exists some confusion between sense II and sense III of the word 'cause'. In support of this interpretation of Mill, he quotes the following passage.

> Since then, mankind are accustomed with acknowledged propriety so far as the ordinances of language are concerned, to give the name of cause to almost any one of the conditions of a phenomenon, or any portion of the whole number, *arbitrarily selected*, without excepting even those conditions which are purely negative, and in themselves incapable of causing anything; it will probably be admitted without longer discussion, that no one of the conditions has more claim to that title than another, and that *the real cause of the phenomenon is the assemblage of all its conditions* [Collingwood's italics].[10]

However, since Mill's concern is primarily to provide a definition of cause as used in theoretical science he does not realize that in sense II conditions are not *'arbitrarily selected'* but are chosen in such a way that *'for any given person the cause in sense II of a given thing is that one of its conditions which he is able to produce or prevent'*.[11]

Collingwood illustrates this proposition by the following well-known passage.

> [I]f my car fails to climb a steep hill, and I wonder why, I shall not consider my problem solved by a passer-by who tells me that the top of a hill is farther away from the earth's centre than its bottom, and that consequently more power is needed to take a car uphill than to take her along the level. All this is quite true; what the passer-by has described is one of the conditions which together form the 'real cause' (Mill's phrase; what I call the cause in sense III) of my car's stopping; and as he has 'arbitrarily selected' one of these and called it the cause, he has satisfied Mill's definition of what the word ordinarily means. But suppose an A.A. man comes along, opens the bonnet, holds up a loose high-tension lead, and says: 'Look here, sir, you're running on three cylinders'. My problem is now solved. I know the cause of the stoppage. It is *the* cause, just because it has not been 'arbitrarily selected'; it has been correctly identified as the thing that I can put right, after which the car will go properly. If I had been a person who could flatten out hills by stamping on them the passer-by would have been right to call my attention to the hill as the cause of the stoppage; not because the hill was a hill but because I was able to flatten it out.[12]

In summary, sense II of 'cause' can be described as *prescribing* the relation between means and end. Thus, in the above example, for the AA man the 'cause' of the car stopping is that it is running on three cylinders, since it is

---

9   E.M., p.301
10 E.M., p.302; Mill, J.S. *A System of Logic* Book III, chapter v, § 3; ed. 1, vol 1, p.403
11 E.M., p.304
12 E.M., pp.302–303

by means of altering this condition that he is able to make the car start. For a giant capable of flattening hills but ignorant of car mechanics, the 'cause' of the car stopping is the hill, since it is by means of flattening the hill that he is able to make the car start. Both the AA man and the giant are concerned with establishing that under certain circumstances x will occur rather than y.

Sense III

Sense III is that used in cases where an attempt is made to understand events as happening independently of human will — as in theoretical science. A 'cause' in sense III is that which necessitates its effect.

> In the necessary world to which sense III belongs a cause is necessary (a) in its existence, as existing whether or no human beings want it to exist, (b) in its operation, as producing its effect no matter what else exists or does not exist. There are no *conditiones sine quibus non*. The cause leads to its effect by itself, or 'unconditionally'; in other words the relation between cause and effect is a one-one relation. There can be no relativity of causes, and no diversity of effects due to fulfillment or non-fulfilment of conditions.[13]

In describing sense III of 'cause', Collingwood has in mind Mill's model of explanation in which the *explanans* consists of (i) a general law (of empirical content) and (ii) a statement of the state of affairs preceding the *explanandum*. According to this model, explanation, takes the form of a deductive argument in which the *explanandum* is logically entailed by: (i) a general law (the major premise), and (ii) the preceding state of affairs (the minor premise).

Causal Explanation

Collingwood's sense III is related to David Hume's reference to a 'cause' as *'an object followed by another, and where all the objects similar to the first are followed by objects similar to the second'*[14] — although, it should be added, that Hume himself was skeptical towards the possibility of deducing an effect from an cause. Hume argued that what is commonly taken to be cause and effect should more accurately be seen as constant conjunction. According to Hume a cause is related to an effect through constant conjunction, contiguity in space and time, and temporal priority. From these relations a necessary connection is inferred, but not observed.

Following the lead suggested by Hume, and followed by Comte and J.S. Mill, Karl Popper developed a model of 'causal explanation' (or 'covering law explanation') in *Logik der Forschung* (1934) and *The Open Society and its Enemies* (1945). Popper defines 'causal explanation' as follows:

---

13   E.M., p.313
14   Hume, David *An Enquiry Concerning Human Understanding* [1777], p.76

To give a *causal explanation* of a certain event means to derive deduc-
tively a statement (it will be called a *prognosis*) which describes that
event, using as premises of the deduction some *universal laws* together
with certain singular or specific sentences which we may call *initial
conditions* ... The initial conditions (or more precisely, the situation
described by them) are usually spoken of as the *cause* of the event in
question, and the prognosis (or rather, the event described by the
prognosis) as the effect.[15]

Carl Hempel has since proposed a more precise formulation of this model,
but although more formally precise, Hempel's model is essentially the
same as that of Mill and Popper. Mill, Popper and Hempel all argue that to
cite a cause is to cite a general law under which regularities occur.
Hempel's account of explanation is as follows:

The explanation of the occurrence of an event of some specific kind E
at a certain place and time consists, as it is usually expressed, in indi-
cating the causes or determining factors of E. Now the assertion that a
set of events — say, of the kinds C1, C2, ... , Cn — have caused the event
to be explained, amounts to the statement that, according to certain
general laws, a set of events of the kinds mentioned is regularly accompanied by an event of kind E. Thus, the scientific explanation of the
event in question consists of
(1) a set of statements asserting the occurrence of certain events C1 ...
Cn at certain times and places
(2) a set of universal hypotheses, such that
(a) the statements of both groups are reasonably well confirmed by
empirical evidence,
(b) from the two groups of statements the sentence asserting the
occurrence of event E can be logically deduced.[16]

Hempel argues that, to the extent that the natural scientist and the historian offer explanations of events, their explanations conform to the above
'deductive-nomological model' regardless of their subject matter. The difference between their two subjects is conceptually insignificant.

Hempel modified this theory in 1965, replacing the claim that particular
events universally substantiate general laws with the claim that less general laws or particular events may be deduced from general laws with sta-
tistical probability. He termed this reformed model of explanation the
'inductive-statistical model'.[17] However he maintains that the fact that the
historian deals with agents' *envisaged* states of affairs makes no difference

15   Popper, Karl *The Open Society and its Enemies* (1945) Vol. II, p.262 The above description is
     reiterated in *Objective* Knowledge, 1972, p.59: 'To give a *causal explanation* of an event means to
     deduce a statement which describes it, using as premises of the deduction one or more
     universal laws, together with certain singular statements, the *initial conditions*.' (Popper argues
     that the problem of induction 'dissolves' once it is realized that the scientist does not *begin* his
     inquiry with induction but with covering laws that are then subjected to empirical tests.)
16   Hempel, Carl 'The Function of General Laws in History' *Journal of Philosophy* 39 (1942), p.36
17   Hempel, Carl 'Aspects of Scientific Explanation' in *Aspects of Scientific Explanation and other
     Essays in the Philosophy of Science*, 1965; similarly, Ernest Nagel advocates 'probabilistic
     explanation' in *The Structure of Science*, 1961.

to the logical structure of historians' explanations. They are essentially of the same form as the natural scientists'. Although the historian relies upon 'dispositional statements'[18] to account for the behaviour of the historical agent, these play the same role as covering laws. Thus although historians' explanations are less precise than natural scientists' they share the same logical form.[19]

With a few notable exceptions,[20] causal explanation has had very few devotees among historians. This is perhaps not surprising for, as William Dray points out in *Laws and Explanation in History* (1957), such theories leave the question unanswered as to whether the study of history has *any* positive distinguishing characteristics. Some covering law theorists claim that it does not. For example, Morton White argues that the fact that history has no unique vocabulary suggests that explanations in history are reliable only insofar as they are taken from those disciplines, such as anthropology and sociology, from which history borrows its more technical vocabulary.[21]

Counterfactual Explanation

After defining a cause as *'an object followed by another, and where all the objects similar to the first are followed by objects similar to the second'* Hume adds that a cause is also *'an object followed by another ... where, if the first object had not been, the second never had existed'*.[22] Collingwood's Sense II is related to the latter statement in that it alludes to 'what admits of being otherwise'. It is this sense of cause that we have in mind when, like the AA man and the giant, we decide how to attain a particular practical end.

Whether Hume intends the latter statement to do more than add detail to his first definition of causation is unclear, but many philosophers have seen the latter as more informative than his first definition. According to David Lewis:

> Hume's 'other words' — that if the cause had not been, the effect never had existed — are no mere restatement of his first definition. They propose something altogether different: a counterfactual analysis of causation.[23]

As such, Hume's second claim can be seen as ancestor not only of Collingwood's Sense II but also of recent work on counterfactual condi-

---

18   This terminology is from Gilbert Ryle's *The Concept of Mind* (1949).

19   Hempel terms historians' explanations 'explanation sketches'.

20   Exceptions include the archaeologists Lewis Binford and David Clarke, both influenced by Carl Hempel, and nineteenth century historian Henry Thomas Buckle, influenced by John Stuart Mill.

21   White, Morton G. 'Historical Explanation' *Mind* 1943, pp.212–29

22   Hume, David *An Enquiry Concerning Human Understanding* [1777], p.76

23   Lewis, David 'Causation' *Journal of Philosophy* 70, 1973, pp.556–67, reprinted in *Causation* ed. Ernest Sosa and Michael Tooley, 1993

tionals and modal logic. As an example of such a theory, I shall here briefly outline J.L. Mackie's 'I.N.U.S.' model of counterfactual explanation and examine its possibility suitability as a model of historians' explanations.[24]

Mackie argues that the idea and use of the word 'cause' involves what he terms 'I.N.U.S.' conditions. For example: in a simple newspaper head-line such as 'Bomb Rumours Cause Panic' we are to understand that rumours of bombs were (in themselves) *Insufficient* to bring panic but that they nonetheless formed a *Necessary* part of a set of conditions, which itself was *Unnecessary* but *Sufficient* to bring about panic. In Mackie's view, a good explanation should make this clear. He takes the example of a short-circuit that is said to be the *cause* of a fire in a house. An explanation will demonstrate this cause as follows.

> At least part of the answer is that there is a set of conditions (of which some are positive and some are negative), including the presence of inflammable material, the absence of a suitably placed sprinkler, and no doubt quite a number of others, which combined with the short-cir-cuit constituted a complex condition that was sufficient for the house's catching fire—sufficient, but not necessary, for the fire could have started in other ways. Also, of *this* complex condition, the short-circuit was an indispensable part: the other parts of this condition, conjoined with one another in the absence of the short-circuit, would not have caused the fire. The short-circuit which is said to have caused the fire is thus an indispensable part of a complex sufficient (but not necessary) condition of the fire.[25]

To be concise, the short-circuit—the so-called cause—is 'an *insufficient* but *necessary* part of a condition which is itself *unnecessary* but *sufficient* for the result'.[26] In this way, in Mackie's view, an informative explanation always makes reference to what might otherwise have been.

The problem with the application of this model to history is simply that the historian does not know what might otherwise have occurred had the *explanandum* not occurred. However, in sense II of 'cause', in practical problem-solving, we do make mental reference to that which might other-wise occur, for example: the AA man might cite a fault in the car's engine as a 'cause' of the car stopping, that is as 'an *insufficient* but *necessary* part of a condition which is itself *unnecessary* but *sufficient* for the result.' Like-wise, according to the same model of explanation, the giant might cite the steepness of the hill as a 'cause'.

24   The idea that historians may make use of counterfactual (or contrastive) explanations is proposed by Michael Scriven in 'Causes, Connections and Conditions in History' in *Philosophical Analysis and History* (ed. W. Dray), 1966, pp.238–64

25   Mackie, J.L. 'Causes and Conditions' [1965], reprinted in *Causation* (ed. Ernest Sosa and Michael Tooley), 1993, p.34

26   Mackie, J.L. 'Causes and Conditions' [1965], reprinted in *Causation* (ed. Ernest Sosa and Michael Tooley) 1993, p.34

Rational Explanation

Collingwood's sense I of 'cause' reaches contemporary philosophy of action and philosophy of history largely via the influence of William Dray. Inspired by Collingwood, Dray provides an alternative account of historians' explanations in opposition to that proposed by Hempel and Popper. According to Dray, historians employ *rational explanations*:

> The goal of such explanation is to show that what was done was the thing to have done for the reasons given, rather than merely the thing that is done on such occasions, perhaps in accordance with certain laws (loose or otherwise).[27]

Dray argues that even though evidence might be found of a trivial covering law in every explanation in history this would still not constitute conclusive evidence that historians work with the same model of explanation as natural scientists. He argues that such covering laws as are found in historians' explanations should more accurately be termed 'inference licences' (a term introduced by Gilbert Ryle).[28] In historians' explanations an inference license, of the form 'if p then q', may be imported from an unknown source: it commits the historian to nothing more than 'reasoning in a similar way in any further cases which may turn up'.[29] Hence, even if a covering law is implicit in every historian's explanation, this does not imply that the historian's explanations are derived *from* those laws.

Dray cites Ryle's *Concept of Mind* to the effect that although 'dispositional statements' about particular individuals may ostensibly take the same form as universal laws, unlike general laws as applied to the natural world, a dispositional statement — whether made of an individual in the present or the past — does not in *any* circumstances entail the ability to predict, with certainty, what an individual will do. This, according to Dray, suggests that the nature of historian's explanation is essentially different from that of the natural scientist.

> The historian must offer explanations that are rationally necessary to explain the actions of the individual but this does not commit the historian to the belief that without that reason the agent had no reason to do what he did.[30]

There is, according to Dray, a 'conceptual connection between understanding a man's actions and discovering its *rationale*'[31] in that, in order to discover the agent's *rationale*, the historian need not interest himself in the

---

27 Dray, W. *Laws and Explanation in History*, 1957b, p.124

28 Ryle, G. '"If", "So" and "Because"' in *Philosophical Analysis* (ed. M. Black), 1950, pp.323–40

29 Dray, W. *Laws and Explanation in History*, 1957b, p.41

30 Dray, W. 'The Historical Explanation of Actions Reconsidered' in *The Philosophy of History* (ed. Patrick Gardiner) 86

31 Dray, W. 'The Historical Explanation of Actions Reconsidered' in *The Philosophy of History* (ed. Patrick Gardiner), 1974, p.69

truth or falsity of the agent's beliefs but he must reconstruct the grounds of the argument underlying the agent's action. The resulting rational explanations are normative in that the reasons they contain:

> if they are to be explanatory in the rational way, must be *good* reasons at least in the sense that *if* the situation had been as the agent envisaged it (whether or not we, from our point of vantage, concur in his view of it), then what was done would have been the thing to have done.[32]

Dray argues that historians tend to use 'rational explanations' to explain 'how possibly', whereas 'causal explanations' (in which sense III of 'cause' is prominent) tend to be used to explain 'why necessarily'.[33] 'Causal explanations' rely upon the absolute presupposition that nature is uniform, but the historian cannot assume that the beliefs of historical agents are uniform, and it is with the reconstruction of these beliefs that the historian is concerned. Sense III of 'cause' is irrelevant to this purpose. Indeed the use of sense III of 'cause' in historian's explanations instead of sense I would set up 'a kind of *conceptual barrier* to a humanistically oriented historiography',[34] for, subsuming the patterns of the agent's actions under covering laws, the historian would be unable to reconstruct beliefs that he does not share.

For the sake of completeness, it should also be mentioned that in the final pages of *An Essay on Metaphysics* Collingwood provides a somewhat elliptical supplementary argument for the logical primacy of sense I of cause, similar to that put forward by Thomas Reid against Hume.[35] However, this argument I shall ignore as it is out of keeping with the aims of his 'metaphysics without ontology'. It is the repercussions of the idea that there are different senses of 'cause' characteristic of different forms of investigation,[36] none of which are fundamental, that will be further explored in the next chapter.

---

32 Dray, W. *Laws and Explanation in History*, 1957b: 126 Reason is 'pleonastic' (Dancy, 2002) or honorific — the use of the term 'reason' itself implies 'good' reason: thus it is said of someone who reasons badly that he is not really thinking. (Similarly, 'art' might also be termed 'criteriological' or 'pleonastic' in that the use of the term 'art' implies 'good' art.)

33 'The essential feature of explaining how-possibly is ... not that it is given of happenings that cannot be brought under law. It is rather given in the face of a certain sort of puzzlement.' Dray, W. *Laws and Explanation in History*, 1957b. My thanks to Chris Rolliston for bringing this passage to my attention.

34 Dray, W. 'Historical Explanation of Actions Reconsidered' in *The Philosophy of History* (ed. Patrick Gardiner), 1974, p.89

35 Reid, Thomas *Essays on the Active Powers of the Human Mind* [1788], 1969, pp.326-38 Michael Beaney provides an exposition of Collingwood's final argument in 'Collingwood's Conception of Presuppositional Analysis' *Collingwood and British Idealism Studies*, vol. 11, no.2, Autumn 2005, pp.41–114.

36 For this idea Collingwood acknowledges a debt to Bertrand Russell's 'On the Notion of Cause' *Proceedings of the Aristotelian Society* 1912-13, reprinted in *Mysticism and Logic*, 1917, pp.118–208 (E.M., p.319).

Chapter XII

Collingwood and Davidson on Action Explanation

In this chapter I use Collingwood's argument that different senses of cause are appropriate to different sorts of explanation in order to show that there is an ontological bias to Davidson's anomalous monism. I argue that this bias is apparent in the privileged and unwarranted metaphysical status that Davidson grants to sense III of cause.

A recurrent theme of Collingwood's philosophy is his repudiation of the mind-body problem as construed in Cartesian terms, in favour of a discussion of the problem in terms of the relationship between different sciences, based upon different absolute presuppositions. As previously mentioned, in Collingwood's view, the mind-body problem as cast in Cartesian terms ('what is the relationship between mind and body?') rests upon a false assumption.

> 2.4. The truth is that there is no relation between body and mind. That is, no direct relation; for there is an indirect relation.
>
> 2.41. 'The problem of the relation between body and mind' is a bogus problem which cannot be stated without making a false assumption.
>
> 2.42. What is assumed is that man is partly body and partly mind. On this assumption questions arise about the relations between the two parts; and these prove unanswerable.
>
> 2.43 For man's body and man's mind are not two different things. They are one and the same thing, man himself, as known in two different ways.[1]

Collingwood argues that the different ways in which man knows himself are embodied in the practices of different disciplines. When the natural scientist studies a man he studies the man's physiology, when the historian studies a man he studies the *rationale* underlying his actions. However, although these two disciplines may overlap, in that they may study the same event, this fact should not lead us to think that we must judge as to which inquiry captures the 'essence' of a particular event.

---

1   N.L., pp.10–11

In order to make clear the different approaches towards the mind-body problem Norman Malcolm poses the following question:

> Take the example of the man climbing a ladder in order to retrieve his hat from the roof. This explanation relates his climbing to his intention. A neurophysiological explanation of his climbing would say nothing about his intention but would connect his movements on the ladder with chemical changes in body tissues or with the firing of neurons. Do the two accounts interfere with one another?[2]

Collingwood's answer would be that the historian provides an intentional explanation and the natural scientist a neurophysiological explanation. Although their different inquiries may overlap, the historian and the natural scientist are interested in different (non-conflicting) aspects of the event. The mind-body problem dissolves in the light of this recognition:

> 2.49. The 'indirect relation between body and mind' (2.4) is the relation between the sciences of body, or natural sciences, and the sciences of mind; that is the relation inquiry into which ought to be substituted for the make-believe inquiry into the make-believe problem of 'the relation between body and mind'.[3]

As has been seen, although Collingwood did not live to complete his project of revealing the absolute presuppositions of history in a definitive manner (i.e. in explicit accordance with his theory of presupposition), in the course of his investigations he notes that the word 'cause' 'has three senses; possibly more; but at any rate three'.[4] As was seen in the last chapter, he categorises these three senses as follows: Sense I, as found in historians' explanations, approximates to 'the means by which an agent is afforded a motive'; Sense II predominates in practical problem-solving, and approximates to 'the means by which we manipulate events in nature'; and Sense III, as found in natural science, approximates to 'necessitates'. He argues, in line with his conception of 'metaphysics without ontology', that these different senses of the word should not be seen as conflicting, for they are based upon different questions asked with different interests in mind. These different questions and interests are ultimately based upon different absolute presuppositions. William Dray defends and develops these ideas in *Laws and Explanation in History* (1957), in which he uses the term 'rational explanation' for explanations reliant upon Sense I of cause, as opposed to 'causal explanation', reliant upon Sense III.

Owing, in some measure, to the work of Collingwood and Dray, the belief grew in the 1950s that the mind-body problem might be dissipated when recast as a legitimate conceptual overlap as opposed to an ontologi-

---

2   Malcolm, Norman 'The Conceivability of Mechanism' *Philosophical Review* 77 [1968]; reprinted in Gary Wilson (ed.) *Free Will*, 1982, p.133

3   N.L., p.11

4   E.M., pp.285–86

cal problem of mental-physical interaction. Gilbert Ryle's widely read *Concept of Mind* (1949), which encouraged the dissolution of previously intractable metaphysical disputes via the device of the 'category mistake', contributed to this consensus. However, the conceptual approach to the mind-body problem has since diminished in popularity in favour of various physicalist approaches to this problem:

> [T]he question of mental causation, as it is asked in contemporary philosophy of mind, is much closer to the way in which Descartes formulated the problem of mind-body dualism: it is a question about how mind can fit in a physical world, and whether the causal over determination of an event by both mental and physical causes threatens physical closure.[5]

Many of these physicalist approaches trace their descent from the publication of Donald Davidson's 'Actions, Reasons, and Causes'[6] in 1963.

In this chapter I provide an exposition of the main argument of Davidson's 'Actions Reasons, and Causes' and the ontology that underlies it, as proposed in 'Mental Events' (1970). Where necessary I have quoted from other essays by Davidson in order to clarify his somewhat tersely expressed arguments. (However, although I do not believe that I have significantly misrepresented Davidson, I have not aimed to provide an exposition of Davidson's arguments that is comprehensive in every detail.) Finally, I reply to Davidson from a viewpoint sympathetic to the conceptual approach to the mind-body problem.

In 'Actions, Reasons, and Causes' Davidson advances the thesis that, although not all valid explanations take the form of natural scientists' explanations, nonetheless:

> rationalization is a species of causal explanation.[7]

By this Davidson means that rational explanation is a subset of 'causal explanation' — which, in his view, relies upon Hume's view of causation:

> [A]n object followed by another, and where all the objects similar to the first are followed by objects similar to the second. Or in other words where, if the first object had not been, the second never had existed.[8]

He states that he advances this position in opposition to Gilbert Ryle's *Concept of Mind* (1949), G.E.M. Anscombe's *Intention* (1959), Stuart Hamp-

5   D'Oro, Giuseppina 'Collingwood's 'Solution' to the Problem of Mind-Body Dualism' *Philosophia* 32 2005d, p.356

6   Davidson, Donald 'Actions, Reasons, and Causes' *Journal of Philosophy* 60 [1963], reprinted in *Essays on Actions and Events*, 1980. The favourable reception of 'Actions, Reasons, and Causes' may in part be accounted for by its apparent accommodation of a frequently made criticism of behaviourism — that behaviourist explanations unavoidably make use of intentional mental terms. See Hempel, Carl *Philosophy of Natural Science*, 1966, p.110

7   Davidson, Donald 'Actions, Reasons, and Causes' [1963] in *Essays on Actions and Events*, 1980, p.3 The terms of this debate are potentially confusing. Davidson uses the term 'rationalisation' where Dray uses the term 'rational explanation'.

8   Hume, David *An Essay Concerning Human Understanding* [1777], p.76

shire's *Thought and Action* (1959), Hart and Honoré's *Causation in the Law* (1959), William Dray's *Laws and Explanation in History* (1957), Anthony Kenny's *Action, Emotion and Will* (1963), and A.I. Melden's *Free Action* (1961).[9]

It is perhaps easiest to understand Davidson's position by firstly reviewing the concessions that he makes to these opponents. He grants that we understand an agent's purpose in performing a certain action by understanding his reason for performing that action; and that when we explain an action we rationalize it. He grants that historians' explanations have a logical form distinct from natural scientists' explanations; and that this is due to the historian's sensitivity to the rationality of his subject matter. He grants that rational explanations are normative (in contrast to laws in natural science). Thus although someone has reasons to do something, he may not in fact do it, no matter how persuasive the reasons - but this does not lead us to blame the rationalisation, rather, it leads us to blame the agent.[10] That is to say, ascribing rationality does not commit the historian to the belief that the historical agent did act with rational purpose, nor does it guarantee the recovery of an agent's thoughts, but it is the historian's way of explaining actions. He agrees that the most comprehensive rationalization of an agent's action takes the form of a practical syllogism: so that for example the explanation of an agent's flipping of a light switch would cite the agent's 'pro attitude' to turn the light on and his belief that flipping the switch would cause the light to switch on.[11] Finally, he agrees that:

> [E]vents as described in the vocabulary of thought and action ... resist incorporation into a closed deterministic system.[12]

But, *against* the above opponents, he argues that if an agent flips a switch to illuminate a room and thereby unintentionally alerts a prowler, although 'to alert a prowler' provides a reason for flipping the light switch, it does not causally explain the flipping of the light switch if the prowler's presence was previously unknown.[13] Thus although Davidson grants that historians' explanations are methodologically autonomous from natural scientists', he also insists that a reason that is correctly identified must also be the cause of the action it explains.

---

9   Davidson, Donald 'Actions, Reasons, and Causes' [1963] in *Essays on Actions and Events*, 1980, p.3f.n.

10 See Davidson, Donald 'How is Weakness of Will Possible?' [1970] in *Essays on Actions and Events*, 1980, pp.21–42

11 Davidson, Donald 'Actions, Reasons, and Causes' [1963] in *Essays on Actions and Events*, 1980, p.5

12 Davidson, Donald 'Psychology as Philosophy' [1974] in *Essays on Actions and Events*, 1980, p.230

13 In Jonathan Dancy's vocabulary, in *Practical Reality* (2000), a rational explanation provides a *reason for* flipping the light switch but not a *reasons why* the switch was flipped.

Davidson argues that were rational explanation wholly unrelated to causal explanation a rational explanation would amount to no more than a *post facto* justification: moreover the order of events described by the explanation would be interchangeable. We might say, for example: 'my reason for alerting the prowler was that I wanted to turn on the light'.[14] In other words, were rational explanations wholly unrelated to causal explanations they would not respect Hume's view of a 'cause' as temporally prior to its effect.

In summary, Davidson argues that, although certain explanations may make use of the ideal of rationality (due to the putative rationality of their subject matter), insofar as a rationalization is judged to be correct it is judged to have been shown to be the *cause* of a physical effect; it is not judged to be correct insofar as it provides a justification of the agent's action. He believes this point to be a crucial amendment to previous descriptions of rational explanations. He argues that without this amendment rational explanation cannot aspire to explain why a particular belief was causally efficacious.

Davidson attempts to expand and clarify the above argument in 'Mental Events' (1970). In this essay Davidson makes clear that he sees his work on the relation between rational and causal explanation as answering the following problem, articulated by Kant:

> [W]e think of man in a different sense and relation when we call him free, and when we regard him as subject to the laws of nature ... It [philosophy] must therefore show that not only can both of these very well co-exist, but that both must be thought *as necessarily united* in the same subject ... .[15]

Davidson's answer to this problem is 'anomalous monism':

> The anomalism of the mental is ... a necessary condition for viewing action as autonomous.[16]

His argument for this thesis proceeds as follows.[17] He claims that an apparent contradiction between rational and causal explanation arises from the following three principles.

P.1 'The first principle asserts that at least some mental events interact causally with physical events. (We could call this the Principle of Causal

---

14 Davidson, Donald 'Actions, Reasons, and Causes' [1963] in *Essays on Actions and Events*, 1980, p.5

15 Kant *Fundamental Principles of the Metaphysics of* Morals, p.76; quoted by Davidson in 'Mental Events' [1970] in *Actions and Events*, 1980, p.225

16 Davidson, Donald 'Mental Events' [1970] in *Actions and Events*, 1980, p.225

17 This exegesis has been aided by Mark Johnston's 'Why Having a Mind Matters' in *Actions and Events: Perspectives on the Philosophy of Donald Davidson* (eds. Ernest LePore & Brian P. McLaughlin), 1985.

Interaction)'.[18] For example, the mental intention to illuminate a room may lead to the physical event of flipping a light switch.

P.2 'The second principle is that where there is causality, there must be a law: events related as cause and effect fall under strict deterministic laws. (We may term this the Principle of the Nomological Character of Causality)'.[19] Such laws (including probabilistic laws) are found in the physical sciences in which, in principle, every event may be described in such a manner as to fall under a deterministic law.

P.3 'The third principle is that there are no strict deterministic laws on the basis of which mental events can be predicted and explained (the Anomalism of the Mental)'.[20] Deterministic laws cannot be framed by the use of mental concepts, for the mental does not constitute a closed system; nor are there psychophysical bridging laws by which mental events are connected to physical events.

He acknowledges that since he is willing to accept all three principles as true he is obliged to offer an explanation of the apparent contradiction between the third of these principles (the absence of psychophysical laws) and the first two. He believes that the solution of this problem will also address Descartes' problem of mental-physical interaction. He attempts to resolve the above three principles as follows.

C.1 Although the distinguishing characteristic of a mental event is that it exhibits intentionality, nonetheless it can be picked out using physical vocabulary alone, for 'an object cannot alter in some mental respect without altering in some physical respect'.[21]

P.4 Any event that has a physical description is a physical event.[22]

C.2 '[A]ll mental events are identical with physical events'.[23] That is to say, even though mental events (events described using intentional vocabulary) remain anomalous, i.e. irreducible to deterministic laws (P.3)[24], it may yet be inferred that they are also physical events—for only causes in Sense III hold between events irrespectively of how they are described. Mental events are therefore, in Davidson's vocabulary, *supervenient* upon physical events.

This conclusion is sometimes expressed as follows: although token mental events are identifiable with token physical events, mental types cannot be identified with physical types—for, in answer to Kant's problem, the

---

18   Davidson, Donald 'Mental Events' [1970] in *Actions and Events*, 1980, p.208
19   Davidson, Donald 'Mental Events' [1970] in *Actions and Events*, 1980, p.208
20   Davidson, Donald 'Mental Events' [1970] in *Actions and Events*, 1980, p.208
21   Davidson, Donald 'Mental Events' (1970) in *Actions and Events*, 1980, p.214
22   Davidson, Donald 'Mental Events' (1970) in *Actions and Events*, 1980, p.211
23   Davidson, Donald 'Mental Events' (1970) in *Actions and Events*, 1980, p.212
24   Davidson, Donald 'Mental Events' (1970) in *Actions and Events*, 1980, p.214

anomalism of the mental (P.3) 'is ... a necessary condition for viewing action as autonomous'.[25]

A Reply to Davidson

The second premise of Davidson's argument is incorrect. For Collingwood, as has been seen, offers two other senses of 'cause': Sense I, in which 'cause' approximates to 'the means by which an agent is afforded a motive'; and Sense II, in which 'cause' approximates to 'the means by which we manipulate events in nature'.[26]

Were it thought that Sense I is ontologically fundamental, an argument might be constructed of the same logical structure as Davidson's but with the conclusion that the physical is supervenient upon the mental. Such an argument would run as follows.

P.1 Some mental events interact causally with physical events.

P.2 Where there is causality an agent must be afforded a motive.

P.3 Physical events cannot be afforded a motive.

C.1 Although the distinguishing characteristic of a physical event is that it falls under a general law, nonetheless it can be picked out using intentional vocabulary alone.

P.4 Any event that can be picked out using intentional vocabulary is an mental event.

C.2 All physical events are identical with mental events. That is to say, even though physical events, falling under general laws, remain anomalous, i.e. irreducible to motives afforded to agents (P.3), it may yet be inferred that they are mental events—for only causes in Sense I hold between events irrespectively of how they are described. Physical events are therefore supervenient upon mental events.

However, it is not apparent that a study of causation favours either the supervenience of the mental or the supervenience of the physical. Rather, in both arguments it is a prior ontological commitment that has dictated the second premise.

Collingwood's argument that it is the context of the investigation that determines the appropriate sense of cause provides support for the idea that it is unnecessary to have recourse to the idea of any fundamental sense of cause. Thus:

> For example, a car skids while cornering at a certain point, strikes the kerb, and turns turtle. From the car-driver's point of view the cause of the accident was cornering too fast, and the lesson is that one must drive more carefully. From the county surveyor's point of view the cause was a defect in the surface or camber of the road, and the lesson is that greater care must be taken to make roads skid-proof. From the

25   Davidson, Donald 'Mental Events' (1970) in *Actions and Events*, 1980, p.225
26   E.M., p.286

> motor-manufacturer's point of view the cause was defective design in the car, and the lesson is that one must place the center of gravity lower.[27]

It is the idea that the context of an investigation that determines the appropriate sense of cause[28] (and that the reasons/causes debate is purely conceptual) that is advocated by Collingwood scholars, against Davidson's identification of reasons with causes.

On Davidson's behalf, the counter-argument might be made that if there is no fundamental sense of cause the relationship between that which is explained with Sense I of cause and that which is explained with Sense III is left in a state of mystery.

This would be true if it were claimed that Sense I and Sense III are used to study different things — rather than the different categories or concepts under which these things fall. But this is not a claim I wish to defend. The claim I wish to defend is that, when metaphysics is confined to the study of other disciplines, as Collingwood recommends, there would appear to be no single sense of cause that is fundamental. Rather, different senses of cause seem to be appropriate to different sorts of explanation.[29]

Without a single fundamental sense of cause the ground upon which anomalous monism is built falls away.

---

27 E.M., p.304

28 Replies to Davidson from this standpoint include: Von Wright, Georg Henrik *Explanation and Understanding*, 1971, pp.118–31; Williams, Bernard 'Internal and External Reasons' [1980], reprinted in *Moral Luck*, 1981; Stoutland, Frederick 'Davidson on Intentional Behaviour' in *Actions and Events: Perspectives on the Philosophy of Donald Davidson* (1985); Baker, Lynne Rudder 'Metaphysics and Mental Causation' in *Mental Causation*, 1993; Burge, Tyler 'Mind-Body Causation and Explanatory Practice' in *Mental Causation*, 1993; Menzies, P. and Price, H. 'Causation as a Secondary Quality' in *British Journal for the Philosophy of Science*, 44, 1993, pp.187–203; Dray, William *History as Re-Enactment: R.G. Collingwood's Idea of History*, 1995; Tanney, Julia 'Why Reasons May Not Be Causes' in *Mind and Language* 1995 vol. 10, no. 1/2, pp.105–28; Hutto, Daniel 'A Cause for Concern: Reasons, Causes and Explanations' *Philosophy and Phenomenological Research* vol. 59, no.2 (June 1999), pp.381-401; D'Oro, Giuseppina 'In Defence of the Agent-Centred Perspective' *Metaphilosophy* 36 2005c, pp.652-67. This group can be divided between those, such as Menzies and Price, who believe that an agent-centred sense of causation underlies all others, and those, such as von Wright, who renounce any attempt to find a sense of causation more fundamental than any other.

29 That is not to say that the historian confines himself exclusively to the use of sense I of cause – he may use both sense I and sense III. Such an overlap is termed by Karsten Stueber 'the dual-explanandum strategy'. (See Stueber, Karsten R. 'Mental Causation and the Paradoxes of Explanation' in *Philosophical Studies* 2005, vol. 22: 243–77.) It is perhaps this dual-explanandum strategy that enables the reader of a historical narrative to enjoy both the forward looking standpoint of the agent and a retrospective standpoint.

Chapter XIII

The Radical Conversion Hypothesis

It is sometimes argued that between the publication of *An Essay on Philosophical Method* (1933) and the publication of *An Essay on Metaphysics* (1940) Collingwood underwent a 'radical conversion' whereby metaphysics and history became merged. It is this hypothesis that forms the basis for a charge of historical relativism. The radical conversion hypothesis divides Collingwood scholars. T.M. Knox, Alan Donagan,[1] Nathan Rotenstreich[2] and Stephen Toulmin[3] support it. L. Rubinoff,[4] James Connelly,[5] L.O. Mink,[6] Giuseppina D'Oro,[7] Tariq Modood,[8] Adrian Oldfield[9] and Rex Martin[10] oppose it.

My aim in this chapter is to defuse this charge. I argue that, although in practice Collingwood did not always carefully distinguish between metaphysics and history it is in principle possible to distinguish between these two disciplines, without a wholesale revision of his metaphysics.

The idea that in the late 1930s Collingwood underwent a 'radical conversion' first appears in T.M. Knox's preface to *The Idea of History* (1946).

---

1 Donagan, Alan *The Later Philosophy of R.G.* Collingwood, 1962, Chapter X

2 Rotenstreich, Nathan 'Metaphysics and Historicism' in M. Krausz (ed.) *Critical Essays on the Philosophy of R.G. Collingwood*, 1972

3 Toulmin, Stephen 'Conceptual Change and the Problem of Relativity' in M. Krausz (ed.) *Critical Essays on the Philosophy of R.G. Collingwood*, 1972

4 Rubinoff, L. 'Collingwood and the Radical Conversion Hypothesis' *Dialogue* 5/1 (1966), pp.71–83

5 Connelly, James *Metaphysics, Method and Politics*, 2003

6 Mink, L.O. *Mind, History and Dialectic*, 1969

7 D'Oro, Giuseppina 'Collingwood and the Radical Conversion Hypothesis' pp.79–87 in *Collingwood and the Metaphysics of Experience*, 2002

8 Modood, Tariq 'The Later Collingwood's Alleged Historicism and Relativism' *Journal of the History of Philosophy* 27 (1989), pp.101–25

9 Oldfield, Adrian 'Metaphysics and History in Collingwood's Thought' in *Philosophy, History and Civilization: Interdisciplinary Perspectives on R.G. Collingwood* (eds. D. Boucher, J. Connelly and T. Modood), 1995

10 Martin, Rex 'Collingwood's Claim that Metaphysics is a Historical Discipline' in *Philosophy, History and Civilization: Interdisciplinary Perspectives on R.G. Collingwood* (eds. D. Boucher, J. Connelly and T. Modood), 1995

Knox claims that Collingwood's 'philosophical standpoint radically changed between 1936 and 1938'.[11] He quotes the following passage, from a letter from Collingwood written in 1936, in support of this view:

> St. Augustine looked at Roman history from the point of view of an early Christian; Tillemont, from that of a seventeenth century Frenchman; Gibbon, from that of an eighteenth-century Englishman; Mommsen, from that of a nineteenth-century German. There is no point asking which was the right point of view. Each was the only one possible for the man who adopted it.

According to Knox the absorption of philosophy by history is also apparent in *An Essay on Metaphysics*. The problem with this work, according to Knox, is that since the metaphysician is inescapably situated within his own particular historical context he is unable to attain the detachment from history that would be necessary to carry out an objective metaphysical analysis. Knox argues that it was this *impasse* that prevented the completion of *The Principles of History*:

> Diminished physical strength, and preoccupation with *The New Leviathan* are two obvious answers. But the true answer is that his project [*The Principles of History*] had become either impossible or unnecessary.[12]

Collingwood himself would have contested the idea of any 'radical conversion' in his work of the late 1930s. From *An Autobiography* it may be inferred that he dates the final formulation of his philosophy of history as having occurred between 1928[13] and 1930.[14] Since Collingwood had begun writing *An Essay on Metaphysics* before he had finished writing *An Autobiography*, were he aware of any 'radical conversion' we might expect to find this recorded.[15]

Collingwood would also contest Knox's suggestion that the effects of illness are evident in his work:

> Whether luckily or unluckily, I have never known any illness interfere with my power of thinking or writing, or with the quality of what I think and write. When I am unwell, I have only to begin to work on

---

11   I.H., *xi*

12   I.H., *xvii* David Boucher gives some credence to Knox's interpretation of events: 'He began writing the book [*The Principles of History*] on 15 February 1939 and had finished the first three chapters by 23 February. Over a month later, on 26 and 27 March, he began chapter four but was unable to formulate his thoughts on the relationship between history and philosophy. At this point he stopped, never to return to the manuscript again.' 'The Significance of Collingwood's *Principles of History*' *Journal of the History of Ideas* 58 (1997), p.310

13   A., p.107

14   A. p.115

15   According to Collingwood's log the last chapter of A. was re-written in March 1939 while on the return trip from Indonesia aboard the SS *Rhesus*; E.M. was begun on the outward journey on 24 October aboard the MV *Alcinous*. E.M.xv–xvii (Rex Martin's introduction).

> some piece of philosophical writing, and all my ailments are forgotten until I leave off.[16]

In the absence of theoretical reasons mentioned by Collingwood, it seems more likely that *The Principles of History* was set to one side in favour of what Collingwood saw as his contribution to the war effort, *The New Leviathan*. This would accord with the conclusion of *An Autobiography*, in which Collingwood records his determination to fight against Fascism and 'the triumph of irrationalism':

> I know that all my life I have been engaged unawares in a political struggle, fighting against these things in the dark. Henceforth I shall fight in the daylight.[17]

Similarly the conclusion of *An Essay on Metaphysics* may also be read as a prequel to *The New Leviathan*:

> When Rome was in danger, it was the cackling of the sacred geese that saved the Capitol. I am only a professorial goose, consecrated with a cap and gown and fed at a college table; but cackling is my job, and cackle I will.[18]

Turning now from an historical account of events to a critical examination of the charge of relativism, it may be useful to ask what is meant by relativism, and by historical relativism in particular. It is a position that is more often mentioned in passing than discussed under an explicit definition.

In the philosophy of history 'relativism' is commonly used to describe three different positions. These are often assumed to be synonymous but they are actually quite different. They are as follows.

1. The idea of a view advanced without a historical context does not make sense.

2. There is nothing beyond our own views.

3. No view is better than another.

Neither 2 nor 3 can be proposed without contradiction. 2 is an ontological claim vulnerable to the same criticism that Collingwood made of Oxford realism: it claims to know what it simultaneously defines as unknown. 3 rests on the premise that 'this view is better than another'.

Neither 2 nor 3 follow from 1 or are presupposed by 1. It is 1, alone, which is advanced by Collingwood in *An Essay on Metaphysics* and *An Autobiography*, in such passages as the following:

> Metaphysics is the attempt to find out what absolute presuppositions have been made by this or that person or group of persons, on this or that occasion or group of occasions, in the course of this or that piece of

---

16   A., p.117
17   A., p.167
18   E.M., p.343

thinking.[19]

Metaphysics ... is no futile attempt at knowing what lies beyond the limits of experience, but is primarily at any given time an attempt to discover what the people of that time believe about the world's general nature; such beliefs being the presuppositions of all their 'physics', that is, their inquiries into its detail. Secondarily it is the attempt to discover the corresponding presuppositions of other peoples and other times, and to follow the historical process by which one set of presuppositions has turned into another.[20]

Although Collingwood does not advance 2 or 3, nor associate them with 1, it might be argued that on the evidence of the above passages Knox's concern is justified: since history and metaphysics do not appear to be distinct disciplines, how is the metaphysician to attain sufficient detachment from his subject matter?

Collingwood seems keen to tell us how metaphysics is similar to history, for example:

Not only has metaphysics quite definite presuppositions, but every one knows what some of them are, for as metaphysics is an historical science it shares the presuppositions of all history; and every one, nowadays, has some acquaintance with the principles of historical thought.[21]

But he neglects to say how metaphysics differs from history. He plainly aims to bring about 'a *rapprochement* between philosophy and history'[22] but, the question arises, does he not rather bring about a merger?

I attempt to allay this concern in the following section. Following James Connelly's lead I shall argue that, although both the historian and the metaphysician presuppose 1, awareness of the fallacy of false disjunction enables a distinction to be drawn between metaphysics and history.

The Fallacy of False Disjunction

James Connelly points out that in *An Essay on Philosophical Method* Collingwood argues that it is a fallacy to identify two disciplines as distinct only in that area in which there is no overlap in their instances (the fallacy of precarious margins).[23] Likewise it is a fallacy to identify two concepts as identical in that area in which their instances coincide (the fallacy of false identified coincidents).[24] These are alternative applications of the fallacy of false disjunction. This consists:

19   E.M., p.47

20   A., pp.65–66

21   E.M., pp.63–4

22   A., p.77

23   Connelly, J. *Metaphysics, Method and Politics*, 2003, p.21

24   E.P.M., p.49

in the disjunctive proposition that any instance of a generic concept must fall either in one or in another of its specific classes.[25]

Connelly recalls Collingwood intention to avoid this fallacy: his resulting first rule of philosophical method is to:

> beware of false disjunctions and to assume that the specific classes of a philosophical concept are always liable to overlap, so that two or more specifically differing concepts may be exemplified in the same instance … The traditional way of referring to this principle is to speak of 'distinction without a difference', that is, a distinction in the concepts without a difference in the instances.[26]

Considering the claim cited by Knox, that 'philosophy as a separate discipline is liquidated by being converted into history'[27], in the light of the fallacy of false disjunction, Connelly concludes that:

> [H]e [Collingwood] never denied the autonomy of philosophy, but he did deny that it could exist as a separate subject, and he did deny that it could be studied separately from its historical instantiations.[28]

It is an instance of the fallacy of false disjunction to assume that when the subject matter of two concepts (in this case two disciplines) coincide there is no conceptual difference between the two disciplines. Accordingly when Collingwood makes the provocative claim that '[a]ll metaphysical questions are historical questions, and all metaphysical propositions are historical propositions'[29] he is not claiming that metaphysics and history are conceptually identical, he is simply claiming that their subject matter coincides and that since metaphysicians are themselves historical agents their pronouncements may be the subject of historians' scrutiny. The historian is at liberty to study metaphysical pronouncements by the same means as he studies all other pronouncements, since, as Collingwood makes clear, all views (including metaphysical views) have an historical context.

However, Collingwood neglects to mention that when the historian studies metaphysical propositions he does so with different interests than the metaphysician. A significant difference is that whereas the metaphysician is interested in absolute presuppositions the historian is interested in predominant attitudes.[30] That is to say, the historian is less interested in the logical commitments of an historical agent than in what the agent, in fact, thought.

That is not to deny similarities between the attempt to recover absolute presuppositions and predominant attitudes: both the historian and the

25   E.P.M., p.49
26   E.P.M., p.50
27   I.H. x; P.H., p.238
28   Connelly, J. *Metaphysics, Method and Politics*, 2003, p.22
29   E.M., p.49
30   I am grateful to Giuseppina D'Oro for this suggestion.

metaphysician ask what questions gave rise to particular actions. Moreover, no piece of thinking is likely to rest upon a single absolute presupposition or a single predominant attitude. Thus, for example, both the historian and the metaphysician might say of an historical agent that in some respects his actions hark back to medieval and classical attitudes, whilst in other respects the agent is typical of his time, whilst in yet other respects he anticipates contemporary attitudes. But ultimately the historian is only interested in the agent's reasoning to the extent that evidence may be found for this reasoning to have affected subsequent events, or to have been affected by previous events: he is not interested in absolute presuppositions *per se*. (Nor need he take an interest in his own absolute presuppositions in order to be a good historian).

Both the historian and the metaphysician presuppose that all views are advanced from particular historical contexts, but this has a different effect upon the metaphysician's work than the historian's. The metaphysician, interested in the absolute presuppositions of particular form of inquiry, must begin his inquiry from commonly agreed examples of good practice within the discipline that he studies, but his ultimate concern is to uncover the distinctive logical structure of historians' explanations. By contrast, the historian's ultimate concern is to employ this logical structure in order to establish, and to better understand, a series of events.

I am not claiming that in practice Collingwood never makes the mistake of confusing metaphysics and history — as will be seen in the next chapter, his law of primitive survivals makes just this mistake — but that, in principle, it is possible for a distinction to be maintained.

Chapter XIV

Critical and Speculative Philosophies of History

My aim in this chapter is to examine certain elements of speculative philosophy that are present in Collingwood's writings. I argue that these are extraneous to the valid core of his critical philosophy of history.

Critical (or analytical) philosophy of history is concerned with the logical structure of historians' explanations. Those sympathetic to Collingwood's philosophy have argued that his work falls within this category. For example, Dray points out that in referring to the inside-outside distinction Collingwood is not reverting to 'traditional' metaphysics, nor is he advocating a methodological precept that guarantees understanding, rather, he is attempting to provide an analysis of the logical nature of historians' explanations. Thus:

> When Collingwood says that historical understanding consists of penetrating to the thought-side of actions—discovering the thought and nothing further—the temptation to interpret this in the methodological way is understandably strong. But there is another way in which the doctrine can be formulated: 'Only by putting yourself in the agent's position can you *understand* why he did what he did'. The point of the 'projection' metaphor is, in this case, more plausibly interpreted as a logical one. Its function is not to remind us of *how we come to know* certain facts, but to formulate, however tentatively, certain *conditions which must be satisfied* before a historian is prepared to say: 'Now I have the explanation'.[1]

Subsequent debates within the philosophy of history have, in general, also tended to focus upon the logical structure of historians' explanations, for example: Hempel's argument that an event is invariably explained by citing the general law from which it follows; and Dray's argument that there is a 'conceptual connection between understanding a man's action and discovering its *rationale*'.[2] Whatever else their disagreements, it is gener-

---

1   Dray, W. *Laws and Explanation in History*, 1957b, p.128

2   Dray, W. 'The Historical Explanation of Actions Reconsidered' in *The Philosophy of History* (ed. Patrick Gardiner), 1974, p.69

ally agreed by the proponents of these views that their debate takes place within critical philosophy of history.

By contrast speculative philosophy of history aims to make explicit the underlying *rationale* of a past course of events.[3] It views the unfolding of a past course of events as an essentially logical process, such that if the *nisus* or *telos* of the process is known the course of past events can be reconstructed. A substantive explanation of the rationality of past events is offered, as opposed to (and at the cost of) an examination of historians' actual practices.

Perhaps the most clear cut examples of speculative philosophy of history are to be found in the work of Hegel and Marx. Hegel's speculative philosophy of history is predicated upon the view that:

> What is rational is actual and what is actual is rational.[4]

Walsh explains the appeal of this form of philosophy as follows.

> If we ask why history was thus thought to constitute a problem for philosophers, the answer is because of the apparently chaotic nature of the facts which made it up. To nineteenth-century philosophical eyes history appeared to consist of a chain of events connected more or less loosely or accidentally, in which at first sight at any rate, no clear plan or pattern could be traced. But to accept that description of history, i.e. to take it at its face value, was for many philosophers of the period a virtual impossibility, for it meant (so they thought) admitting the existence in the universe of something ultimately unintelligible. To persons brought up to believe with Hegel that the real is the rational and the rational the real, this was a very shocking conclusion to come to, one which ought to be avoided if any way of avoiding it could be found.[5]

Speculative philosophy of history is not *wholly* unconcerned with problems of methodology. In the past it was influenced by the hermeneutic tradition, focused upon problems of interpretation — problems that were for much of the history of philosophy a greater preoccupation among continental philosophers than among Anglophone philosophers. This tradition had grown in response to the need to resolve particular legal and theological problems. Thus, for example: Vico was influenced by the legal theorist Grotius, who wrote on the value of cross-examination in the evaluation of testimony. However, it has now become common practice to distinguish speculative philosophy of history from critical (or analytical) philosophy of history.

---

3   'When what we call academic history began to develop, particularly in Göttingen, in the later decades of the eighteenth century, it set itself against this movement.' Butterfield, Herbert *The Origins of History*, 1981, p.219

4   Hegel, Preface to *Philosophy of Right*, 1942, p.10

5   Walsh, W.H. *An Introduction to Philosophy of History*, 1951, pp.119–20.

Karl Popper famously criticizes speculative philosophy of history in *The Poverty of Historicism* (1957) and *The Open Society and its Enemies* (1945).[6] Specifically, Plato, Hegel and Marx are criticized for their conflation of logical and temporal order in the service of teleological explanations. Popper argues that although it *is* possible to depict history as a series of events unfolding towards an inevitable present or future *telos*, such a story, whatever its ending — the dictatorship of the proletariat or the fulfillment of rational freedom — is impossible to falsify, and so is essentially uninformative. That is not to say that all 'retrospective' histories are logically flawed: for example, a history may legitimately investigate 'the growth of the modern state' and begin its account before the advent of any modern state — so long as the growth of the modern state is not explained as having occurred according to an *inevitable* course of events.

Speculative philosophy of history assumes that the course of history unfolds according to intrinsic laws and principles: but, since every historical event is preceded by an indefinitely large number of previous events, the historian can not hope to pick out the 'laws of history' — at best, he can hope to pick out trends that are of particular interest. Popper agrees with Hegel that human history has been influenced by the growth of human knowledge, but he argues that we cannot use this fact as a lodestar by which to provide history with an all-pervasive structure and direction, for we cannot predict how future society will be influenced by human knowledge when we do not know what that future knowledge will be:

> if there is such a thing as growing human knowledge, then we cannot anticipate today what we shall know only tomorrow.[7]

It is to these faults that Popper applies the term 'historicism'.

Historicism

The point has previously been made that where Popper uses the term 'historicism' Collingwood uses the term 'pigeon-holing'.[8] Collingwood agrees with Popper that the historian cannot anticipate future knowledge; for:

> History terminates not in the future but in the present. The historian's task is to show how the present has come into existence; he cannot show how the future will have come into existence, for he does not know what the future will be.[9]

Nonetheless *upon occasion* Collingwood is himself vulnerable to Popper's criticisms of historicism. For despite disparaging the 'late-nineteenth cen-

---

6   See also Berlin, Isaiah 'Historical Inevitability' (1954) in *Four Essays on Liberty*, 1969
7   Popper, Karl *The Poverty of Historicism* (1957) vii
8   P.H., p.19; I.H., p.264 See also Collingwood's criticisms of Hegel found in N.L. 33.85–33.89
9   I.H., p.104

tury identification of history with progress'[10] he seems to endorse the view that 'the basic meaning of history lies in man's developing historical consciousness'.[11]

Collingwood's historicism is perhaps most apparent in his defence of Fichte. In *The Idea of History* he defends what appear to be 'two specially flagrant errors'[12] in Fichte's work:

> (1) the idea that the present state of the world is perfect, a complete and final achievement of all that history has been working to bring about, and (2) the idea that the historical succession of ages can be determined *a priori* by reference to abstract logical considerations. I think it can be shown that in spite of their apparent silliness there is some truth in both these ideas.[13]

Collingwood defends the first of these ideas as follows:

> The present is our own activities; we are carrying out these activities as well as we know how; and consequently, from the point of view of the present there must always be a coincidence between what is and what ought to be, the actual and the ideal ... the aim of every age is to be itself; and thus the present is always perfect in the sense that it always succeeds in being what it is trying to be. This does not imply that the historical process has nothing more to do; it only implies that, so far, it has done what it meant to do, and that we cannot tell what it is going to do next.[14]

The second he defends as follows:

> [I]f it is maintained that temporal sequence and logical implication have nothing to do with each other, historical knowledge becomes impossible, for it follows that we can never say about any event 'this *must* have happened'; the past can never appear as the conclusion of a logical inference. If the temporal series is a mere aggregate of disconnected events, we can never argue back from the present to the past. But historical thinking consists precisely of arguing back in this way; and it is therefore based on the assumption (or as Kant and Fichte would have said, on the *a priori* principle) that there is an internal or necessary connection between the events of a time-series such that one event leads necessarily to another and we can argue back from the second to the first.[15]

Collingwood defends Fichte's 'flagrant errors' by the above arguments, whilst also granting that Fichte may be criticized for not granting any role to empirical evidence.

---

10   I.H., p.99
11   Mazlish, Bruce *The Riddle of History*, 1966, pp.8–9
12   I.H., p.108
13   I.H., p.108
14   I.H., p.109
15   I.H., p.110 See also P.H., p.121: 'What I want to suggest here is that history is the coincidence of logical with temporal order. I mean that the successive events of history form an order which, so far as it is genuinely historical (not all chronological sequences of events in human life are so), is a logical order as well as a temporal one.'

Although in the above passages Collingwood's historicism is not as obvious as that of, for example, Karl Marx, nonetheless he does not avoid the charge of historicism—for no empirical evidence is offered to support the idea that the present 'always succeeds in being what it is trying to be'.

The second of Collingwood's arguments relies upon the idea that, since logic can be used to reconstruct the course of past events, the connection between two neighbouring events is itself in the nature of a logical relation.[16] However, as was argued in Chapter VI, it is doubtful that the study of logic can lead to ontological conclusions. The counter-argument is that it is the conflation of logical and temporal order that allows the unjustified conclusion that 'this *must* have happened'.

The historicist idea that the course of past events is intrinsically rational underlies Collingwood's confusion between the *method* of question and answer (that the metaphysician uses to reveal absolute presuppositions and that the historian uses to reveal predominant attitudes) and what, in *An Autobiography*, he terms the *logic* of question and answer. In *An Autobiography* he implies that if the historian asks the correct question the evidence *must* yield the 'correct' answer. This is a different, and stronger, claim than that the evidence yields answers in relation to the acuity of the historian's questions. The latter more cautious thesis amounts to the claim that although the evidence yields answers it is in relation to the acuity of the historian's questions, nonetheless, however astute the historian, there is no guarantee that answers will be forthcoming—moreover, the answers that are forthcoming may be quite unexpected. In other words, the acuity of the historian's questions is a necessary but not a sufficient condition for the progress of the historian's investigation.

It is perhaps his conception in *An Autobiography* of the method of question and answer as a *logic* that leads Collingwood to make the following astonishing claim:

> Naval historians think it worth while to argue about Nelson's tactical plan at Trafalgar because he won the battle. It is not worth while arguing about Villeneuve's plan. He did not succeed in carrying it out, and therefore no one will ever know what it was.[17]

This argument is invalidated by the simple observation that 'it is often quite easy to characterize (to decode the intention *in*) an attempted but wholly unsuccessful action'.[18] For example, it is possible to decode the intention in Scott's unsuccessful expedition to the South Pole by the same

---

16 Collingwood notes that this is a characteristic of Christian historiography (I.H., p.50). It should be remembered that Collingwood himself wrote on Roman Britain as a *Christian* historian. For Collingwood, the major significance of Roman rule was that it prepared the ground for Christianity.

17 A., p.70

18 Skinner, Quentin 'Meaning and Understanding in the History of Ideas' *History and Theory*, Vol. 8, 1969, p.51

means as it is possible to decode the intention in Nelson's tactical plan at Trafalgar.

Another example of Collingwood's historicism is his law of primitive survivals. A formal definition of this law is provided in *The New Leviathan*, as follows:

> 9.51. *When A is modified into B there survives in any example of B, side by side with the function B which is the modified form of A, an element of A in its primitive or unmodified state.*[19]

Collingwood claims that this law is a feature of the course of history. In *An Autobiography*, he claims to have worked out this law already by 1920.[20] In *The Idea of History* this idea is linked to the idea of re-enactment and the *revival* of acts of thought:

> Because the historical past, unlike the natural past, is a living past, kept alive by the act of historical thinking itself, the historical change from one way of thinking to another is not the death of the first, but its survival integrated in a new context involving the development and criticism of its own ideas.[21]

This law is historicist in that it purports to describe the course of history, and to make history intelligible, but is not offered on the basis of historical evidence — it is not empirically testable. It is unclear whether Collingwood offers it as a philosopher or an historian, or as a 'historiosopher'.[22] It *is* clear however that Collingwood is no longer studying the working practices of historians. He has forsaken critical philosophy of history for speculative philosophy of history.

That is not to say that Collingwood's analysis of historians' practices is thereby invalidated, but it must be admitted that he does not consistently restrict himself to their analysis.

---

19   N.L., p.65

20   A., pp.98–9. In Collingwood's 'Fascism and Nazism' *Philosophy* Vol. XV, 1940, pp.168–76 the law of primitive survivals is used to explain the rise of fascism in Germany and Italy.

21   I.H., p.226

22   This is Isaiah Berlin's term for speculative philosophers of history, such as Hegel, Spengler and Toynbee — 'The Concept of Scientific History' (1960) reprinted in W.H. Dray (ed.) *Philosophical Analysis and History*, 1966, p.23

Chapter XV

Historical Methodology
The Historian and the Detective

In this book I have taken the view that when Collingwood's philosophy of history is read in the light of his arguments in *An Essay on Philosophical Method* and *An Essay on Metaphysics* it becomes clear that his principal concern is with the conceptual project of discovering the absolute presuppositions of history. His remarks on historical methodology are subordinate to this conceptual project.

In order to recover these absolute presuppositions, Collingwood asks how it is possible for the historian to understand the actions of another person—what must the historian presuppose in order to achieve this understanding? He argues that the historian does not offer causal explanations reliant upon a Humean sense of 'cause',[1] rather the historian offers, in Dray's vocabulary, 'rational explanations'—in which the word 'cause' is used to mean 'that which affords the historical agent a motive'.[2] In order to explain an action historically the historian must presuppose that the historical agent, however dubious his motivations or ambitions, may yet be capable of valid reasoning. It is this idea that Collingwood has in mind when he claims that: 'a bad reason is still a reason'.[3] Collingwood's best-known example of historical explanation is to be found in his discussion of the devil-fearers in *The Idea of History*. In this example, the historian's own belief that there are no devils in the mountains is irrelevant to his reconstruction of the devil-fearer's actions.

> The historian says that these are the facts because that is the way in which he has been taught to think. But the devil-fearer says that the presence of devils is a fact, because that is the way in which he has been taught to think. The historian thinks it a wrong way; but wrong ways of thinking are just as much historical facts as right ones, and no less

---

1   E.M., pp.285–86

2   E.M. p.285

3   P.H., p.47

than they, determine the situation (always a thought situation) in which the man who shares them is placed.[4]

It is the agent's 'thought situation' that Collingwood has in mind when he proposes, as the absolute presupposition of history, that 'all history is the history of thought'.[5] By this he does not mean that all history is the history of ideas, nor that the historian should not pay attention to economic and geographical factors, but that consideration of other factors should not over-ride the historian's attempt to reconstruct a situation *as seen by the historical agent*. Thus, Collingwood's answer to the conceptual question 'how is it possible for the historian to understand the action of another person?' is that historical understanding is possible on the presumption that agents are universally rational, in the sense of being capable of reasoning validly from premises to conclusion.

Nonetheless, aside from addressing this conceptual question, there is also a recessive methodological side to Collingwood's philosophy of history, in which he is concerned with the methodological question of how knowledge of past events is acquired.[6] This question is addressed in 'The Limits of Historical Knowledge',[7] in which Collingwood responds to Bernard Bosanquet's 'skeptical' view of history as 'the doubtful story of successive events';[8] and in the first chapter of *The Principles of History* in which Collingwood provides an example of how historical knowledge is attained, in the form of a miniature detective story entitled 'Who killed John Doe?'.[9]

In the first section of this chapter, 'Skepticism about the Past', I provide an exposition of Collingwood's argument in 'The Limits of Historical Knowledge'; in the second section, 'Knowledge of the Past', I provide an exposition of Collingwood's argument in 'Who killed John Doe?'.

In the third section, 'Data and Interpretation', I argue that the analogy between the work of the historian and the work of the detective may be extended further than Collingwood realizes: for it is essential to both the historian and the detective that a distinction is made between data and interpretation.

---

4   P.H., p.100; I.H., p.317

5   A., p.110; I.H., pp.215, 317; P.H., pp.67, 98, 100

6   Recent works focusing upon this aspect of Collingwood's philosophy include Coady, C.A.J. *Testament*, 1992; Couse, G.S. 'Collingwood's Detective Image of the Historian and the Study of Hadrian's Wall' in *History and Theory*, 1990; D'Oro, Giuseppina 'On Collingwood's Conceptions of History' in *Colllingwood Studies*; McCulagh, C. Behan *The Logic of History*, 2004; Pompa, Leon 'Collingwood's Theory of Historical Knowledge' in *Philosophy, History and Civilisation*, 1995.

7   Collingwood, R.G. 'The Limits of Historical Knowledge' *Journal of Philosophical Studies*, 3 (1928), pp.213–22

8   Bosanquet, Bernard *The Principle of Individuality and Value*, 1912, p.79; quoted by R.G. Collingwood in 'The Limits of Historical Knowledge', 1928, p.213

9   P.H., pp.21–8

In the final section of this chapter, I suggest there is a tension between the analogy made in 'Who killed John Doe?' and the rest of Collingwood's philosophy and I suggest alternative ways by which this tension might be removed.

Skepticism about the Past

In 'The Limits of Historical Knowledge' Collingwood responds to Bernard Bosanquet's view of history as 'the doubtful story of successive events.'[10] Collingwood terms this view 'historical skepticism.' Bosanquet's skepticism is epistemological: he is skeptical of historical knowledge not in the sense that he doubts the existence of the past but that he doubts our ability to achieve reliable knowledge of it.

Collingwood sees Bosanquet's skepticism as arising from consideration of the incomplete nature of historical evidence:

> Now — and this is the root of historical skepticism — we only have a strictly limited quantity of evidence concerning any historical question; it is seldom free from grave defects, it is generally tendentious, fragmentary, silent where it ought to be explicit, and detailed where it had better be silent; even at its best, it is never free from these and similar faults, it only refrains from thrusting them indecently upon our notice.[11]

In 'The Limits of Historical Knowledge' Collingwood argues that historical skepticism ceases to be a concern when we reject historical 'realism' — the idea of an exact correspondence between written history and past events — and admit that:

> The past simply as past is wholly unknowable; it is the past as residually preserved in the present that is alone knowable.[12]

In support of this conclusion, Collingwood argues that the questions concerning the past for which there is no available evidence are regarded, by the historian, as not worth asking.

> [E]very historian knows that there are some questions — pseudo-questions rather — into which it is not his business to inquire, because there is no available evidence towards their answer; and that it is no shame to him to be ignorant by what name Achilles was called when he was disguised as a maiden. But historical realism would imply that this is incorrect; that there are no limits whatever to historical knowledge except the limits of the past as past, and that therefore the question what Julius Caesar had for breakfast the day he overcame the Nervii is

---

10   Bosanquet, Bernard *The Principle of Individuality and Value*, 1912, p.79; quoted by R.G. Collingwood in 'The Limits of Historical Knowledge', 1928, p.213

11   'The Limits of Historical Knowledge' *Journal of Philosophical* Studies, 3 (1928), p.214

12   'The Limits of Historical Knowledge' *Journal of Philosophical* Studies, 3 (1928), p.220 Collingwood's argument gives the impression that Bosanquet was a realist: he was in fact an exponent of absolute idealism.

as genuinely historical a problem as the question whether he proposed to become king of Rome.[13]

Collingwood is not here concerned with the ontological status of the past. He is not, for example, concerned with addressing Russell's ontological form of historical skepticism. This form of skepticism, as opposed to Bosanquet's, is expressed in *The Analysis of Mind* (1921) as follows:

> There is no logical impossibility in the hypothesis that the world sprang into being five minutes ago, exactly as it then was, with a population that 'remembered' a wholly unreal past. There is no logically necessary connection between events at different times; therefore nothing that is happening or will happen in the future can disprove the hypothesis that the world began five minutes ago. Hence the occurrences which are *called* knowledge of the past are logically independent of the past; they are wholly analyzable into present contents, which might, theoretically, be just what they are even if no past had existed.[14]

Russell's own response to the hypothesis that the world began five minutes ago is that the non-existence of the past should not be entertained as a serious hypothesis, for: 'Like all skeptical hypotheses, it is logically tenable, but uninteresting'.[15] Presumably, as Ayer says, the skeptical hypothesis is: 'Uninteresting … because although it cannot be refuted, there is equally no reason to believe it'.[16]

Collingwood is not concerned with ontological skepticism but with the epistemological challenge posed by Bosanquet. In answer to Bosanquet's epistemological question, Collingwood's point is that although the historian should not aspire to emulate von Ranke in claiming to know '*wie es eigentlich gewesen war*'[17] [what really happened] it does not follow that all claims to have attained historical knowledge are doubtful. On the contrary, they are convincing if they are demonstrated to follow from the interpretation of present-day evidence. The historian: 'must argue from the evidence he has, or stop arguing'.[18]

Nor should the argument that 'every historian knows that there are some questions … into which it is not his business to inquire'[19] be taken to imply that Collingwood is denying that Caesar either did or did not have breakfast the day he overcame the Nervii.[20] Although questions relating to

---

13 'The Limits of Historical Knowledge' *Journal of Philosophical* Studies, 3 (1928), p.220

14 Russell, Bertrand *The Analysis of Mind*, 1921, pp.159–60

15 Russell, Bertrand *The Analysis of Mind*, 1921, p.160

16 Ayer, A.J. 'Statements about the Past' *Proceedings of the Aristotelian Society* vol. LII, 1951-52; reprinted in *Philosophical Essays*, 1954, p.169

17 from the preface to *History of the Latin and Teutonic Peoples 1494–1514* [1825] in *Varieties of History: from Voltaire to the Present*, (ed. F. Stern), 1956

18 A., p.139

19 I.H., p.220

20 See Chapter 2 of *Truth and Contradiction*

Caesar's breakfast are of little interest, the historian does not discount them from entering into historical discussion at some future date.

Collingwood denies that there is any absolute starting point to historical inquiry, but he argues that it does not follow that historical inquiry is therefore entirely arbitrary. Historical inquiry begins when a certain question 'arises'. The answer that the historian gives to this question is convincing insofar as it is seen to address this question, not insofar as it tells us *'wie es eigentlich gewesen war'*.

As previously mentioned, the question of how the past might be reconstructed from present evidence is taken up again, and answered in greater detail, in one of Collingwood's best-known pieces of writing, 'Who killed John Doe?' This passage appears both in the first chapter of *The Principles of History* and in the Epilegomena of *The Idea of History*. In the Epilegomena 'Who killed John Doe?' is surrounded by passages concerning the conceptual nature of history. It is clearer, in *The Principles of History* that Collingwood's concern — in the case of John Doe — is with the methodological question of how knowledge of the past is acquired rather than with the question of how it is possible to understand the actions of another person.

Knowledge of the Past

Collingwood claims that 'the true theory of experimental science'[21] is correctly summarized in Francis Bacon's epigram, that the natural scientist must 'put Nature to the question'.[22] According to Collingwood, Bacon was here asserting two things at once:

> first, that the scientist must take the initiative, deciding for himself what he wants to know and formulating this in his own mind in the shape of a question; and secondly, that he must find means of compelling nature to answer, devising tortures under which she can no longer hold her tongue.[23]

According to Collingwood, this 'is also, though Bacon did not know this, the true theory of historical method'.[24] By this he means that the scientific historian, like Bacon's natural scientist, reads previous histories as he would read all other evidence, 'with a question in his mind, having taken the initiative by deciding for himself what he wants to find out from them'.[25] His approach is in contrast to that of the scissors-and-paste historian who reads previous accounts of the past in 'a purely receptive spirit'.[26]

---

21   P.H., p.24: I.H., p.269
22   P.H., p.24; I.H., p.269
23   P.H., p.24; I.H., p.269
24   P.H., p.24; I.H., p.269
25   P.H., p.25; I.H., p.269
26   P.H., p.25; I.H., p.269

Collingwood argues that all the *scientific* historian's evidence is sub-jected to critical scrutiny. In this respect the historian is similar to the detective. The fictional vignette 'Who killed John Doe?' is intended to illustrate this.[27] According to Collingwood the hero of the fable, Detec-tive-Inspector Jenkins of Scotland Yard, takes no evidence at face-value, but all is subjected to critical scrutiny ('put to the question') so that, for example, even when the confession of the rector's daughter is known to be false, the Inspector does not abruptly lose interest in her story, but asks what clue is provided by the fact that she told a lie.[28] Collingwood argues that in the same manner, having been subjected to critical scrutiny ('put to the question') no evidence is incorporated into the historian's account of events in its 'ready-made' state.[29]

The knowledge that is thus attained by the historian is not completely final – his evidence may be incomplete[30] – but though it may, in principle, be subject to future revision it is yet rational to believe it.

Collingwood suggests that Jenkins takes after Hercule Poirot. He asks only those questions to which his imagination demands answers – in expectation of constructing a cohesive and compelling account of past events. He suggests that the methods of Sherlock Holmes are by compari-son less scientific, for Holmes seems to have no particular question in mind in his study of the evidence. In contrast to Poirot, Holmes and the non-scientific historian tend to try 'to collect everything, no matter what, which might conceivably turn out to be a clue'[31] – presumably in the hope, or expectation, that previously unrelated data might intuitively 'jump together' in a fortuitous guess in the investigator's mind.

In summary, Collingwood's answer to the question of how the historian achieves knowledge of past events is that the historian – like the detec-tive – traces the logical connections between past events in his own mind. In so doing he is not reliant upon any 'copy theory' of knowledge, rather he is, in Collingwood's vocabulary, reliant upon his '*a priori* imagination':

> Freed from its dependence on fixed points supplied from without, the historian's picture of the past is thus in every detail an imaginary pic-ture, and its necessity is at every point the necessity of the *a priori* imag-

---

27   As it is on record that Collingwood relaxed by reading Agatha Christie novels it is reasonable to suspect that he derived inspiration for this idea, at least in part, from this source (see his log of a voyage to the Dutch East Indies, to be appended to a forthcoming edition of *An Autobiography*). Collingwood first makes use of this analogy in a letter to F.G. Simpson in July 1934 (Van der Dussen, 1981, p.443). Joseph Levine points out that there are similarities between the plot of 'Who killed John Doe?' and Agatha Christie's *Murder at the Vicarage* (1930) – see 'The Autonomy of History: R.G. Collingwood and Agatha Christie' *Clio* 7 1978, pp.253–64.

28   P.H., p.26; I.H., p.270
29   P.H., pp.32–3; I.H., p.277
30   I.H., p.248
31   P.H., p.37; I.H., p.281

ination. Whatever goes into it, goes into it not because his imagination passively accepts it, but because it actively demands it.[32]

Collingwood gives an example of the historian's use of '*a priori* imagination' concerning Caesar's journey from Rome to Gaul:

> ... our authorities tell us that on one day Caesar was in Rome and on a later day in Gaul; they tell us nothing about his journey from one place to the other, but we interpolate this with a perfectly good conscience.[33]

Collingwood argues that history is like mathematics in that, having traced the logical connections between events by means of his *a priori* imagination, the historian is able to *conclusively* justify his claims to knowledge by demonstrating the grounds upon which they are based.

> One hears it said that history is 'not an exact science'. The meaning of this I take to be that no historical argument ever proves its conclusion with that compulsive force which is characteristic of exact science. Historical inference, the saying seems to mean, is never compulsive, it is at best permissive; or, as people sometimes rather ambiguously say, it never leads to certainty, only to probability. Many historians of the present writer's generation, brought up at a time when this proverb was accepted by the general opinion of intelligent persons ... must be able to recollect their excitement on first discovering that it was wholly untrue, and that they were holding in their hands an historical argument which left nothing to caprice, and admitted of no alternative conclusion, but proved its point as conclusively as a demonstration in mathematics.[34]

In the following section I intend to extend (and, to some extent, revise) the analogy between the work of the historian and the work of the detective so as to make a point overlooked by Collingwood: that both the historian and the detective, *but not the mathematician*, must distinguish between data and interpretation.

Data and Interpretation

According to Collingwood any differences between the work of the historian and the work of the detective are due to the fact that their ultimate purpose is not the same:

> A criminal court has in its hands the life and liberty of a citizen, and in a country where the citizen is regarded as having rights the court is therefore bound to do something and do it quickly. The time taken to arrive at a decision is a factor in the value (that is, the justice) of the decision itself.[35]

By contrast:

---

32 I.H., p.245
33 I.H., p.240
34 P.H., p.18; I.H., p.262
35 P.H., p.23; I.H., p.268

> [T]he historian is under no obligation to make up his mind within any stated time. Nothing matters to him except that his decision, when he reaches it, shall be right: which means, for him, that it shall follow inevitably from the evidence.[36]

The latter claim is not entirely accurate. In practice, neither the detective nor the historian is immune to time pressure. Neither can wait until a conclusion can be seen to follow from the evidence with absolute certainty. The factor of time pressure may be different in the work of the detective and the work of the historian, but this is a difference of degree rather than a distinction in principle.

Nor is it justifiable to cite the story of John Doe and the analogy with detective work in support of the idea that:

> History so far from depending on testimony has ... no relation with testimony at all.[37]

For, as C.A.J. Coady points out, there are several instances in the story of John Doe in which Inspector Jenkins does take testimony at face value, for example: the Inspector takes at face value the information that Richard Roe's shoes were muddy; that Richard Roe is a medical student; that the rector always patronises a certain glove shop; and that John Doe is a black-mailer.[38] The Inspector must make some such assumptions if he is to make progress in his inquiries:

> It seems that, just as we cannot dispense with observational and experimental data in natural science, so we cannot do without testimonial data in history.[39]

Leon Pompa makes the related point that the historian is dependent upon historical lemmas — previously established historical facts. Indeed, Collingwood himself may be quoted in support of this point: 'To ask any question ... we must already possess information'.[40] However, as Pompa points out, the acceptance of previously established historical facts need not be equated with the uncritical acceptance of authority such as occurs in scissors-and-paste history: for the acceptance of previously established historical facts is, in scientific history, *revisable*.[41] Crucially, the historian is able to revise the conclusions of his predecessors when historical sources

---

36 P.H., p.24; I.H., p.268

37 I.H., pp.202–3

38 Coady, C.A.J. *Testimony: A Philosophical Study*, 1992, pp.241-2. Whilst critical of Collingwood's philosophy of history, Coady's book is sympathetic to non-foundational 'positive epistemology'. According to Coady, 'positive epistemology takes it that the challenge of scepticism is somehow overcome, or sidetracked, and proceeds to investigate the structure (or absence of structure) to be found in human knowledge or in that body of belief which can, scepticism aside, lay reasonable claim to that title.' *Ibid.*, p.3

39 Coady, C.A.J. *Testimony: A Philosophical Study*, 1992, p.248

40 S.M., p.79

41 Pompa, Leon 'Collingwood's Theory of Historical Knowledge' in *Philosophy, History and Civilization: Interdisciplinary Perspectives on R.G. Collingwood*, 1995, p.180

(or data) are distinguished from interpretation. This distinction, between data and interpretation, is also characteristic of the detective's report. The significance of this distinction (unmentioned by Collingwood) is explored below.

Collingwood fails to note that there are two separate stages to both the historian's work and the detective's: investigation and summation. He is correct to note that investigation starts in response to a question that has 'arisen'; and that during the investigation further questions are asked at various junctures in response to the interpretation of the evidence. But he fails to note that, in response to the historian's questions, his sources (or data) are (or should be) collected in 'a purely receptive spirit', so as to allow for the revision of those questions. During this stage of his work, insofar as time and interest allow, the detective and the historian collect everything that 'might conceivably turn out to be a clue'.[42] The methods of Poirot and Holmes are therefore not, in principle, incompatible.

As the historian alternates between investigation and summation, he will alternate between respectively the present tense (all evidence is, after all, present day evidence) and the past tense. (By contrast the philosopher, unless he strays purposely or otherwise into the historian's field, will present his predecessors' arguments only in the present tense).

That the historian (and the detective) retains a distinction between data and interpretation is not due to an underlying commitment to 'realism' but is so that when a final interpretation (a summation) is presented it will still be possible to distinguish between the historian's interpretation and his 'ready-made' data. This allows his data to be reused by other historians with other questions. In the discipline of history, this characteristic first appears in the work of Herodotus, in the following statement:

> It is my principle that I ought to repeat what is said; but I am *not* bound always to believe it — and that may be taken to apply to this book as a whole.[43]

In following this principle, Herodotus' reliability is lent further support in the following instances. He recounts the belief that the Nile flood is due to the melting of mountain snow, although he is disinclined to believe this himself, for:

> How *could* there be snow in the hottest part of the world?[44]

Likewise, he recounts the reports of the Phoenicians whom circumnavigated Africa at the command of the Pharaoh Necoh, as follows:

> These men made a statement which I do not myself believe though others may, to the effect that as they sailed on a westerly course round

---

42 P.H., p.37; I.H., p.281
43 Herodotus *The Histories* VII, 152
44 Herodotus *The Histories* II, 22

the southern end of Libya, they had the sun on their right—to the northward of them.[45]

Herodotus perhaps formulated his principle for aesthetic motives, not wanting to miss out any 'good stories' — Eusebius of Caesaria independently rediscovered this principle and in his *History of the Church* used it as a means of paying homage to his predecessors: but regardless of the motives of Herodotus and Eusebius the value of the principle remains. It supports history as a collaborative enterprise intent upon the cumulative accretion of reliably cross-referenced knowledge.

In contrast to Herodotus (at his best), Roman historians tended *not* to attempt to separate data from interpretation. Instead they relied upon the concept of *inventio*:

> [Inventio] is not 'invention' if by that we imply some degree of imaginative creation. It is simply the 'discovery' of what requires to be said in a given situation (*ta deonta heurein*), the implied theory being that it is somehow already 'there' though latent, and does not have to be made up as a mere figment of imagination ... The nature of ancient *inventio* and its difference from modern invention are of the first importance. Not only did the concept circumscribe the poet in ways we find surprising, but it actually liberated the historian, by giving him very much the same range; this is why most ancient historians feel free to fill out the tradition with speeches, standardised accounts of embassies or battles, likely motivations, and other manifestations of *to eikos*. Both poet and historian operate within rules which were originally rhetorical.[46]

That Roman historians did not draw a distinction between data and interpretation has greatly impeded subsequent generations of historians. Thus for example, in Tacitus' account of Caratacus' speech before the emperor Claudius,[47] and in his account of Boudica's speech to her warriors,[48] Tacitus may have reconstructed propositional attitudes that he himself did not share; but, since no distinction between data and interpretation is apparent, subsequent historians are uncertain as to what parts (if any) of these speeches are attributable to Caratacus and Boudica. (In such cases as these, it is the details that are incidental to the writer's purpose that seem most trustworthy — in exposing these, the historian works, as it were, against the grain).

Although, like all historians, Herodotus clearly relishes 'a good story' his approach to history is, at times, more rigorous than that of Tacitus. We tend to give credence to his history due to the distinction drawn between

---

45   Herodotus *The Histories* IV, 42 Collingwood relates Herodotus' account of the circumnavigation of Africa in order to make the point that Herodotus is in some measure a critical historian (P.H.: 45). However, he does not comment on the significance of Herodotus's separation of data and interpretation.

46   Russell, D.A. 'Rhetoric and Criticism' *Greece and Rome* 14 (1967), p.135

47   Tacitus *Annals* 12, 27

48   Tacitus *Annals* 14, 35

data and interpretation. This distinction is not obscured by his own thoughts as to the veracity of his witnesses' reports and the motivations that may have given rise to such reports. The same is true of a detective's report: in order for it to be found convincing, the distinction drawn between data and interpretation, that was originally drawn during the detective's investigation, must remain clearly visible in his summation.[49]

This distinction is found in the work of the detective and the historian but is not found in the work of the historical novelist or the historical illustrator. For the historical novelist and the historical illustrator (and the re-enactors of the Sealed Knot Society and the Ermine Street Guard) use *fixed* (not revisable) points in order to hang a particular story or to depict a particular scene.

The separation of data and interpretation allows the historian the means by which he may demonstrate that his expectations have not dictated his conclusions – the reader is afforded the means to follow the historian's reasoning, and to compare rival interpretations for their 'fit' against the data.[50] By these means *previous interpretations can be modified in the light of new data*. To the historian, this is the most valuable consequence of Herodotus' principle.

The fact that a distinction is drawn between data and interpretation does not cast doubt on the idea that the historian should use his '*a priori* imagination' in order to reconstruct what happened in the past. Nonetheless, the distinction between data and interpretation does cast doubt upon the clear-cut analogy that Collingwood draws between history and mathematics.

In *The Principles of History* Collingwood attempts to minimize the difference between history and mathematics by classing the gathering of data as, at most, an 'essential preliminary'[51] to the study of history. However, the collection of data is more than simply a preliminary to the study of history. For not only must the historian have in mind the distinction between data and interpretation from the start of his investigation but he must also remember it in composing his final summation. Admittedly this distinction is less important in popular histories, which are often presented in a

---

49   Historians of the detective story have pointed out that the *genre* only became possible after the judicial system began to accord priority to the gathering of evidence rather than the extraction of confessions. With this in mind, Collingwood's description of the historian imitating Francis Bacon's example of putting the evidence 'to the question' (i.e. to torture) seems singularly inappropriate.

50   This process is further explored in Gilbert Harman's article 'The Inference to the Best Explanation' *Philosophical Review* 74 1965, pp.88–95 and in Peter Lipton's *Inference to the Best Explanation*, 1993.

51   P.H.: 52

purely summative form,[52] but the maintenance of this distinction is commonly agreed to be good practice in any work that aspires to be taken seriously as new research.

Granted that the historian's '*a priori* imagination' plays a role in his reconstruction of events, it remains the case that his data are not self-evident. In this respect the data from which the historian begins his inquiry are different from the unrevisable fiats from which the mathematician works—'let AB = BC' *etcetera*.

The historian cannot question all his data at once, and so must rely to some extent upon previously established historical facts. These facts, his historical data, remain in principle, empirically revisable. Thus the historian's distinction between data and interpretation does not rely upon a copy theory of knowledge, but upon the idea that:

> all history is in some respects false, but what these respects are we can never know.[53]

And, conversely, all history is in some respects true, but what these respects are we can never know.

In sum, the historian's knowledge of the past comes about through reliance upon revisable fixed points. This is both its strength and its weakness. It allows for the cumulative accretion of ever more reliable knowledge, but it also implies that certainty is impossible.

The Philosophy of History and the Philosophy of Action

Collingwood does not make explicit the difference between the thesis developed in 'Who killed John Doe?' and 'The Limits of Historical Knowledge', and that developed in the rest of his philosophy of history. I shall attempt to draw out this difference in this final section.

For Collingwood history is, above all, the study of mind. This is a more significant feature of history than the fact that it deals with past events. Thus to the extent that other sciences understand agents by reconstructing their thought processes they may be termed historical sciences. For example:

> In anthropological science man is trying to understand man; and to man his fellow-man is never a mere external object, something to be observed and described, but something to be sympathized with, to be studied by penetrating into his thoughts and re-enacting those for oneself. Anthropology—I refer to cultural, not physical anthropology—is an historical science, where by calling it historical as opposed to natu-

---

52   Likewise the two distinct stories presented in detective stories, the story of the crime and the story of its discovery, merge together in thrillers and suspense novels—see Todorov, Tzetan *The Poetics of Prose*, 1977, pp.47-50.

53   S.M., p.235

ralistic I mean that its true object is to get inside its object or recreate its object inside itself.[54]

For the same reason, according to Collingwood, palaeontology is not an historical science.[55] For although the palaeontologist deals with past events and arranges artefacts in chronological order, these similarities are not so significant as the difference, that the historian reconstructs thought processes and the palaeontologist does not. This is made clear in the following passage:

> The archaeologist's use of his stratified relics depends on his conceiving them as artifacts serving human purposes and thus expressing a particular way in which men have thought about their own life; and from this point of view the palaeontologist, arranging his fossils in a time-series, is not working as an historian, but only as a scientist thinking in a way which can at most be described as quasi-historical.[56]

In Collingwood's view, even though the palaeontologist reconstructs past events he is not a historian for he does not study the mind. Likewise, although he acknowledges that geography, geology and astronomy deal with historical problems,[57] and that Darwin resolved the problems of biology into historical problems,[58] he is only willing to grant these sciences the title of 'pseudo-history':

> A pseudo-history is an account of changes, whether geological, astronomical, social, or any other kind, where the person giving the account does not re-enact in his own mind the thoughts of the person or persons by whose action these changes came about.[59]

According to the conception of history outlined above the historian is primarily concerned with understanding the historical agent's *rationale*. Collingwood assumes that in the case of rational agents this is synonymous with discovering what happened. But, a closer inspection of the similarities between historical research and detective work suggests that the historian shares another fundamental principle not only with the detective but also with the geologist and palaeontologist: in order to acquire knowledge of past events, he must maintain a distinction between data and interpretation.

Does this discovery undermine the rest of Collingwood's philosophy of history? Arguably a conflict exists only if the subject matter of the philosophy of *history* is identified with the subject matter of the philosophy of

---

54 P.E., pp.153–54
55 In contrast to Collingwood, William Whewell classed palaeontology with geology, biology, cosmogony and history, as 'palaetiological sciences'.
56 I.H., p.212
57 S.M., p.187
58 S.M., p.53
59 P.H., p.245

action. Collingwood's claim that 'all history is the history of thought'[60] assumes that the subject matter of the philosophy of history and the subject matter of the philosophy of action are indistinguishable. However, if this absolute presupposition is recast as 'the agent's reasoning should be recovered whenever possible' (as argued in Chapter VIII) and if action explanation is seen not as the sole goal of the historian, but as one of several, then the tension between 'Who killed John Doe?' and Collingwood's philosophy of *action* is removed.

To the same effect, we might also draw a conceptual distinction between history and archaeology—the primary concern of the historian being w the question of '*why* this happened?' and the primary concern of the archaeologist being identical to the detective's, namely, '*what* happened?'.[61]

---

60   A., p.110; I.H., pp.215, 317; P.H., pp.67, 98, 100
61   I owe this suggestion to Professor Leo S. Klejn, who has explored the similarities between archaeology and detection in many different works over the last forty years. See, for example, 'Metaarchaeology' in *Acta Archaeologica* (special issue), 2001.

Chapter XVI

Conclusion

This book began with a description of what I see as the valid foundation of Collingwood's philosophy — philosophy's 'reversible direction'. It was from this ground, rather than Collingwood's ontological argument, that I examined Collingwood's 'metaphysics without ontology'; and, in particular, his attempt to recover the absolute presuppositions of history.

Collingwood's approach was found to reveal different senses of cause appropriate to different forms of inquiry, with no single sense of cause more fundamental than any other. I argued that this discovery undermines Donald Davidson's anomalous monism and, by implication, much of the contemporary physicalism that Davidson inspired. This argument stands, notwithstanding the criticisms of Collingwood raised in the previous chapter.

Bibliography

Anselm *Proslogion: with the replies of Gaunilo and Anselm* (trans. Thomas Williams), Indianapolis: Hackett, 1995

Aristotle *Metaphysics* (2nd ed.) (ed. W.D. Ross), Oxford: Clarendon Press, 1928

Aristotle *Physics* (ed. W.D. Ross), Oxford: Oxford: Clarendon Press, 1930

Ayer, A.J. *Language, Truth and Logic* (1936), 2nd rev. ed. New York: Dover Press, 1946

Ayer, A.J. 'Statements about the Past' *Proceedings of the Aristotelian Society* vol. LII 1951-52: i–xx; reprinted in *Philosophical Essays*, London: Macmillan, 1954

Ayer, A.J. *Part of My Life*, London: Collins, 1972

Ayer, A.J. *Philosophy in the Twentieth Century*, London: Weidenfeld and Nicolson, 1982

Baker, Lynne Rudder 'Metaphysics and Mental Causation' in *Mental Causation* (eds. John Heil and Alfred Mele), Oxford: Clarendon, 1993

Berlin, Isaiah 'Historical Inevitability' (1954) in *Four Essays on Liberty*, Oxford: Clarendon Press, 1969

Berlin, Isaiah 'The Concept of Scientific History' *History and Theory* I, 1 (1960) 19, reprinted in *Philosophical Analysis and History* (ed. W. Dray), New York: Harper, 1966, pp.5–53

Berlin, Isaiah 'The Purpose of Philosophy' in *Concepts and Categories* (ed. H. Hogarth), Hogarth Press, 1982

Bergmann, G.A. *The Metaphysics of Logical Positivism*, New York: Longmans Green, 1954

Blackburn, Simon 'Collingwood, Robin George' in *The Routledge Encyclopaedia of Philosophy* (ed. E. Craig), 1998

Bosanquet, Bernard *The Principle of Individuality and Value*, London: Macmillan, 1912

Boucher, David '*The Principles of History* and the Cosmological Conclusion to *The Idea of Nature*' in *Collingwood Studies* Vol.II 1995, pp.140–74

Boucher, David 'The Significance of Collingwood's *Principles of History*' in *Journal of the History of Ideas*, 1997, vol.58, no.2, pp.309–30

Bradley, F.H. *The Presuppositions of Critical History* (1876) reprinted in *Collected Essays*, Oxford: Clarendon Press, 1976

Breeze, David J. and Brian Dobson *Hadrian's Wall*, Harmondsworth: Penguin 4th ed. 1999

Browning, Gary K. *Rethinking R.G. Collingwood: Philosophy, Politics and the Unity of Theory and Practice*, Basingstoke: Macmillan, 2004

Burge, Tyler 'Mind-Body Causation and Explanatory Practice' in *Mental Causation* (eds. John Heil and Alfred Mele), Oxford: Clarendon Press, 1993, pp.97–120

Butterfield, Herbert *The Origins of History*, London: Eyre Methuen, 1981

Carlyle, Thomas 'On Heroes, Hero-Worship, and the Heroic in History' (1840) in *The Varieties of History* (ed. Fritz Stern), London: Macmillan, 1956

Carnap, Rudolf 'Pseudo-Problems in Philosophy' (1928) in *The Logical Structure of the World and Pseudo-Problems in Philosophy* (trans. R.A. George), London: Routledge, 1967

Coady, C.A.J. *Testimony: A Philosophical Study*, Oxford: Clarendon Press, 1992

Collingwood, R.G. Unpublished 'Lectures on the Ontological Proof of the Existence of God' Written 1919 for delivery Hilary Term 1920', Bodleian Library, Dep. 2

Collingwood, R.G. 'The Purpose of the Roman Wall' in *The Vasculum* 8 (1921), pp.4–9

Collingwood, R.G. 'Hadrian's Wall: A History of the Problem' in *The Journal of Roman Studies* 11 (1921), pp.37–66

Collingwood, R.G. *Roman Britain*, London: Clarendon Press, 1923, rev. ed. 1932

Collingwood, R.G. *Speculum Mentis*, Oxford: Clarendon Press, 1924

Collingwood, R.G. 'Some Perplexities about Time: with an attempted solution' *Proceedings of the Aristotelian Society* 26 (1925–26), pp.135–50

Collingwood, R.G. *A Guide to the Roman Wall* (1926), Newcastle upon Tyne: Reid, 2nd ed. 1932

Collingwood, R.G. 'Reason is Faith Cultivating Itself' in *Hibbert Journal*, vol.26 (1927), reprinted in *Faith and Reason: Essays in the Philosophy of Religion* (ed. Rubinoff L.), Chicago: Quadrangle, 1967

Collingwood, R.G. 'The Limits of Historical Knowledge' *Journal of Philosophical Studies* 1928 vol.III, pp.213–22

Collingwood, R.G. 'Roman Signal-stations on the Cumberland Coast' in *Transactions of the Cumberland and Westmorland Antiquarian Society* 29 (1929), pp.138–65

Collingwood, R.G. 'Town and Country in Roman Britain' in *Antiquity* 3 (1929), pp.261–76

Collingwood, R.G. Unpublished Introduction to Moral Philosophy Lectures, 1929, Bodleian Library, Dep. 10

Collingwood, R.G. *The Archaeology of Roman Britain*, London: Methuen, 1930 Collingwood, R.G. 'Hadrian's Wall, 1921–30' in *Journal of Roman Studies* 21 (1931), pp.36–64

Collingwood, R.G. Unpublished Introduction to Moral Philosophy Lectures, 1932, Bodleian Library, Dep. 7

Collingwood, R.G. *An Essay on Philosophical Method* (edited and introduced by James Connelly and Giuseppina D'Oro) Oxford: Clarendon Press, 2005

Collingwood, R.G. 'An Introduction to the Prehistory of Cumberland, Westmorland and Lancashire north of the Sands' in *Transactions of the Cumberland and Westmorland Antiquarian and Archaeological Society* 33 (1933), pp.163–200

Collingwood, R.G. 'The Romans and Britain' and 'The Conquest of Britain' in S.A. Cook *et al* (eds.) *Cambridge Ancient History*, Vol. 10, 1934

Collingwood, R.G. Unpublished 'Central Problems in Metaphysics, lectures written April 1935, for delivery T[rinity] T[erm] 1935', Bodleian Library, Dep. 20

Collingwood, R.G. & Myers, J.N.L. *Roman Britain and the English Settlements*, Oxford: Clarendon Press, 1936

Collingwood, R.G. 'The Latin West: Britain' *Cambridge Ancient History*, vol. 11, 1936, pp.511–25

Collingwood, R.G. 'Roman Britain' in T. Frank (ed.) *An Economic Survey of Ancient Rome* vol.3 Baltimore MD: John Hopkins University Press 1937, pp.1–118

Collingwood, R.G. Unpublished Notes on Causation (1937?), Bodleian Library, Dep. 19

Collingwood, R.G. 'King Arthur's Round Table' in *Transactions of the Cumberland and Westmorland Antiquarian and Archaeological Society* 38 1938, pp.1–31

Collingwood, R.G. 'On the so-called idea of causation' in *Proceedings of the Aristotelian Society*, 38 (1937–38), pp.85–112

Collingwood, R.G. *The Principles of Art*, Oxford: Clarendon Press, 1938

Collingwood, R.G. 'Britain' in *Cambridge Ancient History*, vol. 12, 1939, pp.282–96

Collingwood, R.G. *An Autobiography*, Oxford: Clarendon, 1939

Collingwood, R.G. *First Mate's Log of a Voyage to Greece in the schooner yacht 'Fleur de Lys' in 1939*, Oxford: Oxford University Press, 1940

Collingwood, R.G. *An Essay on Metaphysics* (revised edition, with an introduction by Rex Martin), Oxford: Clarendon Press, 1998

Collingwood, R.G. *The New Leviathan* (1942), revised edition, edited and introduced by David Boucher, Oxford: Clarendon Press, 1992

Collingwood, R.G *The Idea of Nature*, Oxford: Clarendon Press, 1945

Collingwood, R.G. *The Idea of History* (revised edition, with an introduction by Jan van der Dussen), Oxford: Clarendon Press, 1993

Collingwood, R.G. and R.P. Wright *The Roman Inscriptions of Britain with Addenda and Corrigenda by R.S.O. Tomlin*, 2nd ed. Stroud: Sutton, 1995

Collingwood, R.G. *The Principles of History*, (edited by W.H. Dray and Jan van der Dussen) Oxford: Clarendon Press, 1999

Collingwood, R.G. *The Philosophy of Enchantment: Studies in Folktale, Cultural Criticism, and Anthropology* (eds. D. Boucher, W. James & P. Smallwood) Oxford: Clarendon Press, 2005

Collini, Stefan and Bernard Williams ' R.G. Collingwood' in *The Dictionary of National Biography*, 2004, pp.677–81

Connelly, James 'Metaphysics and Method: A Necessary Unity in the Philosophy of R.G. Collingwood' in *Storia, Antropologia e Scienze del Linguaggio* 5/1-2 (ed. Bulzoni), Rome, 1990

Connelly, James *Metaphysic, Method and Practice*, Exeter: Imprint Academic, 2003

Connelly, James 'New Metaphysics for Old', unpublished

Couse, G.S. 'Colllingwood's Detective Image of the Historian and the Study of Hadrian's Wall' *History and Theory* Beiheft 29 no.4 1990, pp.57–77

Croce, Benedetto *The Philosophy of Giambattista Vico* (trans. R.G. Collingwood), London: Howard Latimer, 1913; reprinted with a new introduction by Alan Sica, New Brunswick, New Jersey: Transaction, 2002

Croce, Benedetto *An Autobiography* (trans. R.G. Collingwood), Oxford: Clarendon Press, 1927

Dancy, J. *Practical Reality*, Oxford: Clarendon Press, 2002

Danto, Arthur C. *Analytical Philosophy of History*, Cambridge: Cambridge University Press, 1965

Davidson, Donald 'Actions, Reasons and Causes' *Journal of Philosophy* 60 1963, reprinted in *Essays on Actions and Events*, Oxford: Clarendon Press, 1980

Davidson, Donald 'Causal Relations' *Journal of Philosophy* 64 1967, republished in *Essays on Actions and Events*, Oxford: Clarendon Press, 1980

Davidson, Donald 'The Individuation of Events' in *Essays in Honour of Carl G. Hempel* (ed. Nicholas Rescher & D. Reidel) 1969, reprinted in *Essays on Actions and Events*, Oxford: Clarendon Press, 1980

Davidson, Donald 'Mental Events' in *Experience and Theory* 1970 (ed. Lawrence Foster & J.W. Swanson), reprinted in *Essays on Actions and Events*, Oxford, Clarendon Press, 1980

Davidson, Donald 'How is Weakness of Will Possible?' 1970, reprinted in *Essays on Actions and Events*, Oxford, Clarendon Press, 1980

Davidson, Donald 'Radical Interpretation' *Dialectica* 1973; 27, pp.313–28, reprinted in *Inquiries into Truth and Interpretation*, Oxford: Clarendon Press, 1984

Davidson, Donald 'Psychology as Philosophy' in *Philosophy of Psychology* (ed. S.C.Brown) 1974, reprinted in *Essays on Actions and Events*, Oxford: Clarendon Press, 1980

Davies, Martin and Stone, Tony 'Simulation Theory' in *The Routledge Encyclopaedia of Philosophy* (ed. E.Craig), London: 2000

De Ruggiero, Guido *Modern Philosophy* (trans. R.G. Collingwood and Howard Hannay), London: Allen, 1920

De Ruggiero, Guido *The History of European Liberalism* (trans. R.G. Collingwood), Oxford, Clarendon Press, 1927

Dilthey, Wilhelm *Selected Works/ Volume I. Introduction to the Human Sciences* Princeton: Princeton University Press, 1989

Dilthey, Wilhelm *Selected Works/ Volume IV. Hermeneutics and the Study of History* Princeton: Princeton University Press, 1996

Donagan, Alan *The Later Philosophy of R.G. Collingwood*, (1962) Oxford: Clarendon Press, 1985

D'Oro, Giuseppina 'On Collingwood's Conceptions of History' *Collingwood Studies* Vol. VII 2000, pp.45–69

D'Oro, Giuseppina *Collingwood and the Metaphysics of Experience*, London: Routledge, 2002

D'Oro, Giuseppina 'Collingwood and Ryle on the Concept of Mind', *Philosophical Explorations* vol. 6, 2003, pp.18–30

D'Oro, Giuseppina 'Re-Enactment and Radical Interpretation' *History and Theory* 43 2004b, pp.198–208

D'Oro, Giuseppina 'Collingwood, Psychologism and Internalism', *European Journal of Philosophy* 12:2 2004c, pp.163–77

D'Oro, Giuseppina 'Idealism and the Philosophy of Mind' *Inquiry* vol.48, no.5, 2005b, pp.395–412

D'Oro, Giuseppina 'In Defence of the Agent-Centred Perspective', *Metaphilosophy* 36 2005c, pp.652–67

D'Oro, Giuseppina 'Collingwood's 'Solution' to the Problem of Mind-Body Dualism', *Philosophia* 32 2005d, pp.349–68

Dray, William H. 'R.G. Collingwood and the Acquaintance Theory of Knowledge', *Revue Internationale de Philosophie* 11 1957a, pp.420–432

Dray, William H. *Laws and Explanation in History*, Oxford: Clarendon Press, 1957b

Dray, William H. 'Historical Understanding as Rethinking', *University of Toronto Quarterly* 27 1958, pp.200–15

Dray, William H. 'Historical Explanation of Actions Reconsidered', originally in S. Hook (ed.) *Philosophy and History*, New York: New York University Press, 1963; reprinted in *The Philosophy of History* (ed. Patrick Gardiner), Oxford: Clarendon Press, 1974

Dray, William H. *Philosophy of History*, Toronto: Prentice-Hall, 1964

Dray, William H. *History as Re-Enactment: R.G. Collingwood's Idea of History*, Oxford: Clarendon Press, 1995

Dray, William H. 'Philosophy and Historiography' in *Companion to Historiography* (ed. Michael Bentley), London: Routledge, 1997

Dreisbach, Christopher *R.G. Collingwood: A Bibliographic Checklist*, The Philosophy Documentation Center, Bowling Green, OH: Bowling Green State University, 1993

Emmett, Dorothy *Philosophers and Friends: Reminiscences of Seventy Years in Philosophy*, Basingstoke: MacMillan, 1996

Fischer, David Hackett *Historians' Fallacies: Towards a Logic of Historical Thought*, London: Routledge, 1971

Foster, M.B. 'Christian Theology and Modern Science of Nature' (I & II) *Mind* vol. XLIV 1935, pp.439–66 & XLV 1936, pp.1–27

Frege, Gottlob 'On Sense and Reference' (1892) in *Translations from the Philosophical Writings of Gottlob Frege* (eds. Geach, P. and Black, M.), Oxford: Clarendon Press, 1960

Gardiner, Patrick *The Nature of Historical Explanation*, Oxford: Clarendon Press, 1952a

Goldstein, Leon J. 'Collingwood on the Constitution of the Historical Past' in *Critical Essays on the Philosophy of R.G. Collingwood*, ed. M. Krausz, Oxford, Clarendon Press, 1972

Gordon, Robert 'From Folk Psychology to Cognitive Science' *Mind and Language* 1986 1, pp.158–71

Harman, Gilbert 'The Inference to the Best Explanation', *Philosophical Review* 74 1965, pp.88–95

Harris, E.E. 'Mr Ryle and the Ontological Argument', *Mind* vol. XLV, October 1936, pp.474–80

Heal, Jane 'Replication and Functionalism' in *Language, Mind and Logic*, ed. J.Butterfield, Cambridge: Cambridge University Press, 1986

Hegel, Georg Wilhelm Friedrich *Philosophy of Right* (trans. T.M. Knox), Oxford: Clarendon Press, 1942

Hegel's Logic, Oxford: Clarendon Press, 1975

Heizer, Robert F. *Man's Discovery of his Past* (1962), Palo Alto, California, Peek Publications, revised ed. 1980

Hempel, Carl 'Problems and Changes in the Empiricist Criterion of Meaning', *Revue Internationale de Philosophie* 4 1950, pp.41–63

Hempel, Carl 'The Function of General Laws in History', *Journal of Philosophy* 39 1942, pp.35–48

Hempel, Carl 'Aspects of Scientific Explanation' in *Aspects of Scientific Explanation and Other Essays in the Philosophy of Science*, New York: Free Press 1965, pp.447–53

Hempel, Carl *Philosophy of Natural Science*, Englewood Cliffs: Prentice Hall, 1966

Hennig, Martin *The Art of Roman Britain* London: Routledge, 1997

Herodotus *The Histories* (trans. Aubrey de Sélincourt, revised with an introduction by A.R. Burn), Harmondsworth: Penguin, 1972

Hume, David *An Enquiry Concerning Human Understanding* [1777], Oxford: Clarendon Press, 1975

Hutto, Daniel 'A Cause for Concern: Reasons, Causes and Explanations' *Philosophy and Phenomenological Research* vol. 59, no. 2 (June 1999), pp.381–401

Ignatieff, Michael *Isaiah Berlin: A Life*, London: Chatto & Windus, 1998

Johnston, Mark 'Why Having a Mind Matters' in *Actions and Events: Perspectives on the Philosophy of Donald Davidson* (ed. Ernest LePore & Brian P.McLaughlin), Oxford: Basil Blackwell, 1985

Johnstone, W.M. *The Formative Years of R.G. Collingwood*, The Hague: Nijhoff, 1967

Joynt, Carey B. and Rescher, N. 'The Problem of Uniqueness in History' in History and Theory vol.1, 1961, pp.150–62

Joynt, Carey B. and Rescher, N. 'On Explanation in History' *Mind* vol.68, July 1959, pp.383–88

Joynt, Carey B. and Rescher, N. 'Evidence in History and in the Law' *Journal of Philosophy* vol.56, June 1959, pp.561–77

Kant, I. *Critique of Pure Reason* (translated by Norman Kemp Smith), London: Macmillan, 1933

Kim, Jaegwon 'Causes and Events', *American Philosophical Quarterly* 2/4 1965, pp.245–64; reprinted in *Causation* (ed. Ernest Sosa & Michael Tooley), Oxford: Clarendon Press, 1993

Kim, Jaegwon *Supervenience and Mind: Selected Philosophical Essays* Cambridge, Cambridge University Press, 1993

Klejn, Leo S. 'Metaarchaeology' in *Acta Archaeologica* (special issue), Copenhagen: Blackwell-Munksgaard, 2001

Kobayashi, Chinatsu 'Collingwood on Re-Enactment: Understanding in History and Interpretation in Art', unpublished PhD thesis, University of Ottawa, 2003

Krausz, M. 'The Logic of Absolute Presuppositions' in M. Krausz (ed.) *Critical Essays on the Philosophy of R.G.C. Collingwood*, Oxford: Clarendon Press, 1972

Langford, C.H. 'Comment' in *The Philosophy of G. E. Moore* (ed. P.A. Schilpp),1942

Levine, Joseph 'The Autonomy of History: R.G. Collingwood and Agatha Christie' *Clio* 7 1978, pp.253–64

Lewis, David 'Causation', *Journal of Philosophy* 70 (1973), pp.556–67, reprinted in *Causation* (eds. Ernest Sosa & Michael Tooley) Oxford: Clarendon Press, 1993

Lipton, Peter *Inference to the Best Explanation*, London: Routledge, 1993

Locke, John *An Essay Concerning Human Understanding* (ed. P. Nidditch), Oxford: Clarendon Press, 1975

Mackie, J.L. 'Causes and Conditions', *American Philosophical Quarterly* 2 (1965), pp.245–55 & 261-4, reprinted in *Causation* (Ernest Sosa & Michael Tooley) Oxford: Clarendon Press, 1993

Mackie, J.L. *The Cement of the Universe*, Oxford: Clarendon Press, 1974

Malcolm, Norman 'The Conceivability of Mechanism' *The Philosophical Review* 77 1968, pp.45–72, reprinted in *Free Will* (ed. Gary Watson) Oxford: Clarendon Press, 1982

Martin, Rex 'Collingwood's *Essay on Philosophical Method*', *Idealistic Studies* 4 1974, pp.224–50

Martin, Rex *Historical Explanation: Re-enactment and Practical Inference*, Ithaca: Cornell University Press, 1977

Martin, Rex 'Collingwood's Claim that Metaphysics is a Historical Discipline' in *Interdisciplinary Perspectives on R.G. Collingwood* (eds. D. Boucher, J. Connelly, T. Modood) Cardiff: University of Wales Press, 1995

Mazlish, Bruce *The Riddle of History*, New York: Harper & Row, 1966

McCulagh, C. Behan *The Logic of History*, London and New York: Routledge, 2004

Menzies, P. and Price, H. 'Causation as a Secondary Quality' *British Journal for the Philosophy of Science* 1993, 44, pp.187–203

Mill, J.S. *A System of Logic* (1843), Toronto: University of Toronto Press (ed. J.M. Robson), 1973

Millett, Martin *The Romanisation of Britain: An Essay in Archaeological Interpretation*, Cambridge: Cambridge University Press, 1992

Milne, A.J.M. 'Civilization and the Open Society: Collingwood and Popper' in *Philosophy, History and Civilization: Interdisciplinary Perspectives on the Philosophy of R.G. Collingwood* (eds. D. Boucher, J. Connelly, T. Modood) Cardiff: University of Wales Press, 1995

Mink, Louis O. *Mind, History and Dialectic*, Bloomington, IND: University of Indiana Press 1969; republished by Middletown, CONN, 1987

Mink, Louis O. 'Collingwood's Historicism: A Dialectic of Process' in *Critical Essays on the Philosophy of R.G. Collingwood* (ed. Michael Krausz), Oxford: Clarendon Press, 1972

Modood, Tariq 'The Later Collingwood's Alleged Historicism and Relativism', *Journal of the History of Philosophy* vol.27 no.1 Jan.1989, pp.101–25

Modood, Tariq 'Collingwood and the Idea of Philosophy' in *Interdisciplinary Perspectives on R.G. Collingwood* (ed. D. Boucher, J. Connelly, T. Modood), Cardiff: University of Wales Press, 1995

Oakeshott, M. *Experience and its Modes* (1933), Cambridge: Cambridge University Press, 1986

Oldfield, Adrian 'Metaphysics and History in Collingwood's Thought' in *Philosophy, History and Civilization* (eds. D. Boucher, J. Connelly and T. Modood), Cardiff: University of Wales Press, 1995

Oppy, Graham *Ontological Arguments and Belief in God*, Cambridge: Cambridge University Press, 1995

Patrick, James *The Magdalen Metaphysicals* Macon, GA.: Mercer University Press, 1985

Platinga, Alvin 'The Ontological Argument' in *God, Freedom and Evil*, London: Allen and Unwin, 1974

Plato's Meno with essays ed. Brown, Malcolm, trans. W.K.C. Guthrie, Indianapolis: Bobbs-Merrill Company, 1971

Pompa, Leon 'Collingwood's Theory of Historical Knowledge' in *Philosophy, History and Civilization* (eds. D. Boucher, J. Connelly and T. Modood), Cardiff: University of Wales Press, 1995

Pompa, Leon 'Some Problems of Re-Enactment', *Collingwood Studies* vol. 9 2002, pp.31–44

Popper, Karl *The Open Society and its Enemies* (1945), London: Routledge, 1990

Popper, Karl *The Poverty of Historicism*, London and New York: Routledge, 1957

Popper, Karl *Conjectures and Refutations: The Growth of Scientific Knowledge*, London: Routledge, 1963

Popper, Karl 'A Pluralist Approach to the Philosophy of History' (1967), reprinted in *Roads to Freedom: Essays in Honour of Friedrich A. von Hayek* (ed. E. Streissler), London: Routledge, 1969

Popper, Karl *Objective Knowledge: An Evolutionary Approach* (rev. ed.), Oxford: Clarendon Press, 1979

Priest, Stephen 'Subjectivity and Objectivity in Kant and Hegel' in *Hegel's Critique of Kant* (ed. Stephen Priest), Oxford: O.U.P., 1987

Pritchard, H.A. *Kant's Theory of Knowledge*, Oxford: Clarendon Press, 1909

Quine, Willard van Orman *The Ways of Paradox* (rev. edn.) Cambridge MA: Harvard University Press, 1976

Quine, Willard van Orman *Pursuit of Truth* Cambridge MA: Harvard University Press, 1992

Rescher, Nicholas *Conceptual Idealism*, Oxford: Blackwell,1973

Rescher, Nicholas *The Primacy of Practical Reason*, Oxford: Blackwell,1973

Rescher, Nicholas 'Idealism' in *The Cambridge Dictionary of Philosophy* 2nd ed. Cambridge: Cambridge University Press, 1999

Rescher, Nicholas *Philosophical Reasoning: A Study in the Methodology of Philosophising*, Oxford: Blackwell, 2001

Richmond, I.A. 'Appreciation of R.G. Collingwood as an Archaeologist', *Proceedings of the British Academy* 29 1943, pp.478–9

Ridley, Aaron *R.G. Collingwood*, London: Phoenix, 1998

Ross, William David *The Right and the Good* (1930), Indianapolis, IN: Hackett, 1988

Rotenstreich, N. 'Metaphysics and Historicism' in M. Krausz (ed.) *Critical Essays on the Philosophy of R.G. Collingwood*, Oxford: Clarendon Press, 1972

Rubinoff, L. 'Collingwood and the Radical Conversion Hypothesis', *Dialogue* 5/1 (1966), pp.71–83

Rubinoff, L. *Collingwood and the Reform of Metaphysics: A Study in the Philosophy of Mind*, Toronto: University of Toronto Press, 1970

Russell, Bertrand 'On the Notion of Cause', *Proceedings of the Aristotelian Society* 1911–12, pp.85–112; reprinted in *Mysticism and Logic*, London: Longman, 1918

Russell, Bertrand *The Analysis of Mind*, London: George, Allen and Unwin, 1921

Russell, D.A. 'Rhetoric and Criticism', *Greece and Rome* 14 1967, pp.130–44

Ryle, Gilbert 'Mr Collingwood and the Ontological Argument', *Mind* vol. XLIV, April 1935, pp.137–51

Ryle, Gilbert 'Back to the Ontological Argument', *Mind* vol. XLVI, 1937, pp.53–7

Ryle, Gilbert *The Concept of Mind* (1949), London: Penguin Books, 1990

Ryle, Gilbert "'If', 'So' and 'Because''' in M. Black (ed.) *Philosophical Analysis*, Ithaca, New York, 1950, pp.323–40

Saari, Heikki *Re-enactment: A Study in R.G. Collingwood's Philosophy of History*, Åbo: Åbo Akademi, 1984

Salas, Charles G. 'Collingwood's Historical Principles at Work' *History and Theory* Vol. 26no.1, 1987, pp.53–71

Salmon, N. 'Existence' in *Philosophical Perspectives* (ed. J. Tomberlin), vol.1 *Metaphysics* Atascadero, Calif.: Ridgeview, 1987

Scriven, 'Truisms as the Grounds for Historical Explanations' in *Theories of History* (ed. P. Gardiner), London: Collier MacMillan, 1959

Scriven, Michael 'Causes, Connections and Conditions in History' in *Philosophical Analysis and History* (ed. W. Dray), 1966, pp.238–64

Skagestad, Peter *Making Sense of History: The Philosophies of Popper and Collingwood*, Oslo, Bergen and Tromsö: Universitetsforlaget, 1975

Skinner, Q. 'Meaning and Understanding in the History of Ideas', *History and Theory* (1969) 8, pp.3–53

Stich, Stephen *From Folk Psychology to Cognitive Science*, Cambridge MA: MIT Bradford, 1983

Stoutland, Frederick 'Davidson on Intentional Behaviour' in *Actions and Events: Perspectives on the Philosophy of Donald Davidson* (eds. Ernest Le Pore & Brian P. McLaughlin) Oxford: Blackwell, 1985

Stroud, Barry 'Transcendental Arguments' *Journal of Philosophy* 65 (1968), pp.241–256

Tacitus *Annals* (trans. Michael Grant), Harmondsworth: Penguin, 1976

Tanney, Julia 'Why Reasons may not be Causes' *Mind and Language* 1995 vol.10 no.1/2, pp.105–28

Todorov, Tzvetan *The Poetics of Prose* (trans. R. Howard) Oxford: Blackwell, 1977

Toulmin, Stephen 'Conceptual Change and the Problem of Relativism' in *Critical Essays on the Philosophy of R.G. Collingwood* (ed. M. Krausz), Oxford: Clarendon Press, 1972

Van der Dussen, J.W. *History as a Science: The Philosophy of R.G. Collingwood*, The Hague: Martinus Nijhoff Publishers, 1981

Van der Dussen, J.W. 'The Philosophical Context of Collingwood's Re-Enactment Theory', *International Studies in Philosophy* 1995 XXVII, pp.81-99

Van Fraasen, Bas C. *The Scientific Image*, Oxford: Clarendon Press, 1980

Vanheeswijck, Guido 'R.G. Collingwood on Metaphysics, History and Cosmology' *Process Studies* vol.27, fall-winter 1998, pp.215–36

Vico, G. *The New Science of Giambattista Vico* (trans. Thomas G. Bergin and Max H. Fisch), Ithaca: Cornell University Press, 1968

Von Hayek, Friedrick *Individualism and Economic Order*, London: Routledge & Kegan Paul, 1949

Von Wright, G.H. *Explanation and Understanding*, London: Routledge & Kegan Paul, 1971

Von Wright, G.H. 'Explanation and the Understanding of Actions' in *Contemporary Action Theory*, Vol. 1, Holstrum-Hintikka G. and Tuomela R. (eds.) Kluwer Academic Publishers, Dordrecht, 1997

Vrijen, Charlotte 'Ryle and Collingwood: Their Correspondence and its Philosophical Context', *British Journal for the History of Philosophy*, vol. 14, no.1, Feb. 2006, pp.93–131

Walsh, W.H. *An Introduction to the Philosophy of History* (1951) London: Hutchinson, 1958

White, Allan R. *Methods of Metaphysics*, London: Croom Helm, 1987

White, Morton G. 'The Logic of Historical Narration' in *Philosophy and History: A Symposium* (ed. Sidney Hook), New York: New York University Press, 1963

White, Morton G. 'Historical Explanation' *Mind* 1943, pp.212–29

Whitehead, A.N. *The Function of Reason*, Princeton: Princeton University Press, 1929

Whitehead, A.N. *Modes of Thought* New York: MacMillan, 1966

Williams, Bernard 'Internal and External Reasons' in *Moral Luck: Philosophical Papers 1973–1980*, Cambridge: Cambridge University Press, 1981

Williams, Bernard *Truth and Truthfulness*, Princeton: Princeton University Press, 2002

Williams, Bernard *In the Beginning was the Deed* (ed. Geoffrey Hawthorn), Princeton: Princeton University Press, 2005

Williams, Bernard *Philosophy as a Humanistic Discipline* (ed. A.W. Moore), Princeton: Princeton University Press, 2006

Williams, Bernard 'An Essay on Collingwood' in *The Sense of the Past* (ed. Myles Burnyeat), Princeton: Princeton University Press, 2006

Winch, Peter 'Understanding a Primitive Society' *American Philosophical Quarterly* vol.1, no.4, Oct. 1964, pp.307–24

Wittgenstein, Ludwig *Tractatus Logico-Philosophicus* (trans. D.F. Pears and B.F. McGuiness), London: Routledge, 1961

Wittgenstein, Ludwig *On Certainty* (ed. G.E.M. Anscombe & G.H. von Wright) Oxford: Blackwell, 1969

Wittgenstein, Ludwig *Philosophical Occasions 1912–51*, Indianapolis and Cambridge: Hackett, 1993

Wright, Crispin 'The Verification Principle: Another Puncture, Another Patch', *Mind* (1989) 98, pp.611–22

Index

References to Writings by Collingwood

Books

Articles

Unpublished Manuscripts

Correspondence